TECHNOLOGY MANAGEMENT IN FINANCIAL SERVICES

Palgrave Macmillan Finance and Capital Markets Series
For information about other titles in this series please visit the website
http://www.palgrave.com/business/finance and capital markets.asp

Also by Ross McGill

THE NEW GLOBAL REGULATORY LANDSCAPE with Terence Sheppey
SARBANES-OXLEY – Building Working Strategies for Compliance with Terence Sheppey
GLOBAL CUSTODY AND CLEARING SERVICES with Naren Patel
INTERNATIONAL WITHHOLDING TAX – A Practical Guide to Best Practice and Benchmarking
RELIEF AT SOURCE – An Investor's Guide to Minimising Internationally Withheld Tax

Technology Management in Financial Services

ROSS McGILL

palgrave
macmillan

First published in 2008 by
PALGRAVE MACMILLAN
Houndmills, Basingstoke, Hampshire RG21 6XS and
175 Fifth Avenue, New York, N.Y. 10010
Companies and representatives throughout the world.

PALGRAVE MACMILLAN is the global academic imprint of the Palgrave Macmillan division of St. Martin's Press, LLC and of Palgrave Macmillan Ltd. Macmillan® is a registered trademark in the United States, United Kingdom and other countries. Palgrave is a registered trademark in the European Union and other countries.

ISBN-13: 978–0–230–00679–9 hardback
ISBN-10: 0–230–00679–5 hardback

This book is printed on paper suitable for recycling and made from fully managed and sustained forest sources. Logging, pulping and manufacturing processes are expected to conform to the environmental regulations of the country of origin.

A catalogue record for this book is available from the British Library.

A catalog record for this book is available from the Library of Congress.

10 9 8 7 6 5 4 3 2 1
17 16 15 14 13 12 11 10 09 08

Printed and bound in Great Britain by
CPI Antony Rowe, Chippenham and Eastbourne

To Kathryn
Late nights are finally over. At least for the present.

Contents

List of Tables ix

List of Figures x

List of Case Studies xi

List of Abbreviations xii

Preface xv

Acknowledgements xvii

About the Author xviii

Introduction 1

PART I THE ROLE OF TECHNOLOGY IN FINANCIAL SERVICES

1 Morphology 5

2 Environment 13

3 Technology Management Issues 21

4 Technology Strategy – Best Practice 26

5 Front, Middle and Back Office Explained 32

6 Communications, Standards and Messaging 43

7 Open Source in Financial Services 56

PART II TECHNOLOGY ACQUISITION AND MANAGEMENT

8 Build 77

9 Buy 91

10 Bureau 96

11 Outsource 100

PART III DELIVERING VALUE FROM TECHNOLOGY

12 Disruptive Innovation – Threat or Opportunity 109

13 Documentation 128

14 Testing and Quality Control 153

15 Benchmarking Value 182

PART IV REGULATION AND COMPLIANCE

16 The Role of Regulation and Global Regulatory Impact 197

17 IT Governance in Financial Services 201

18 Conclusion 221

Appendix 1 Template Request for Proposal 222

Appendix 2 Typical Business Continuity Policy Statement 230

Further Reading 234

Index 237

List of Tables

7.1	Financial companies using OSS	58
7.2	OSS Areas of use	58
7.3	OSS FAQ	64
8.1	Summary of factors for management in technology deployment	79
12.1	Characteristics of a disruptive innovation	122
14.1	Types of risk	171
14.2	Risk rating	172
14.3	Test metrics	179
16.1	GRIA Stage 1	199
16.2	GRIA Stage 2	199

List of Figures

1.1	Morphology of financial services	8
2.1	Business process model for financial services	18
2.2	Modelling content flows for technology solutions	19
3.1	Impact of age on adopter stance	22
3.2	Layering of technology	23
4.1	Effect of extended planning for cost benefit analyses	28
6.1	Current tax processing practice by financial firms	49
6.2	V-STP management model	52
6.3	V-STP in practice	53
6.4	Implementation process	54
PII. 1	Strategic options for delivery of technology projects	74
PII. 2	The macro-technology cycle	74
12.1	Low-end disruption: the innovators' dilemma	116
12.2	Moore's Law	120
14.1	Testing phases	155
14.2	Defect detection by phase	161
14.3	Defect tracking process	169
14.4	Risk evaluation	173
14.5	Defect tracking	180
15.1	Benchmarking management performance	184
15.2	Benchmarking and improvement cycles	186
15.3	Value delivery perception by consitituency	191

List of Case Studies

1	Lessons from the FMCG sector	9
2	V-STP – a lesson in corporate actions automation	49
3	Lessons of a retail pensions build project	88
4	Lessons in managing bureau providers	97
5	Lessons in outsourcing	101

List of Abbreviations

ACH	Automated Clearing Hose
ADBIC	Additional Destination BIC
ADR	American Depositary Receipt
AML	Anti-Money Laundering
AP	Assimilation Plateau
ASP	Application Service Provider
ATM	Automated Teller Machine
AUT	Application User Testing
BI	Business Intelligence
BIC	Bank Identifier Code
BKE	Bilateral Key Exchange
BoB	Best of Breed
BPM	Business Process Management
BPR	Business Process Reengineering
BSD	Berkley Software Distribution License
BSP	Business Services Provider
CERT/CC	CERT Coordination Center
CFO	Chief Financial Officer
CIO	Chief Information Officer
CoA	Constraints on Action
COBIT	Control Objectives for Information and related Technology
COTS	Common Off The Shelf software
CRM	Customer Relationship Management
CSD	Central Securities Depository
CTO	Chief Technology Officer
CUG	Closed User Group
DDP	Defect Detection Percentage
DFP	Defect Fix Percentage
DiD	Defence in Depth

DTCC	Depository Trust & Clearing Corporation (see also DTC)
DR	Disaster Recovery
DR	Depositary Receipts (by context)
EMEA	Europe, Middle East and Africa
ERP	Enterprise Resource Planning
EU	European Union
FFIEC	Financial Institutions Examination Council
FI	Financial Intermediary
FISMA	Financial Services and Markets Act
FMCG	Fast Moving Consumer Goods
FOSS	Free Open Source Software
FTE	Full Time Employee
FOI	Freedom Of Information
FSA	Financial Services Authority
GPL	General Public License
GRIA	Global Regulatory Impact Assessment
HR	Human Resource
IC	Improvement Cycle
ICSD	International Central Securities Depository
IFRS	International Financial Reporting Statndards
IPR	Intellectual Property Rights
ISMS	Information Security Management System
ISO	International Standards Organisation
ISP	Internet Service Provider
ITGI	IT Governance Institute
IVCAF	Insurance Value Chain Architecture Framework
IVN	Industry Value Network
KAP	Key Analysis Points
KPI	Key Performance Indicators
MCD	Maintenance Control Document
MiFiD	Markets in Financial instruments Directive
MLR	Money Laundering Regulations
MTx	Message Type x
MUG	Message User Group
MVC	Management Version Control
NHS	National Health Service
NPW	Not Proceeded With
NYSE	New York Stock Exchange
OAT	Operational Acceptance Testing
OFR	Operating & Financial Review
OS	Operating System
OSI	Open Source Initiative
OSS	Open Source Software

PDA	Personal Digital Assistant
P&L	Profit & Loss
RAS	Relief At Source
RFID	Radio Frequency ID
RFP	Request For Proposal
ROCE	Return On Capital Employed
ROI	Return On Investment
SAP	Systeme Anwendungen und Produkte in der Datenverarbeitung (transl. Systems Applications & Products in data processing)
SCARPS	Structured Capital-At-Risk Products
SEC	Securities & Exchange Commission
SEG	Securities Evaluation Group
SEPA	Single European Payments Area
SIG	Special Interest Groups
SIV	Special Investment Vehicle (also SPV special purpose vehicle)
SOA	Service Oriented Architecture
SOX	Sarbanes–Oxley
SSADM	Structured Systems Analysis and Design Method
STP	Straight Through Processing (see also V-STP)
SWIFT	Society for Worldwide Interbank Financial Telecommunications
TPI	Technology Partners International
TTT	Trust Through Test
TVC	Technical Version Control
UAT	User Acceptance Testing
UCITS	Undertakings for Collective Investments in Transferable Securities
VAR	Value Added Re-Seller
VC	Value Delivery Curve
VPN	Virtual Private Network
V-STP	Virtual Straight Through Processing (see also STP)

Preface

Financial services firms will spend over $5 trillion on technology in the next three years, yet how such technology deployments are managed is rarely addressed or benchmarked in terms of its efficiency and the value they can provide to the business. Much of the money spent will be wasted on unnecessary projects, projects that over-run in time and/or budget and projects that don't achieve their business objectives. The management of technology is therefore of fundamental importance. More efficient management and attention to some of the issues that senior executives face in understanding the complexities involved are vital for the continued success of our industry.

This book is not about technology per se. I will delve at times into specific technologies in order to provide a more easily understandable view of a particular concept. There are also specific technologies that change paradigms and therefore need some particular attention. I have however, tried to retain the focus that the title of this book implies. The book is about the management of technology in financial services. How is management structured to deal with the issues. How well can they identify the issues involved – and in this respect I've tried to highlight a few that most often get missed altogether.

Management of technology has a vital role to play in today's financial services environment and that's because the technology itself is fundamental to our global financial economy. It's strange therefore that there has not been any great treatise providing some guidance for the managers involved in business. Too often, business managers have business skills and technologists have technology skills. Yet there is a discipline that combines the two and has sufficient depth to be worthy of attention in its own right.

In this book I seek to give some guidance, based on many years in both business and technology. Some of my experiences in technology have given me insights into the kind of mistakes business people can make either through assumption or presumption. Equally, my experience in business, hopefully has taught me how to understand technologists and avoid some of the pitfalls that are associated with the lack of understanding of the granular details of technology.

If this book provides business people or technologists with some enlightenment or an idea that makes a deployment more successful, it will have succeeded in its intent.

Acknowledgements

I would like to thank the following for their invaluable contributions to this book and their support during its writing.

Tim Durham, for his contribution to Chapter 14 on Testing and Quality Control.

Tom Foale, Sales Director, Urban Wimax plc for his contribution to Chapter 12 on disruptive technologies.

Martin Foont, CEO, and **Len Lipton**, VP both of Globe Tax Services Inc. for their approval to use certain case studies and their contribution to Chapter 5 on back and front offices.

Terence Sheppey, CEO, Precision Texts Ltd for his contribution to Chapter 17 on IT governance.

About the Author

Ross McGill, graduated with Honours in Materials Science and Education in 1978. Since graduating, he has held key management posts with major international companies. He ran his own consultancy practice helping financial services firms become more competitive and efficient. Ross has since worked for 11 years in the wholesale financial services sector and was, until 2002 Group Managing Director of five software companies. He is particularly well known in the industry for his public work with the Society for Worldwide Interbank Financial Telecommunications (SWIFT), the US Treasury, IRS and global custodians dealing with the practical effects of new regulatory structures. He now works as CEO of TConsult Ltd a UK based strategic technology management consultancy and is also managing director for US based Globe Tax Services Inc., leading business process outsourcing of withholding tax processing in the UK and EMEA where he advises financial intermediaries on best practice in business process enhancement.

Ross was co-chair of SWIFT Market Practice Group on US 1441 NRA regulatory issues for ISO standard messaging and co-chaired an Operational Impact group with the IRS, US Treasury and Deloitte & Touche LLP from 1999 to 2001. Ross also serves as the UK expert representing Service Bureaux on ISO20022 Securities Evaluation Group (SEG) Committee TC68.

Ross's published works include

1. Published by Euromoney Books

   - *International Withholding Tax – A Practical Guide to Best Practice and Benchmarking* (2003)

   - *Relief at Source – An Investor's Guide to Minimising Internationally Withheld Tax* (2004)

2. Published by Palgrave Macmillan

   - *The New Global Regulatory Landscape* – co-authored with Terence Sheppey (2005)
   - *Sarbanes Oxley – Building Working Strategies for Compliance* – co-authored with Terence Sheppey (2006)
   - *Global Custody and Clearing Services* – co-authored with Naren Patel (2008)

Introduction

Technology is now firmly embedded in most parts of our western civilisation and nowhere more so than in financial services. The industry simply could not exist without it. Therefore by inference, any systemic failure or determined attack on our financial services industry today is likely to be aimed at technology and, if successful, has the capacity to bring most of the day-to-day activities of our civilisation to a standstill. Ergo what technology we use, how we use it and how we manage it are all critical issues for the industry and critical concerns for everyone who is a beneficiary of its work. It should be self-evident therefore to anyone in financial services that these issues must be continually reviewed and discussed. We can't afford the consequences of not doing so.

This book does not seek to be an exposition of technology per se, which would of course be not only impossible, but futile as one of the key characteristics of modern technology is the speed with which it evolves. The printed book can never hope to keep up. Happily, the management of technology evolves at a slower pace. That's not a bad thing, it's a good thing. To keep up with the pace of technological developments, we need a management system that is capable of bridging the generational gap, to be parental so to speak, so that the technology can grow to meet our needs. But, rather like a Mobius strip, technology does have some effect on management by providing new issues to think about and new problems to solve. We shall look at some of these in the following pages.

This book is segregated into four parts to make referencing easier:

1. The role of technology in financial services

2. Technology acquisition and management

3. Delivering value from technology

4. Regulation and compliance

WHO SHOULD READ THIS BOOK AND WHY

This book is designed and written to be read by an audience with a wide variety of skills, experience and knowledge. Parts of the book are extremely technical, designed for expert practitioners to understand some of the detailed complexities of some modern technologies; for example, open source, SOA etc. Many parts of the book, on the other hand are designed and written for different management levels, where knowledge of technology may be an advantage, but is not a requirement. Readers are likely to be in technology delivery functions, junior, middle and senior management and compliance and legal functions in both retail and wholesale financial services.

PART I

The Role of Technology in Financial Services

In this part of the book we will be looking at some of the general issues that need to be considered at strategic level in the management of technology. These include:

- Morphology – the way in which technology is placed within a wider business framework;
- Environment – the way in which technology is affected by and affects its environment;
- Strategy – explaining best practice at strategic level;
- Interactions – an explanation of front, middle and back offices for the new entrant;
- Communications, Standards and Messaging – discussing the most important elements in any modern deployment;
- Open Source – a look at one specific market model in context as a precusor to a discussion of options in later parts

As the management of technology is relatively underdeveloped at strategic level, and, some may say, overdeveloped further down the chain, this part of the book is important because it establishes some of the key principles that must be considered at strategic level before any lower level deployment can take place and be effective.

CHAPTER 1

Morphology

I mentioned in the Introduction that technology today evolves quickly and that management of technology evolves more slowly. The rather indirect association to biology was intentional. Technology language today has adopted many terms from the biological sciences, some of which we are unfortunately only too aware of, for example, viruses. We can continue the metaphor to good effect here by using the concept of morphology, or the analysis of form and structure, to help us begin to think about how a fast moving organism like financial services can be controlled and managed effectively by a slow moving one like management theory.

The morphology of financial services is that of a somewhat amorphous aggregation of 'corporate entities'. We know those entities as financial services firms acting in a fast moving environment. As with any organism, several different methods of surviving evolve. The largest differentiator today is the gulf between retail financial services and wholesale. There are different 'natural' factors at work in different ways on both communities. Similarly both communities have a degree of overlap.

Retail financial services sits in an extremely fast moving environment akin to the fast moving consumer goods market (FMCG). While it has no real comparison with FMCG, because it operates in the retail environment, many of its management traits are formed by the same pressures that form classical retail businesses.

RETAIL

The retail financial services industry has to appear to be very flexible and move very quickly being perhaps more of an early adopter of technology than its wholesale counterparts. It also engages different kinds of technology – mobile, internet and so on to a much greater degree and is more likely to be involved with so-called disruptive technologies – FaceBook, Plaxo and so on. Of course, both retail and wholesale operate in a dynamic environment that is also reflexive, that is, it receives feedback on its activities that, to some extent, form the basis of future policy and activity. This is clearly visible over the last ten years as we have seen the continual erosion of the branch structure of most banks in favour of ATMs and internet banking. Some of these activities not only benefit our changing lifestyles but they also serve the interests of the financial institutions themselves, for example by reducing costs. Some of course have negative feedback. In the UK for example, the recent trend to outsource customer services to lower-cost India has created a backlash in the market that has even led one bank to use its UK-based customer services operation as the lead in its TV advertising campaigns. Regulation in the retail financial services sector is of a very different kind than that in wholesale. There is some overlap, but in the main, retail financial institutions are more affected by consumer regulation. There are some notable exceptions. Both are subject to data protection regulation, yet failures in wholesale banking go largely unreported while the availability of one retail bank's customer records on a street corner in Mumbai in 2006 is now recognised by most commentators as having been the tip of the iceberg.

We must also not fall into the trap of presuming that retail financial services equals banking services. As the term implies, retail financial services also encompasses a range of other services including, for example, mortgage broking and pensions. The focus of all these sectors however is founded on getting at and securing a flow of product to the retail population. Technology therefore has much more to do in this sector, with controlling the route to market for product and the ability to deliver a very fast cycle time to sale and customer maintenance. The former means that technology systems need to be designed and delivered to meet a highly variable set of needs. Flexibility is the key. Customer fashions change rapidly, available technology is essentially 'faddish', but woe betide the institution that misses out on something like a Google or a FaceBook which can go from a few users to millions relatively overnight. The trick for technology management in retail financial services has more to do with keeping pace with available technologies and having a review and implementation process that can keep up with and identify the successful ones, all in the context of a consumer base that expects its suppliers to be both conservative and stable at the same time.

WHOLESALE

From a consumer perspective, wholesale financial services is essentially invisible except when some major breakdown occurs, for example, Societe

Generale (2008). Wholesale financial services represents the activities that either support the retail financial services industry directly, for example mortgage processing; or the activities of banks with respect to each other as buyers and seller of services otherwise known as 'intra-market'.

Wholesale financial services is fundamentally concerned with risk mitigation, cost reduction and the creation of straight through processing (STP) as we'll see in Chapter 2. Lowering transaction costs and error rates in order to support a rapidly expanding interconnected network of institutions requires a focus on stability, standards and scalability in the management of technology. Wholesale financial services also faces challenges of course. The market fluctuates in a similar macro cycle to that of retail. Where retail services functions through humanist (large branch networks, many staff technology in support role) and through technologist (no branch network, all on-line, technology-driven) phases wholesale's macro cycle consists of consolidation (small businesses aggregating into large ones and new utilities being set up) and fragmentation (creation of centralised and decentralised business units). So for example in 2008, we have a number of historical transactions and events taking place that put us firmly into the consolidation phase of that cycle. Bank of New York's acquisition of Mellon to form Bank of New York Mellon, Turquoise, Global Crossing and so on all support the case. Creating centralised global functions is not necessarily an end point in itself, that is. this is not a linear process at the macro level. These are very much cycles. Most commentators represent financial services globally as being 'on a knife-edge'. There are so many factors that can affect the industry, that can push the entire industry into a different model. The difference is that, unlike any other industry, financial services underpins every other industry on the planet. If it wobbles, so does everything else. If the money system fails, we all go back to the stone age.

So, it is vitally important to understand the morphology – structure – of financial services. The factors that affect those structures are embedded in the success or failure of the system. Since technology is employed in both retail and wholesale financial services, it stands to reason that technology and its management are of fundamental importance.

When we talk of morphology to understand how technology can be managed in this environment we need to have some picture about how the different parts look and are related to each other. As with any biological system, financial services has many different structures, the two top-level structures being those we've already described. Figure 1.1 shows, at the secondary level the available structures that support the industry. From a technology management viewpoint, these are essential to understand because they affect the way in which any given technology will be approached, considered, deployed and maintained. The equivalence to our biology metaphor is that the retail and wholesale environments are akin to

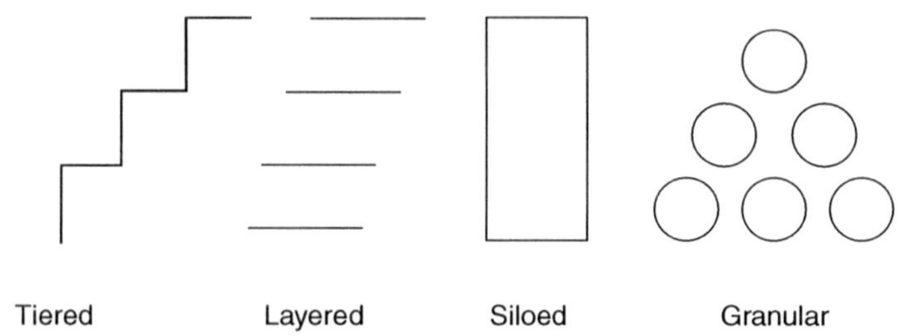

Figure 1.1 Morphology of financial services
Source: Author.

the organs, where the body is the total environment. This lower-level morphology represents the cell structure supporting the activities of the organs. From a metaphorical viewpoint, this is useful because, for a technologist, its all too easy to get drowned in the detail of producing technology for technology's sake. The biological model forces managers to think about the wider context in which their work occurs.

There are four basic types of structure:

- Tiered
- Layered
- Siloed
- Granular

These can represent, among many others, business structures, departmental structures and market structures.

Each of these structures has the possibility to communicate with any of the other types either

- physically as in a branch structure,
- managerially as in a reporting hierarchy or
- technologically as in a communications network.

So, when considering the management of any technological deployment, apart from thinking about the technology itself, its just as important to consider the environment (see Chapter 2) as well as the morphology in which the technology will operate.

TIERS

In a tiered structure the activities in any one tier are directly connected to those of other tiers. In a managerial context this may be a branch structure at the lowest level, with a regional structure above it topped off by a head office and ultimately a holding company. In this scenario, a deployment of technology related to financial reporting for example would have to take account of a regulatory issue such as Sarbanes–Oxley, in a completely different way than in a layered, siloed or granular structure. A technology deployment that leverages say, customer relationship management (CRM), would have to take account of the qualities of the layers as well as the qualities of the connections between them to be successful.

LAYERS

In a layered environment there are either no connections between the layers or, if there are, the connections are very weak or of no real business consequence. At its most obvious, this occurs with the two top layers of retail versus wholesale banking but there are many more examples, the most important example being market sector. The challenge for technology managers in these environments is that typically value is derived from technology when there are connections between things. In a layered environment, value is usually restricted to within the layer and the value is either not recognisable in the other layers or of no use. So, for example hedge fund calculation and statistical analysis engines are invaluable within the hedge fund layer (market sector), but of virtually no interest or use elsewhere in the industry. This example highlights one of the general dangers in business, that of being blind-sided by the restricted use of any one of these models. I made a presumption in stating that there was no use for statistical engines used by hedge fund managers anywhere else in the industry, that is they are layer-specific technologies that must leverage their value from a very narrow usage base. The reality is that this *may* not be the case. Management, while deciding what technology to use, must be open minded enough to categorise what the available technology can do without restricting its freedom of movement.

Case study 1 Lessons from the FMCG sector

I always like to cite the 'What do we do' scenario. This is a technology management anecdote. It relates to a company that makes drills. Sales were falling and the board met to discuss what to do about it. They decided to bring in a team of consultants, who then visited customers, branches and staff to find out how and why the business was failing. They reported back to the board with a statement and a question. The statement was that sales of drills were definitely falling and that this was a market trend they could not buck. The second was a question designed to solve the problem. It was this: 'What do you actually do as a business?'. The more flippant board members said 'we make and sell drills of course'. The consultants smiled and said 'No you don't. You make electric motors with different uses. You just happen to be focusing on only one use so far.' Cutting a long story short, the firm now produces drills, leaf suckers, lawn mowers, saws, planes (woodworking variety) and many other DIY tools based on the model of an electric motor with different attachments. The result – a diversified, more resilient company with increasing sales.

From a technology management viewpoint this case study is important because it reminds us that each of the morphology elements has drawbacks and advantages. We can't assume that one model will work on its own, and in fact, doing so will create a very unstable structure that might work for a while but will eventually create risk. I use this anecdote as a touch stone whenever I'm discussing technology management. There are many existing technologies already deployed in financial services. We often have no need to reinvent the wheel. Often we fail to consider these technologies because they are in different layers, tiers, siloes or granules where we can't easily access the ideas let alone the knowledge.

One final point in this section, for managers: it may not just be that the technology exists – even where technology does exist and someone identifies it. One of the most dangerous things about technologists (as opposed to technology managers) is that they can often fall into the trap of deploying 'new' technology simply because its new, rather than because it's the right technology to deploy. I see this effect gathering great pace as the technology managers of the future are coming up (certainly in western cultures if not in middle or eastern ones) in environments based on 'instant gratification' and the need for a bigger better 'bang for the buck'. There are occasions where an existing technology that has not previously been adopted in a particular place, is a good solution. We drop what works for what is new and shiny, far too often.

SILOES

In a siloed environment, the emphasis is on the vertical and not the horizontal. This is most widely seen in departmental structures within financial services. Trade, Clearing, Settlements and Payments, Back Office Processing are all examples in wholesale financial services, of a siloed environment. There are connections between these, more so in recent years, but historically, each of these activities has been a stand-alone or one with weak interactions. So, while there are experts in payments, experts in back office processing and experts in trading *and* each one is dependent to a certain extent on all the others for the whole to work, it is rare to find anyone, at the managerial level, with cross-silo experience or knowledge.

It is notable, for example, that most of the board of the Society for Worldwide Interbank Financial Telecommunications (SWIFT) has its experience base predominantly in the payments area despite the fact that its current focus is on other areas of financial connectivity such as corporate actions or back office processing. This will clearly change over time, but this does highlight one of the dangers inherent in managing technology. If senior management experience and focus are not closely aligned with the changes in the market and business, it can lead to projects which should be delivered but which aren't because management either has no understanding of the need or imperative or has no interest. Equally, it can result in projects which don't reflect market need. At this level, perfect alignment is often not possible. The alignment always lags behind the need and it is one of my benchmarks to calculate the differential between the market need and the alignment to the market. This tells me, at a glance, the likelihood that the business is (i) moving in the right direction and (ii) that the management is at the right stage of development to both understand and implement any given technology for the benefit of the business. So, you can see that management of technology in financial services is not just about who puts the specifications together and what technology is deployed. It is affected fundamentally at board level where the interaction of the environment (the market) and the skill set (the board) come together to create technology imperatives.

GRANULES

In a granular environment there are no vertical or horizontal connections between elements. This can often occur in wholesale banking at the brand level. I often come across businesses which share the same brand name, that is, I think I'm talking to someone in Firm A. Firm A is actually a business unit of Institution A, so they share the same name. It is dangerous to assume however, in a granular structure, that any one element is either connected to, or even knows of the existence of, any of the other elements. I've found this on a number of occasions. Discussions with Firm A reveals that there are Firms B through D, but, even though they share the same name, none has anything to do with any of the others and often don't even know they exist. The most common manifestation of this is geography-based. For many medium sized financial firms the cost of managing a connection between an office in Sydney and New York is just too great, so the Sydney office is given an initial directive and from then on responds directly to its customer base within its own region or market with little or no connection back to the parent except at a financial reporting level. Clearly this has impacts on management of technology where a typical deployment would want to be or even be mandated to deliver some kind of connectivity at one of the three levels (technological, managerial or physical).

As I said before, we must not assume that any one of these models represents the totality, for example, of any one organisation, department or market. These are tools to look at the environment in which technology is going to be managed and it is highly likely, in my experience, that when a deployment is being considered, more than one of these models will apply at any one given time to parts of the management discussions.

I mentioned earlier that, tiers, levels, siloes and granules operate in three ways – physical, technological and managerial. Do not make the mistake of believing that this book relates only to the second of these three.

At the point of developing a technology strategy, the issue for business managers is to consider the morphology of their business as well as their environment. A typical wholesale provider for example may well have some parts of its business in a tiered structure for example, it may have relationship management based in branches so that it can be 'close to its customers'. It may have parts of its business and branch structure so geographically remote that it essentially makes them independent in a layer – some parts of its operations, often the back office specialist functions, siloed so that it can bring together its expertise in an easily manageable, centralised way. Finally, it may separate business units in a granular way, for example by market activity, direct custody, wealth management, alternative investments and prime brokerage and so on where each of the units has no real interaction with the others. In this scenario technology managers must be able to model their businesses from a technology strategy viewpoint, in a way that leverages the most value irrespective of the morphology of the business.

CHAPTER 2

Environment

The single most important message of this chapter is that technology does not stand alone outside the influence of its users or its creators. Often the siloed approach of many financial services firms leads to the view that technology is something ‘over there’, somehow outside the system, outside the rules that govern everyone else. We are users of technology, ‘they’ are the producers of technology and never the twain shall meet. We all sit within the same system. We are all part of the same environment and that environment acts like a self-regulating system with reflexive effects caused by events outside our control as well as those within it.

Our industry will spend over a trillion dollars on technology in the next five years. If we had to categorise that spend in order to figure out what the main technology management issues are, the list might look something like this:

1. Cost reduction
2. Risk mitigation
3. Resilience and disaster recovery
4. Regulatory compliance
5. Product development
6. Customer satisfaction

Some may argue that the order should be different, but with such a wide scope to look at, there will be differences for readers based on where you are in the world, the culture of financial services in that region, your firms’ particular history and commercial outlook. So research into the order of such lists is less important in my view than what is actually on the list.

What is clear is that technology is, and will remain, at the forefront of innovation in the financial services sector, driving new products and new services. It is also seen as the only way for many firms to remain in the business at all. Even with that level of prewarning, if warnings were needed, many will still fail to innovate or invest enough.

Already the separation of the larger financial institutions from the smaller 'boutique' firms is polarising the community as has, in technology terms, the separation of retail from wholesale banking. The advent of new disruptive technologies such as the semantic web (otherwise known as Web 2.0) is about to hit the financial services markets in the same way that the Internet did a few years ago. Financial services is particularly vulnerable to such threats because of its endemic conservatism and resistance to change.

It is therefore not only vital, but mission-critical that those who develop and manage technology in the financial services sector have a clear picture of the role of technology and its management in one of the fastest moving environments we face.

This creates a dichotomy for financial services which is historically ultra-conservative and resistant to leading-edge change. But those who do not embrace this new approach will increasingly be left with 'modern' yet obsolete systems.

There are three fundamental questions we need to answer in order to begin the process of managing technology:

1. Meaning

2. Principles and

3. Context

We need to know what we mean by the term technology – what it is and just as importantly what it is not. Second we need to have an understanding of the principles underlying the decision to deploy a particular technology; in other words, whether and when to use it and finally we need to understand the context in which any given technology may be acceptable to a financial services company.

MEANING

Technology refers to any tool we use to enhance our ability to survive in a corporate environment. To that extent, in the eighteenth century a quill pen was the equivalent of today's computer and quite clearly 'technology' and paper, the equivalent of today's electronic files. The same issues were faced then too. Disaster recovery was having more than one copy of the books available in case of fire. How books were printed, bound, stored and made available to people – the equivalent to today's data protection policies. Each book's subject matter, given the cost of production, was effectively a new product in a new market. When someone built a new printing press, that was technology changing and adapting to new needs.

So, the fact is that we've been managing technology for a long time. As far as issues are concerned, there's really nothing new under the sun. But there are two big psychological differences between then and now. In earlier days, books were not viewed as an end in themselves, they were clearly a tool, a means to achieve an end, not an end in themselves. Second, because of the scarcity of books and the lack of mass reading skills, no-one could rely on books alone for their success. Books were one tool out of many available to financial professionals in those days.

Today, there are two pervasive modern business myths about technology, particularly in financial services. The first is that technology equals 'IT'. The second is that technology can solve any problem and will naturally deliver both a business benefit and a market benefit. Both are not only untrue, but dangerous precepts from which to work.

Blind adherence to these two precepts has caused more late deliveries, budget overruns and projects that either don't do what was intended or a technology that has been superceded while being built than almost anything else.

Interestingly, every industry I have worked in seems to be full of people who are convinced that their industry is 'different', that somehow, unless you've been immersed in it since birth, usually more, you can't possibly be credible, because you just won't understand it. Today, the pace of change and level of education are both so high that its just as likely, more so perhaps, that someone with absolutely no knowledge of the industry will find an application of technology that those with the blinkers of too much experience could never see, because they've always done it the old way. So, it is important to start off this book not by learning something but by un-learning what you thought your knew. Someone once said 'Thinking you know something is the biggest barrier to learning' and they were right.

Financial services is a business. It make things, sell things and makes a profit. As such technology has only one role – to make a difference to one of those three fundamentals. It has to enable us to make new things and update old things. It has to help us sell things by making them easier to understand, more appropriate to our needs and make them more accessible to us. It has to help reduce costs or increase the saleability (price and volume) so we can make more profit. That's it. There is no more. Thinking in this way, the first thing to unlearn, is that technology is not an end in itself. It's a tool.

Its also a very common error to think of technology just in terms of software applications. To be sure these are the most ubiquitous and obvious manifestations of technology, but they are very far from the absolute description of the term. In very broad terms, technology sits in three-layered and interconnected tiers:

- Systems – the connectivity that allows business processes to interact
- Servers – the business elements that are connected by systems and which allow applications to operate
- Applications – the processes that we use to aggregate data into information and decisions, often collectively known as products

If we had not unlearned our approach earlier in this chapter, it would be very easy to misread the above list as follows:

- Systems – connectivity
- Servers – hardware
- Applications – software

Clearly, the former definition keeps our options open to deploy an appropriate solution for any given business need.

PRINCIPLES

The principles of technology management in financial services are to deliver solutions that

1. meet or exceed business needs;
2. are delivered within budget and on time or before;
3. support (rather than drive) regulatory compliance; and
4. have durability and resilience.

These may sound obvious but it is unfortunately a truism in both government and financial services projects that less than 50% of the above ever get delivered.

Meeting business needs is most often missed because of a lack of well-defined objectives and/or loose management allowing IT departments or suppliers to define the deliverables in their own terms, which don't always coincide with the business's. Delivering to budget and on time is down again mostly due to loose control of the management process from both directions. IT departments and suppliers need to have definitive limits but business managers, renowned for either making it up as they go along or changing the rules as the business environment changes, also create problems by being too definitive and not making allowances while budgeting and time-scheduling for resource or market issues. If it was easy, this book wouldn't exist.

One of the most important elements of any project in financial services these days is to either ensure or assure regulatory compliance. If its not the core objective of the project, it will still be there as a second tier. Ensuring compliance means that it is the reason for the development. Assuring means that, as a second tier benefit, the development will also support more general compliance requirements, as well as its basic objective.

We must of course remember from earlier in this chapter that a development or a project need not, and often isn't, a software application. The development may be of hardware, connectivity or application.

Durability and resilience are often missed entirely from the deliverable. This can either be hidden or overt. If its hidden, the deliverable is stated as being durable and resilient because it uses or 'sits' on other technology whose durability is deemed to 'rub off' onto the project in hand. An example would be a software application designed to run on a Windows operating system. In a business case, the application will have a durability and resilience attached to it by virtue of the development cycles of Windows or the expected obsolescence of the hardware on which the application runs. While partially relevant, the resultant expectation may be inaccurate because the durability of the project may be affected by changes in the market. The resilience may be affected by changes in the landscape of security threats. So business managers need to be aware of not just the top level requirements but also the underlying technology issues that can impact projects and their delivery.

CONTEXT

So, in order to succeed, each financial firm needs to develop propositions that make sense for clients and which permit the delivery of profit to the shareholders. This usually means finding and delivering a differentiating characteristic to a client. Differentiating characteristics can come from only two sources – finding a new product or service that no-one else has thought of or finding a way to deliver an existing product or service in a way that no-one else can. This can be simplified into a matrix of 'The Four "Ps"':

- Product – product structure is different from others
- Price – it is cheaper
- Place – it is delivered into a market where no-one else is
- Promotion – it is promoted to clients in a different way

Figure 2.1 shows the basic business structure of the financial services community. This may not look familiar because it doesn't reflect the complexity of relationships that exist in the industry. It doesn't need to for the purposes of defining a context for technology.

The structure of financial intermediaries (FIs) is shown as the combination of back, middle and front offices which is increasingly how modern financial services firms are viewing themselves. Links to external connections include all connections, in its broadest sense, to other 'suppliers' in the investment chain. This might include depositories, regulators, counterparties, qualified (and non-qualified) intermediaries, exchanges, market reference data vendors and other agencies – anyone with whom the firm has a relationship, other than a client, and whose objective is to help the firm get its product to its clients.

While pertinent to later discussion, the internal granular structure of the FI below (back, middle and front office) is irrelevant at this stage.

Each box in the triumvirate essentially has input and output, whether that be electronic, paper-based or verbal. In between the input and the output,

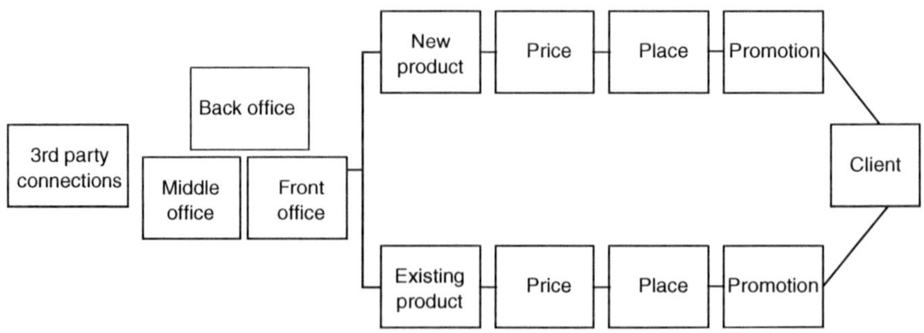

Figure 2.1 Business process model for financial services

Source: Author.

each function must add value in some way to make the delivery of the four Ps effective. That is their one and only function.

It may seem simplistic to be stating this in a book such as this. In order to understand the context of technology, the reader must come out of technological tunnel vision back to basic principles.

We should also be clear that, in the twenty-first century, what constitutes technology is changing. Where we would have separated out the content from the delivery mechanism in the past, now content is an integral part of any technology solution. In fact, when PCs were first invented it was common for people to have no idea of what they could do with the box even after they had it. It was effectively a solution looking for a problem to solve. These days, life is very different. The need to deliver content drives solutions just as much as problems and business issues. It is a different way of looking at business processes that reduces financial services in particular to a giant computer network whose objective is to deliver content from one point to another where that content is in some way enhanced, amended or simply recorded (usually for regulatory purposes).

Figure 2.2 demonstrates a typical model designed to form the basis of a technology solution. Its interesting that there are no lines between any of the

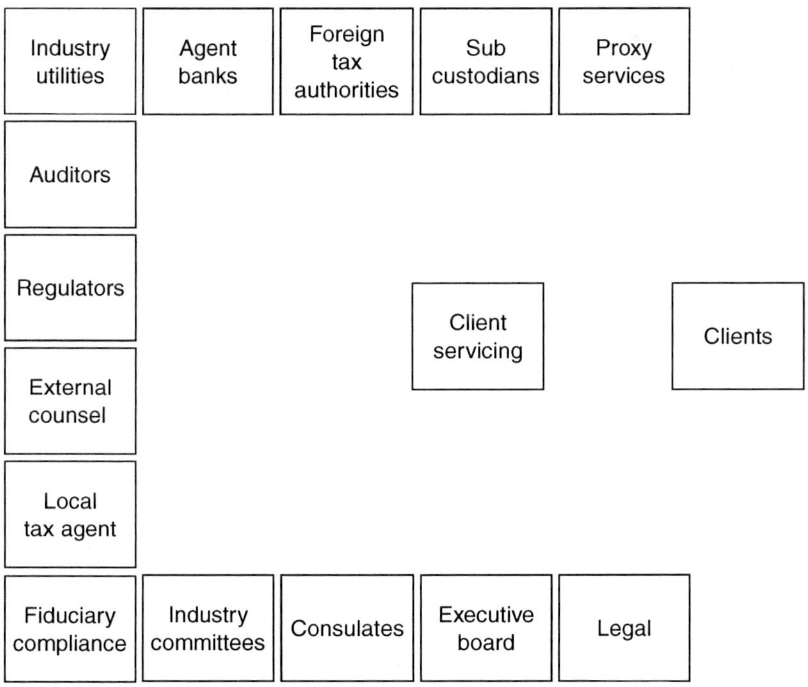

Figure 2.2 Modelling content flows for technology solutions

Source: Author.

boxes at this stage. The positioning of the boxes tells a great deal about the attitude of the firm towards its clients and towards those with whom it has a relationship. One the one hand, this model can evolve positively by reminding us that the client is the key to the whole and the relationship management is the point guard of that principle. Everyone else may have one's own roles and responsibilities but they are ultimately subservient to the survival objective – without that client, none will exist for long. However, and unfortunately much more common, this model is used negatively to define roles and responsibilities that must take place before, or as part of, any service delivery to the client. This latter interpretation leads to inward looking technology solutions.

The model itself is a silo type model but is useful because it allows many overlays to be created. Overlays can reflect different processes within the business, for example tax documentation, where some elements play no part and some are mission-critical. The overlay model can identify both content as well as routing mechanisms which together make up the most modern thinking for such systems.

So, we see that managing technology in a financial services environment is no easy task. It is certainly not as simple as buying software as many more factors and approaches need to be taken into account.

CHAPTER 3

Technology Management Issues

In this chapter we will review not only the basic issues of technology management such as cost, delivery and quality, but also some of the more peripheral issues such as the convergance and geopolitical influences, attention to which can make the difference between good technology management and excellent technology management.

Most people's cosy view of technology is that a department somewhere is responsible for technology and that somehow there's a plan and technology will somehow fit and be a natural evolution of some technology we already have. This is only partly true. Yes, there are departments full of technology professionals, but there's no plan. Managing technology today is mostly about managing change. To manage change effectively we have to consider the basics of resource, cost and benefit, but also some of the more exotic issues that can impact the process.

ADOPTER STANCE

Financial services has historically been, and is still to a large extent, an extremely conservative profession. Financial Services is not typically 'early adopters' of technology. The market in which we work involves people's money and they want to know that we look after it in a sober and controlled fashion. Although this philosophy continues to exist, the time difference between an early adoptive technology and a mature technology is becoming much shorter. The effect is that banks can now appear, if they're not careful, as if they are early adopters, and that can have impacts on their customer's perceptions. Early adopters, by definition, are used to taking more risks; they accept a certain level of pain in order to get at the supposed gain – which could be a more efficient process or just as likely a competitive advantage through having a particular image.

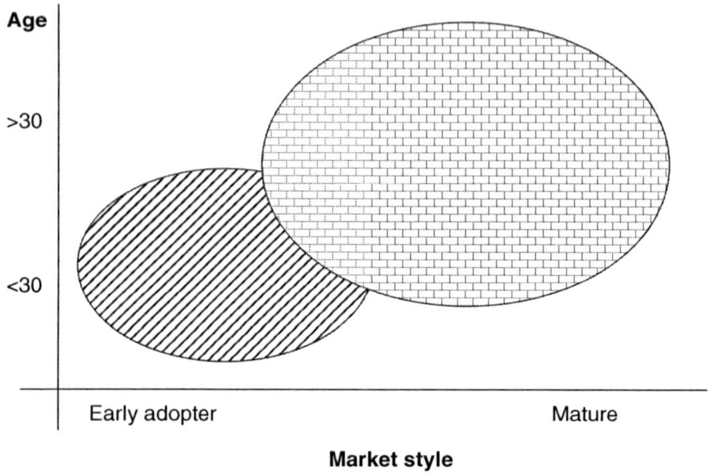

Figure 3.1 Impact of age on adopter stance
Source: Author.

Mature market participants don't have the same characteristics. So banks with 'early adopter' styles tend to have younger customer bases within the retail segment. There is also a similar correlation to market segment. Retail financial services are more aligned to early adopter methodologies while wholesale financial services are more aligned to mature market methodologies and technology. This has major impacts on the types of technology that each is prepared to deploy and hence on the management of deployment. The role of the technology strategist within the firm is therefore to

- Understand the business environment,
- Identify new technologies,
- Understand new technologies,
- Identify how the business can benefit,
- Engage change management and
- Engage process management.

Now the other side of this coin is to look at the levels of technology involved. This will vary depending on the size of the firm. For small retail-oriented financial services firms, the available resources and expertise will be quite different from those of a large wholesale bank. However in both, managers will need to take account of the following (see Figure 3.2):

1. Systems,

2. Servers and

3. Applications.

So, we've now begun to see that managing technology is not just about running a software implementation project. Strategically, we have only just begun. Before we can get to actual implementation we have to understand the style of the organisation both in terms of its customer base, their expectations and the people who work in it. The philosophy and market style of the organisation will determine whether they are early adopters or mature users. That decided, the decision moves on to the resources available. Early adopter or disruptive technologies (see Chapter 12) are generally more expensive. It is also true in the current environment that, particularly in the applications field, technology is more viral in nature. The result is that when planning resources, technology strategists will need to take account of almost logarithmic potential growth, compare with FaceBook. Keeping up with these kinds of growth trends is by no means easy and is often forgotten. For every FaceBook, there were at least ten similar concepts that failed.

GEOPOLITICS

We've talked a lot about 'applications' so far, because that's the most obvious face of technology for many of us, but technology is about much more

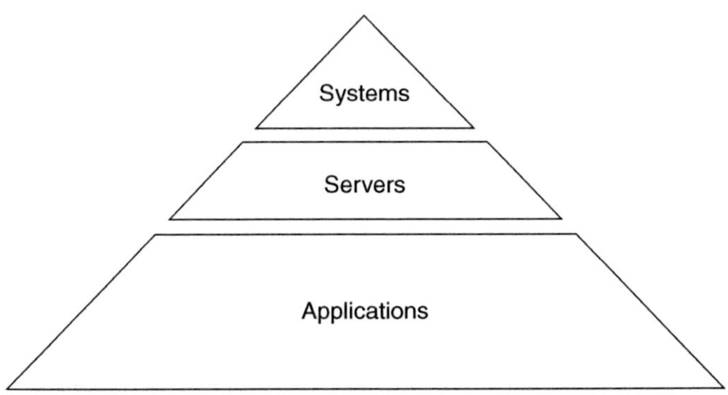

Figure 3.2 Layering of technology

Source: Author.

than that. Servers and Systems are also important. These facets of technology change much more slowly because they don't have the same 'retail' type pressures that applications do and because they are the backbone of what allows the application layer to work. The events of September 11, 2001 give a good example of how event-driven technology decisions are taken. While it wasn't surprising that one of the world's major banks had one of its primary mainframes in one of the twin towers; from where we stand today it is inconceivable that its disaster recovery mainframe was in the other one. In New York today disaster recovery systems must be at least 35 miles away from primary systems. So, geopolitical issues affect how technology is deployed. In the same vein, 'mirroring' of systems has increased significantly since 2001. It is not enough, in the wholesale banking industry, to be able to cut over to a disaster recovery site within 24 hours by switching servers, re-routing communications then bringing yesterday's back-up on line. Our 24 × 365 trading cycles mean that even 24 hours is too long and billions of dollars can be lost in that time. So, in systems and communications, technology projects have focused to a large degree on improving resilience and making disaster recovery almost transparent to users. Naturally, when asking the question 'When should technology be deployed', the answer would be 'Before it is needed' especially in the circumstances described above.

CONVERGENCE

We need also to consider an effect, not mentioned so far – convergence. Convergence is the effect of bringing the way in which technology is accessed into a smaller and smaller number of channels. Yesterday, I could access my bank account using the internet by sitting at my computer. Today I can do the same thing on my mobile phone. In wholesale financial services, document management used to be a manual process and as such was possible with great effort. Now document management systems allow customers, the bank as well as third parties and regulators to access them simultaneously and with strong security. Also in wholesale, the growth of utilities in the form cross-border trading platforms demonstrates convergence. Normally convergence is part of a cyclical effect also known as consolidation. A consolidation cycle will eventually fragment under market pressure. Nevertheless, the consolidation occurs because the market favours lower costs and large competitive organisations can buy up smaller players, keep their brand image and access a greater overall market share. Eventually consolidation breaks down because the niche players' skills don't match the larger organisation's ethos and the boutique or 'souk' mentality reasserts itself. Convergence is different. First convergence has not yet shown any signs of being cyclical in nature. Ever since the first ape used a bone to kill its food, technology has converged with each tool being used to accomplish more than one thing. Second, convergence supports the consolidation/fragmentation cycle while not being a part of it. The impact of convergence on technology management is that it affects the choices available at any one time effectively restricting them. While this may be good for reducing costs, it places much more emphasis on disaster recovery in the back office while cutting off alternative routes to market. The corollary can be seen in the retail banking world with the reduction in branches for many banks in favour of automated teller machines (ATMs) followed by the increase in the use of internet banking. Outside the United States, which is still a cash-focused society, ATMs and branches will increasingly be seen as important but marginal.

CHAPTER 4

Technology Strategy – Best Practice

The best all round phrase I can think of to establish whether any given technological deployment is going to succeed is 'appropriate response'. This term encapsulates many themes. The easy ones are

1. Cost/benefit analysis

2. Testing cycle resilience

3. Redundancy and resilience protection

4. Benchmarking

However, as we've seen, there are 'hidden extras' which bring an adequate strategy to the level of an exemplary or 'best-practice' strategy. These include

1. Geopolitical resilience

2. Regulatory compliance

There may be others. The intent here is not to be exhaustive, especially given the scale and scope of the world's financial services industry, but to point the way and open up new areas of strategic thought.

Cost/Benefit – This is the cost of the deployment outweighed by the benefit. This must be taken in context to short-, medium- and long-term plans. One of the shortcomings of many firms today is the focus on 'short termism'. Results must be immediate or at worst short term; pay-backs in the region of 18 months are common constraints from the business to the technology staff. Such short termism is generally counter-productive, but often technologists have difficulty getting the message across to the business management. My advice to technologists in this area is to learn the language. The greatest difficulty for many technology projects is the lack of mutual understanding or worse, the perception that you do understand the other half of the business. This is most often found in the lack of understanding at C level of any technology detail. Technologists are equally guilty; their insistence on a coded language full of abbreviations does not achieve what it should. What started out as the use of abbreviations, to make otherwise-long complex terms more understandable, breaks down when more than 30% of any sentence is composed of such abbreviations – it becomes a linguistic sub-set in its own right. The result is either that C level staff don't understand the terminology (but are afraid to allow that to be seen) or that technologists use it increasingly to try to maintain an aura of mystique around what they do (purportedly to protect their position and status). If technologists either did not use or explained their terminology better business management would understand the case better, allowing some flow of dialogue between the two regarding the scale of cost/benefit analyses. In particular, technologists should not be afraid of asking senior management to explain how they came to their conclusions about the time-scale of cost/benefit analyses nor the other assumptions underpinning those constraints. C level staff on the business side are equally to blame. Business language has followed the technologists in the use of often confusing or complex terms. So, we end up with two sets of people trying to communicate in different linguistic codes – and that's before we think about layering in the possibility of different real-world languages for the larger multi-country organisations. In the light of this, for the most successful large-scale implementations, consultants, usually viewed as the bane of projects, can be extremely useful as 'interpreters'.

Returning briefly to cost/benefit analyses, the issue is what is the appropriate benefit for the cost concerned and over what period can that benefit be delivered. This is generally not as simple a task as it first looks. In my book *The New Global Regulatory Landscape* for instance I identify 24 sets of global regulations together with the areas in which they overlap from a compliance perspective. Those overlaps can have one of three statuses: destructive, constructive and neutral impact. A destructive overlap between say EU Data Protection Directives and Sarbanes–Oxley means that the nature of the two sets of regulation results in technology solutions that do not have any commonality. So in order to comply with each regulation, separate costs are incurred. Constructive overlaps, as will be obvious, occur when the nature of the overlap allows for both sets of regulation to be complied with from one set of costs. The difficulty is that the benefit from one technology deployment may not become apparent in the same time frame as the benefit from another. So, best practice in the area of cost/benefit analyses is to avoid the tempting idea of simplifying the analysis so that 'even business people can understand it' but to plan out the cost/benefits into short, medium and long term. Figure 4.1 below demonstrates this for a constructive overlap scenario.

The initial high cost is rewarded soon after deployment with a short-term benefit. As time goes by and the deployment 'beds in' the cost to comply with a different set of regulation is reduced and the benefit increases. Finally, in the long term, the benefits of complying with multiple constructive overlap regulatory regimes mean a more integrated system, lower costs and therefore a higher long-term benefit than even the short-term predictions allowed for.

Testing Cycle Resilience – We will return to this theme again and again in this book, particularly in Chapter 14 because it is one of the fundamental technology management issues.

The main differentiator in many technology projects is the degree to which testing is authenticated. For internal builds, the organisation may have control of the testing facility directly (or indirectly if outsourced); however, in most cases, cost constraints or time constraints put in place by the business management create problems for technologists. This usually ends up in a vicious circle when deployments don't work as the business expected because internal testing was not as rigorous as it might be. Similarly however, technologists must be aware that there is no such thing as a perfect system and that testing must be 'appropriate' to the overall need. Business-critical deployments clearly need much stronger testing and retesting than deployments that are neither business- nor time-critical. Outsourcing of technology or buying in a technology that already exists

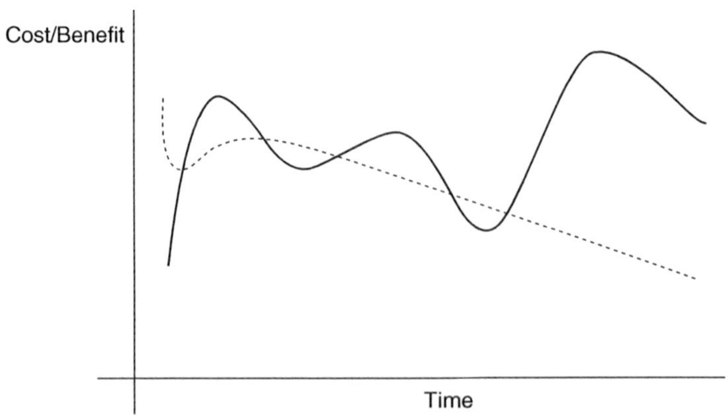

Figure 4.1 Effect of extended planning for cost benefit analyses

Source: Author.

may seem to obviate those issues. However, this is not always the case. As financial services companies continually seek the market advantage and a narrow window in which to exploit it, we must recognise that well over half of the third-party application providers for instance, are relatively small in comparison to their customers. Many do not have strong enough testing and quality assurance (QA) processes if they have them at all. I know of one software company selling to wholesale banks that, for the first ten years of its existence, had absolutely no QA at all. The programmer that wrote the code also tested the code and released it to market. When you use an external supplier for a technology development, while the delivery time may be shortened, the apparent cost reduced and the available 'functionality' increased, the reality is that many of those 'savings' will be lost either though the process of due diligence on their testing facilities or by failures post-contract.

Redundancy and Resilience Protection – It is fascinating to watch financial services firms from a 'high' vantage point. We spoke earlier about the morphology of the industry and its many comparison to biological forms. This might be viewed as a pointless exercise but actually, you can easily map out the large reactions of the industry whether that be to regulatory or technological change, and see how the industry displays most of the chacteristics of the animal kingdom. We react, as an industry, from instinct, not really from any ability to plan long term. All our sociological and political structures are short term, even our governments change every few years with who knows what consequences. As a result, we don't really have a long-term strategic view. The net result is that we have to spend far more than we would expect on resilience and redundancy. Resilience is the ability of a technology deployment to operate as planned, and keep operating. Redundancy is the plan that takes effect if resilience fails. Best practice in managing any technology deployment is to have both issues covered and included in cost analyses.

Benchmarking – In the same way that benchmarking for corporate actions processing has not really existed until relatively recently, benchmarking for best practice in technology management is also woefully absent from our combined agendas. The difficulty is that the issue doesn't really sit completely within any one discipline – management or technology. Technologists focus on whether the deployment meets the required objectives and constraints; for example, whether an application meets its functional specification. Managers focus on whether the deployed solution meets the business requirements of delivery time frame, budget etc. Neither of these add any value to the process of technology management which is strange given that if no attention is given to it, no improvements can be made. As I hope to have demonstrated by the end of this book, attention to the management of technology as a combined discipline can add significant value to a financial services firm over the medium to long term.

As with my very first book, *International Withholding Tax – A Practical Guide to Best Practice & Benchmarking*, I am happy to suggest some basic benchmarks. As those in my earlier work have now become the de facto standards for the industry, I hope that readers will find those provided here a good staring point.

CONFIDENCE

On the retail side of financial services, delivery times are usually much faster because the competitive nature of the market demands us to forever be one step ahead of the competition. The down-side to this is that solutions are usually not really at the 95% confidence limit. The 95% confidence limit is a statistical expression of the readiness of the solution to be deployed. In the case of the Internet for instance it may be the level to which the security protection at the website is strong enough to keep systems secure. At the application level, it may be the proportion of the functionality that has passed testing. This latter may seem strange but most applications today have to be released with a number of both known and unknown bugs. Technicians continue to work on the code to eradicate known bugs and wait for users to find the rest. So managing technology in this environment has more to do with mechanisms which minimise the hassle for the user – by having the main functionality operative, and a reporting-fix-patch cycle that gives users confidence to keep the applications.

The 95% confidence limit is defined in the business specification for the project as a key numeric deliverable. In other words, it is a constraint on the technologists and in particular quality control, not to release the project to its users until it can meet certain expectations. Again, in application delivery this might, for example, be a screen response speed. For the technologists this would translate into systems and server architectures – how fast are the connections over which the application must run; how fast are the processors as well as how the application itself is structured. If it is a database for instance, the way in which tables are structured can affect performance in indexing and access. Any one of these or a combination can cause a failure in quality assurance and resultant overrun on either budget or time frame of both. Business people can only articulate in resultants; hence common 95% confidence statements such as 'sub-second response time required'. Of course, any business person is going to come up with end-point suggestions 'I want instant response'. It's the job of the technologists and in particular the project manager to evaluate and communicate the balance between what the business wants and what the cost is. The result on the retail side is a methodology known as the domino effect. This occurs when a solution does not meet the 95% confidence limit and is released anyway. The solution does not immediately fail; nor does it fail catastrophically, but it does fail just enough to tip the project into a reactive stance. Proactive stances are commonplace in most technology developments in financial services. Software versioning is a typical example. This allows the technologists to indicate that the product has more developments or improvements to come which will be delivered as different versions. Reactive stances are unfortunately just as common. These show up as 'un-foreseen' failures that result in technologists having to 'shoe-horn' new releases into a series of releases as 'bug fixes' or 'patches'. In non-application level developments these may evidence themselves as changing suppliers (because connectivity resources failed) or non-standard 'testing' and 'roll back' of servers out of the normal sequence. All tip the next domino, putting the standard development methodology onto a knife-edge of always trying to catch up. Resources that were well planned to deal with a strong development are now not enough to deal with the domino effect with everyone running around trying to fix things and get ahead of the curve at the same time.

So, best practice is primarily about communication. Unfortunately the two parties concerned rarely speak the same language and need interpreters, more commonly known as project managers.

Best practice, almost by definition, requires benchmarking. As we've seen earlier in this chapter however, best practice is not always something that easily lends itself to the numeric side of benchmarking.

CHAPTER 5

Front, Middle and Back Office Explained

So far, the discussion in this book has been a fairly high-level overview of technological concepts in the financial services industry. Now, in order to contextualise the issue and really dig into discussing the benefits of managing and implementing technology, we will focus on what have traditionally been the three basic divisions of a financial services company and how technology plays a role in the way each of these areas functions. The terms front, middle and back office have traditionally been used to describe how assets are managed from end to end within the financial services community. Traditionally because, these days, in the age of outsourcing and 'best-of-breed' suppliers, the front, middle and back offices may in fact all belong to different organisations.

The front office is commonly used to describe the client-facing side of a financial services firm. The relationship managers or sales people are included in this group as are typically the executive personnel and corporate finance. Also, the asset management and trading functions of an organisation are the front office. In other words, the front office is (or should be) a profit centre of an organisation. Functions of the front office will include things happening in the pre-trade environment right up to the time when the trade is executed. This will also include things like pre-trade analytics and research and will generally be the point of contact for all things up to the point of pre-settlement. Technology often used in the front office environment will include things like the client-facing technology of the websites managed by the company whether corporate or client-only interfaces for trading and self-directed research. In a study published by Technology Partners International (TPI) in 2006, they estimate that 90% of US-managed assets and 95% of mutual funds use third-party service providers for custody services. What that really means is that economies of scale do work here. For many small and mid-sized organisations, it is far more efficient to outsource the post-trade processing and corporate functions out of a firm's area of responsibility, if having it done somewhere else will reduce both cost and liability as well as provide a better, more efficient service for our clients.

Of the three basic areas, the middle office is probably the most recently developed. In the beginning of modern financial services, front office functions included (much like today) trading, research and sales and administration. The back office was essentially everything else. Since the advent and implementation of technology in the financial services community, the middle office has sprung up as the place where pre-settlement activity now takes place. As the role of technology in the world of financial services has grown, the middle office has been taking an increasingly larger role in the processing of securities and the financial services firm's overall operations as well as managing the implementation of technology across the whole organisation.

I mentioned above, that the middle office is involved in pre-settlement activity. But what does that mean? Pre-settlement activity includes tasks such as risk management, profit/loss calculations and netting as well as decisions regarding and implementation of IT resources in all three (front, middle and back) segments of the firm. This is because the one in the middle of the flow, hence called the middle office, is the department with the best overall view of how the different systems and technologies will interact with each other and the segment that best understands the needs of the other departments. The middle office's job has really become preparing the information flow for the back office and the life cycle of the security through settlement and post-settlement processing activities. The middle office is also most often where the risk management personnel and systems are located. This is where the responsibility lies to advise the executive leadership and the front office that overly aggressive behaviour in search of profits needs to be intelligently balanced and managed. It is also where risk is managed for the post-trade settlement process. More and more, the middle office are the people who ensure that the back office has the necessary tools and mechanisms in place to deal with the increasingly complex nature of the securities being sold and processed at the speed demanded by the firm's clients and the competitive environment in which these firms are operating. One of the primary ways to accomplish this is by allocating resources, specifically, to enable the required speed and efficiency for back-office processing. Another way in which this is done is by ensuring that the firm is in a position, based on the way that the three areas operate, to implement not only technology for efficiency but that the process is flexible and scalable enough so that if one or multiple pieces of the process can or should be outsourced, they can be with minimal disruption to the rest of the organisation.

The back office is the area where settlement occurs and all post-settlement activity is managed. This is the area, traditionally, where outsourcing has been most prevalent. The back office carries out activities like settlements, clearances, record maintenance, entitlements calculations, income processing, regulatory compliance and accounting. One of the back office's ongoing struggles is the chore of keeping up with what the front office is doing. As financial services firms continue to create, sell, service and manage increasingly complex financial instruments, for example derivatives, the back office is often playing 'catch up' once these instruments have been issued and sold. This is because, they are the ones responsible for managing the asset and subsequently processing any corporate action having to do with that security. In the next few pages, we will examine in more detail how these three areas of a financial services firm work together to satisfy the needs of their customers and how they continue to work towards a fully Straight Through Processing (STP) environment for the processing of corporate actions for securities.

The landscape in the United States changed in the late 1990s. Earlier, investment legislation, dating back to the wake of the stock market crash in 1929, distinguished banks from investment banks and insurance companies with regard to who could do what. Almost 65 years of established law ended in 1998 shortly after Citicorp and Travelers merged creating Citigroup. This was the beginning of a convergence model in the US market that has had wide-ranging implications. One such impact has been the adoption and common use of the term 'financial services' to describe the US (and latterly global) banking and investment industries. Some will argue that this was a necessary evolution given the global nature of the banking and investment industries today and that the United States had to adjust their laws in order to remain competitive in the modern era. The historic distinction of banks versus investment companies was due to the Glass–Steagall Act, passed in 1933 during the Great Depression. Officially named the Banking Act of 1933, the legislation introduced the separation of banks according to their business type (commercial or investment banking). In 1999, the Gramm–Leach–Bliley Act was enacted, which repealed the Glass–Steagall Act of 1933. One impact of this repeal is that certain advisory activities of the banks are now regulated by the Investment Act of 1940. It also enabled investment and insurance firms like Travelers (which owned the investment firm Salomon Smith Barney) to combine their operations with traditional commercial and retail banks like that of Citicorp. This merger was just the beginning. While there are other examples of firms from either side of the industry combining, the merger of Citicorp and Travelers was the first and remains one of the high-profile mergers. The trend continued with other banks either merging with, or building their own investment and trading businesses, and traditional investment firms either combining with, or starting their own banks. This activity has ushered in an era of combined, one-stop shops for 'financial services'. This began, in the United States, a dichotomic trend in which there was on the one side a creation of financial supermarkets and on the other side, particularly for the smaller firms, a growth in the trend of outsourcing the back office.

The trend of convergence which began with the Citicorp Travelers merger, while spurring tremendous development in the financial services industry has also served to create many challenges for the financial services industry. By removing the limitations of banks, insurance companies, investment banks, private banks, custody banks, commercial banks and brokers on their operations, the landscape has become more complex. At SWIFT's annual SIBOS conference in Boston in 2007, Michael Clark, then Executive Vice President-CEO of Global Security Services of JP Morgan Chase, said that the term custodians or global custodians doesn't really describe the function of what they do anymore and suggested that a more accurate designation would be to call them, 'global asset servicers'. Mr Clark was on the panel at the Securities plenary session and during the discussion suggested that there are many 'elements of change' which are driving the direction of the way the front, middle and back offices interact with each other. These elements include global investment and trade, new product development and the increasing complexity of investment instruments. Mr Clark described the need for real-time pricing and processing, and competitive pricing by the asset servicers necessitates the need for scale to provide a comprehensive, compliant and efficient middle and back office. He was joined on the panel by Jay Hooley, Vice Chairman and Head of Global Securities servicing at State Street who cited an article from the *Economist* entitled, 'Is the middle office, the new back office', the premise of which was to discuss how the traditionally back-office functions of settlement and clearing, as well as the processing of post-trade corporate actions like proxy voting and claims processing, were the areas most likely to be outsourced. Now that is being mirrored in the middle office environment of risk management, pre-settlement activity like netting and IT implementation as these functions are more and more being handled by outside technology and other service providers.

The difference from the current landscape is that, the spending Mr Hooley advocates on 'client-facing technology' will also serve to assist the middle and back office in processing. To remain competitive, the technology will need to be able to extract data from both the middle and back office in order to accurately report information to customers and will be judged on various benchmarks within the post-trade arena and those processes having to do with managing the flow of corporate actions and other asset servicing activities.

Another change in the landscape has been the rise of the alternative investment space. This has led to the creation of more new instruments and ways to trade than any thing since the mutual fund boom of several decades ago. Given the success that this group has had overall, they possess the resources necessary to stay on the cutting edge with regard to order management systems and the like, and since they must continue to innovate in order to remain competitive, IT spending in the front office will continue to outpace that of the middle and back offices.

Many smaller firms have been outsourcing the back-office functions for many years due to the economies of scale in that arena. Given the relative maturity of outsourcing in back-office functions for somewhat commoditised services such as custody, fund accounting, fund administration and transfer agency activity, and the fact that by definition, you are your front office as that is how a company derives revenue and profit, what is to become of the middle office?

One result of front-office spending and investment in IT outpacing that of the middle and back offices is that financial services firms are often stuck with legacy middle- and back-office processing systems that do not communicate with each other. With the innovation in new financial products and the different ways that the front office is developing to interact with the market and drive revenue, middle and back offices are often not aware of new developments on the client-facing side of the business. It is then difficult to deal with potential issues that exist in processing increasingly complex instruments. Clearly, this makes processing of trades and other corporate actions difficult and often leads to breaks in the process, necessitating manual intervention at different points which subsequently can become a drag on costs. The costs here are not only because of the labour costs relative to employing a person to perform a task rather than a machine but also because the likelihood of transcription errors increases whenever processing corporate actions in which manual intervention is necessary. Even more troublesome can be the fact that because a manual process exists within the corporate action lifecycle, certain segments of data are not reported in the same manner as other sets of data. For example, a global custodian receives dividend information regarding a particular security held by multiple clients who are residents in different domiciles and are also various types of beneficial owners (pensions, corporations, individuals, etc.). The various clients are entitled to multiple rates of taxation on this dividend, typically the statutory rate, favourable (treaty) rate or full exemption from tax. One rate, usually the most prevalent, is passed through into the back-office reporting system. The other rates, due to limitations of the system have to be input manually. In addition to transcription errors this can cause reporting errors as entire segments of this data may fail to be reported to the tax department, which calculates and arranges to file reclaims. Many of these issues can be attributed to the limitations of the technology of the middle and back office. Continued pressure on dealer margins through the demand for lower costs in the middle- and back-office settlement process have also contributed to the present state of affairs. Again, this is why the issue of scale in the realm of asset servicing is not going to go away. Another reason that this issue is not likely to go away is also suggested by Mr Clark, when he said, 'don't underestimate the power of client-facing technology'. He continued to discuss that asset servicers should endeavour to, 'streamline the customer/client interface'. In essence, he seemed to endorse an environment in which the front office spending on IT will continue to outpace that of the middle and back office while advocating improved end-to-end communication flows in the asset servicing life cycle.

The problem described in the preceding paragraph might have been avoided with a comprehensive and scalable system – something I will note is rare to find within the major global custodians (or asset servicers) because they have grown in part through acquisition. The acquisitive growth model often creates an awkward environment because again the legacy systems do not mesh in anything resembling an elegant or even harmonious structure. This is one reason for the recent success of the Application Service Provider (ASP) model reflecting growing demand within the financial community, in part, because of the advantages an ASP system has, such as accessibility, speed, flexibility and reduced cost for the user. Cost is the critical issue for most users who are more and more inclined towards software leasing because of the expense level associated with a firm going out and buying or building their own unique system. It's important to note that when we talk about cost, it is not just the upfront cost of implementing a software solution whether it is buy, build or lease. The real cost is only realised over time as it relates to system and IT maintenance as well as the cost associated with having a unique system. Simply put, the financial services community does not operate in a vacuum. Virtually all major players interact regularly with a multitude of counterparties on a wide range of transactions and must be able to communicate effectively. Subsequently, if a financial firm builds their own system based on their daily routine and communications today, it will be outdated and unable to cope with the new developments and changes of tomorrow. This is because no matter what the developments or new products and services are, change is inevitable. So, in terms of cost, particularly for small and mid-size firms, but for large also, it is often better to have the software managed by an outside, semi-neutral party who can view the industry from a vantage point so that they can take into account the needs and direction of multiple customers. When they are developing their solutions, all of their clients will benefit from the cumulative experiences of the other clients.

In other words, there is a clear need for standards. Standard message types greatly diminish the chance for miscommunication and errors. When we talk about cost, there are several issues – buying or building your own systems and IT infrastructure, labour costs and errors. Errors account for a significant percentage of unforeseen costs to firms every year and it would seem that of the costs listed here, the error rate is the one where a proactive effort is likely to add benefit and reduce cost. It is for this reason that several firms now offer a comprehensive IT solution from the outset. ASP providers are now offering to manage all technology from the front office all the way through the processes managed by the middle office and manage the data flow in such a way that the back office is getting a uniform and complete (standardised) set of files from which to manage their processes. These systems do not yet manage all processes in the back office because some of the tasks sitting in the back office environment are not yet automatable. However, there is movement towards a comprehensive solution here too. Another trend which ASP providers are moving towards is signing with partners who are themselves 'best-of-breed' outsourcing providers for complex corporate actions. This model then allows for the back office to offload complex manual tasks to a specialist who will manage the process more efficiently from both a cost and risk perspective. All the while, the user remains involved and in control of the process as they are the users of the ASP system. The major advantage of this model is that users are free to focus on their business and only have to deal with a single interface for all their services.

For smaller institutions, and others who have real weakness in the back office segment of their operations, they might consider a Business Services Provider (BSP) with which to begin a relationship. This way, rather than the ASP model the institution completely outsources their investment and trust operations and implements the BSP's solutions as a whole. These banks rely on the provider's investment processing technology and entrust them with the actual management and processing of client transactions – often called the 'back-office' operations. By relying on the provider's expertise, these banks and trust institutions can reduce risk and achieve operational efficiencies, thereby improving the quality of services. This will also generally lead to a reasonable reduction in head count of back-office personnel, because most of their jobs will have been outsourced to the BSP. Labour costs being what they are, this again goes back to the issue of reducing cost. So, the benefits are operational efficiency, reduction of risk, reduced labour cost and a presumably scalable environment in which the user of the BSP is free to go out to innovate and generate new business with confidence that the solutions to deliver are in place. It is important not to underestimate the value of reducing risk within the process. As security types become ever more complex, trading volume increases and total value within the markets continues to rise, the importance of risk management rises too. One mistake in processing, settlement, classification of security, a break in the processing, miscalculation of entitlement, missing an election for mandatory and optional events and failing to file entitlement claims (i.e., tax and class actions) can be extremely costly. The benefit for an institution that isn't able or doesn't want to manage these processes themselves is that they can outsource them. Then, you have to pick the right provider. The same principles apply to picking a provider as they do to picking a system. Scalable and comprehensive are the keys to a successful relationship with a BSP; and also some flexibility in pricing, logically based on the volume and relative complexity of the work involved. Most firms should opt for variable pricing as it will give incentive for the BSP to provide better service knowing that since they are managing your technology and providing a majority of the back office support, the better you (their client) perform the more business there will be.

For smaller firms and arguably some mid-size firms, the BSP model is catching on. Given the operational efficiencies to be found in the back office from volumes, it is much more efficient for a small firm to send that portion of the work out. When it comes to larger firms, there seems to be a bit more reluctance towards this comprehensive, BSP-type solution. This is particularly true of the bulge-bracket firms. The members of the Association of Global Custodians, the top ten investment banks largely, are not interested in outsourcing their processing, in part, because they already take advantage of operational efficiencies given the size of their own operation. However, this one benefit of being big and doing it yourself is often used to justify the traditional inclination towards building rather than buying. The view is that, 'I know my business better than anyone else, so I can build the best system'. Although intimate knowledge of one's business is certainly important when implementing IT to improve efficiencies within it, often an outside eye which may take the customer's, a counter party's and even a regulator's view is likely to provide insights that prove to be just as valuable to the system being built as the business owner's. The most dangerous thing a large firm with a 'not built here' complex can do is to fail to consult with outside sources of knowledge. This is not to say that one of the institutions that belong to the groups listed above is not capable of building its own systems; it is just caution that never should they be so arrogant in their development process that they fail to consult with others who have the ability to provide advice and insight. For these types of firms, which in part have grown through acquisition, the issue isn't limited to reaching outside for a better view of the process; it is also that they are literally stuck with multiple legacy systems. Major custodians and investment banks often are running on one platform for New York, a different one for London, sometimes a different system still for individual branches and even multiple platforms in the same physical location due to a merger at some point in the past. The sad thing about this is that very often, the merger didn't take place last week, last month or even last year. In several examples I can think of, which will remain nameless to protect the innocent, the mergers which gave rise to multiple platforms within an institution occurred over a decade ago. Does this mean that in the last 10 or so years a solution hasn't been devised to flatten the back-office process, that most if not all organisations would greatly benefit from the reduction in cost and economies of scale from using one standard system across an organisation? The answer, of course is, Yes!

The issue at hand is finding or building and implementing a system which will support an ever-growing range of securities with comprehensive reference data, unique and illiquid transaction types, regulated and industry-standard accounting calculations and process automation which streamlines the management of complex instruments, and this should be the goal for any and especially a large global alternative investment manager. Probably the most important issue when building or selecting such a system is: Is it scalable? If the answer is 'no,' keep looking. Because if you don't, you will find yourself at some point in the not too distant future, looking at another solution to either replace or to patch the system you have. In this context, scalable also means able to take an input from a legacy system so that the processing, at least going forward, can be migrated from legacy to a comprehensive enterprise-wide solution.

The difference here, given the continued change in the financial world, are the types of financial products now available for trade which must subsequently be settled and serviced. Many of these are rather esoteric further complicating the process. For example, prior to the advent of fully scalable multi-currency platforms, accounting for different currencies within the same portfolio was a complex chore requiring a patchwork of systems and manual data transfer, which slowed the process and increased the risk of error. Global hedge funds operate in many currencies and their strategies also involve a wide variety of equity, fixed-income instruments, derivatives and Special Investment Vehicles (SIVs). These firms invest in a myriad of currencies and instruments, often through multiple brokers. As such, they require an accounting system with the ability to manage the complexities of global hedge funds 24/7. Managers need systems which allow for comprehensive instrument coverage and true multi-currency processing, not to mention, streamlined and accurate reconciliation between fund managers and their brokers. Real-time multi-currency processing on a single scalable framework means that global investment management companies can reap the benefits of using a comprehensive portfolio management and fund accounting solution to support their global operations, administrative and accounting services to the alternative investment industry.

Another issue rising from the growth of the alternative investment industry is that traditional custody also often doesn't work for these types of funds as they have different needs. Primary among these is a need for leverage. Since the traditional custodians as banks are not able to provide the level of service required in this area, the business has been managed by the prime brokers at the larger brokerage firms. However, the prime brokers are not used to providing many traditional custody services. This often catches the clients unaware and they then must scramble to put a solution into place because it is something that they just assumed the prime broker would take care of as the custodian. In particular, there are some corporate actions where the prime broker is either unwilling or unable to provide services. Typically in the US market these will be corporate actions where proof of beneficial ownership is required. Due to confidentiality issues that fund managers must contend with and the fact that the funds are most often organised as partnerships, the necessary limited partner beneficial owner information cannot be transmitted to the prime broker necessitating that the fund manager implement alternative solutions.

Implementing alternate solutions as you may have gathered by now is not necessarily as simple as picking up the phone book and searching under back office support. Given the issues that hedge funds have with regard to services not provided by their prime brokers, in order to ensure successful operations, they need to address two primary issues. First, make sure that your financial institutions have a way in which to extract standard trading, settlement and corporate actions data from their system and deliver it in a flexible format. Due to the variations in data with each corporate action, even with 65 standard ISO messages for specific corporate actions a sizable portion of the announcements passed this way contain a narrative field with instructions unique to a particular event. The point is, you want the group or system receiving the data to immediately know what to do with it and not have to spend time with queries so that they can get on with processing the event. Second, the fund manager's documentation and client (partner) communications process must be robust enough to support the gathering of additional documents. Gathering additional documents may be necessary as they may not be held all in one central location as with a traditional custodian. The fund manager may have some, a third-party administrator may hold some and other data will need to be gathered from the prime broker. In order to better service their clients, some of the major prime brokers now have a business services (also called client services) unit which is there to help the fund manager find appropriate solutions and service providers for value added services that the prime broker does not provide. These can be administrators, claims specialists, software vendors and even concierge services – essentially, the prime broker in the context of the business services unit fills the role of the middle office.

As we've discussed, there are certain activities which the back office has where there is simply no way to automate the process. One of these is client documentation and how original documents are collected from clients, stored, retrieved (or generated) and distributed when necessary. Quite simply, paper and STP are diametrically opposed. So, given these tasks having to do with clients' beneficial owner documentation, the question becomes, who is responsible for what? Document management is a critical area to get right if your organisation is going to fulfil fiduciary responsibility to clients by managing the documentation effectively so that proper asset servicing can occur. For some global custodians the account manager is the person responsible for managing the client's documentation requests both from the bank for account opening and management procedures and from external sources; regulators, claims and proxy administrators, tax consultants, legal counsel and others. For all of this to sit with the account manager is probably not the best use of them as a resource. A better model would be one which leverages technology to minimise the intervention necessary at the account manager level. This way, the various parties who will need access to the documents from time to time will be; registered as users of the system, given a login ID and have rights assigned based on what the individual user's needs are to properly service the client. A claims administrator for instance will have different needs than a proxy administrator. Logically, the system will also have a user interface for the client so that they too can have access to the documents that they may need for their own records. A truly proactive and comprehensive system will include features which assist clients in managing process of renewing any documentation requiring update. This will in turn free the account manager up to manage more accounts more effectively than before. As with many other things, if everyone is looking at the same screen then the process becomes much easier and more efficient to manage.

It is certain that back, front and middle offices have much to coordinate, not least technologically. Their different perspectives create different needs in the management functions.

CHAPTER 6

Communications, Standards and Messaging

One of the most visible signs of technology deployment in financial services is the way in which interconnectivity has thrived in the last few years. Communications have improved both in quality and volume both on the retail and wholesale sides of the industry. In retail, mobile telephony is forming the core of convergence for many banks with television, once the expected winner, being a poor third. In wholesale, the industry cooperative Society for Worldwide Interbank Financial Telecommunications (SWIFT) continues to dominate although few recognise its multiple roles in the industry, and its foothold in the US geographically and in funds from a market perspective are still embryonic.

Information is key, but to be more accurate information sharing is key. Today's banking world relies on information being shared in ways that were never imagined even five years ago.

I have already mentioned SWIFT. The Society for Worldwide Interbank Financial Telecommunications has two functions in the financial services world both on the retail and wholesale side. First it is appointed by the International Standards Organisation (ISO) to be responsible for standards setting and management. Second in its capacity as an industry-owned cooperative, it also operates a unique computer network between its members, all of whom are financial institutions. The combination of guardian of standards and provider of message routing places SWIFT in a very powerful position.

Virtually any major technology deployment tioday will need to take advantage and note of standardisation of messaging. In the wholesale area, most banks are now following ISO15022, the previous standard being ISO7775. However, the process of continual improvement goes on and even now, ISO20022 is being engineered and messages and processes worked on by industry members. There are several issues to take note of here.

First, and rather ironically, the technologists have to take into account not only the standards in place at any one time, but also the development of future standards, thereby increasing potential costs. But of course, at the same time, those standards themselves are changing and being managed. This may sound difficult enough, but the word standard itself may be giving a false sense of security to the business managers involved.

The issue is that, even when a standard is issued, and even when there is general agreement of the specification and use of messaging, the reality is that there is enough leeway and enough pressure from within to make the delivery of a real standard almost impossible. Take an example. In securities processing there is a suite of messages called corporate actions messages. They are designed within ISO15022; the detail of how messages in this suite are configured, laid out and sent between counterparties is laid down in a 'Standards Release'. Essentially, any institution sending messages should conform to these standards and layouts. The reason for the standards is to enable cost reductions and efficiency improvements (often referred to as Straight Through Processing or STP) by having 'certainty' that the data in a message can be interpreted at the receiving party in a way that enables that data to be translated straight into electronic systems. Yet, when canvassed, it becomes clear that, even with the standard published and in place, there are up to a hundred different variants of any given message being used at any one time. Some of these variants, but importantly not all, are dealt with by having sub-groupings of SWIFT members where the individual variations are serparately codified between the correspondents so that they can gain their own particular benefits from the standardisation while still, presumably, being able to compete in terms of service delivery. These groups – Message User Groups (MUGs) and Closed User Groups (CUGs) – do allow for the system to work to an extent. Part of the reason this can happen is the level of validation being performed on behalf of the sender and recipient by SWIFT.

I would argue that the minor benefits gained by having multiple variants of interpretation of a standard would be far outweighed by the cost reductions if all the members agreed to a much higher level of consistency (and thus reduction in variations) in their message formats. Variants, if they do exist for rational business purposes, should be codifiable into the normal cycle of standards development.

This does serve to highlight that both technologists and business managers must have sufficient knowledge of both the theory and the practice to be able to make intelligent decisions.

Of course communication need not be interpreted simply as messaging. Nor is SWIFT the only player in that arena. BT Radianz also provides network connectivity and several of the larger trade and settlement support utilities have their own proprietary systems to support their members.

Certainly the Internet has provided the opportunity for increased resilience and redundancy in communications. There are effectively a plethora of ways to get information from point A to point B including

- Manual (paper)
- Fax
- Email
- Ftp
- Virtual Private Network (VPN)
- SWIFT

And so on.

Its worth highlighting that in SWIFT's management of the change between ISO15022 and ISO20022, one of the key changes is the ability for institutions, or groups of institutions, to sponsor a business process. So where individual messages were agreed between members in ISO15022, now a group can identify and sponsor a complete business process. That process might include existing messages and also define new messages, the aggregate of which forms the process. The copyright in the business process belongs to the firms sponsoring the process although part of the arrangement with SWIFT is that as soon as a process is approved under ISO20022, the licensor (the sponsoring group) provides a free unlimited license to all other SWIFT members to use and access that business process.

While this is a good thing, in that it brings the business level of thinking into the management of what is otherwise an excruciatingly detailed technical exposition, it naturally stifles an otherwise competitive market. Why would I, having identified a unique application of standards, messaging and data, that could give my company a market and financial advantage, immediately give that advantage away to my competitors. At the annual symposium of SWIFT members, the reason most often heard is that it is all about collaboration for the common good. This would be believable if everyone were implementing their standards consistently, but we already know that they are not. So, to deny the natural instincts of competitive firms seems to me to be counter-productive. It would be more logical to allow processes to be designed and sponsored by groups with an interest in doing so and for subsequent licensing to be at a cost determined by SWIFT under generally accepted guidelines – one of which would be a stronger element of network validation. In this scenario, there would be far more appetite for firms to find and develop new and better ways to do business as they could gain the benefit directly from having invested in the process improvement within their organisations and also get paid royalties (or deductions from traffic fees) by SWIFT for having assisted in a general improvement.

This highlights one of the issues in managing technology today. The cost of improving a process or deploying a technology is very often hidden, with specific aspects overlooked. Combined with a very high absolute cost anyway, returns on investment that are marginal to the business can often be material to the considerations at board level.

I mentioned earlier that SWIFT is a cooperative and that messages pass between members who are all financial institutions. This, rather closed loop view is not strictly accurate for our purposes here. There are many software vendors, outsource agents, governmental authorities, auditors and so on that have an interest in the way that communications are structured and how they are sent between parties. Managing this large-scale technology platform is a major factor in most financial services firm's planning. Rather like outsourcing a business function to a third party, the cooperative assures, within limitations, that business planners can assume certain things about their technology platforms with some degree of safety. Unfortunately, again because of a widely held belief, this can cause problems.

By way of introduction to this issue, SWIFT's network is guaranteed to be secure through a strong process of authentication, currently using hardware and password 'keys'. This means that a message can be created at one point but only sent to another destination on the network if the 'keys' for sender and destination have been swapped by authorised parties at each firm – so called Bilateral Key Exchange or BKE. While in transit, SWIFT performs no other role than (i) perform limited validation of certain fields within each message and (ii) ensure that what leaves point A arrives at point B without anyone being able to access the message contents en-route. This would be a major factor in any business-level consideration of a technology deployment.

In 2007, following concerns expressed by the US security industry (in this case security as in safety rather than equity) SWIFT granted access to message contents to support the US investigations into terrorist activities. This caused uproar in the community not least because of the long-term implications for security of banking information and the limitations this puts on data protection principles.

Messaging electronically in financial services creates an opportunity for any firm to generate a business advantage by automating processes and removing the manual, error-prone, costly elements represented by humans. So, it would come as some surprise to those outside the industry that all the efforts to automate a chain of activity between multiple counterparties, can be stopped and started within the chain by human intervention caused by outdated approaches to security. For instance, if a bank receives a message from a data provider that a dividend is about to be announced (MT564), the recipient can easily automate that process so that the implications of the event are automatically flowed through the business. For example, if the dividend is not domestic, systems will take the data from the message and automatically calculate whether any of its customers are impacted in terms of taxation of the dividend and if so, spin off a separate process to recover some of that tax. When the dividend is actually paid (MT566) however, the typical scenario is that the message is first printed out, then sent for approval, presumably because it involves the transfer of funds. Once approved, an entirely new message is created, manually (no cut and paste) and then sent out to the recipient. It does not take much analysis to figure out that while the existence of the standards and message layouts works to give the opportunity for reduced costs and reduced risks, the manual processes still in-built into management systems and thinking eradicate any cost reduction or risk mitigation.

So, apart from the fact that members can vary the content and layout of messages away from the envisioned standard; apart from the fact that management of new processes does not necessarily allow for a freely competitive market or reward the developers adequately; apart from the fact that absolute security of the message contents is assumed (but can't really be delivered) and apart from the fact that a supposedly STP-system exists that starts and stops through manual intervention, it's a pivotal system that cannot fail.

This is not meant to be critical of SWIFT. By no means. For any organisation which essentially is a grouping of competitors, developments in standards and message processing are always going to have some level of compromise and the world is not perfect. The examples above were cited to highlight, in the context of the subject matter of the book, that even when you have many thousands of people all looking to achieve the same objective with the same tools, it is not easy. SWIFT does a great job and should be congratulated for what it has achieved. Is there room for improvement?; yes, of course. But readers of this book will be concerned to understand the opportunities and limitations inherent in messaging and standards and to apply those into the management of their own projects.

Of course, one of the key lessons of this book is that you can't take any one chapter in isolation. Messaging is an element within automation standards and should apply across the board and many of the issues here could be mitigated or processes made more efficient depending on whether the technology deployment is built, bought or outsourced (Chapters 8–11). If a technology deployment is designed to be disruptive as a competitive advance or is a reaction to a disruptive technology then this will have an impact on other areas (Chapter 12). Overarching all of these are of course the issues of budget planning and testing (Chapters 13 and 14).

So at this point, it would be useful to look at the concepts discussed already, to see what the practical effects are of a technology deployment in the twenty-first century. We will outline, with the permission of GlobeTax Services Inc., a US-based services provider of withholding tax solutions, a semi-disruptive technology which uses messaging and standards as its platform. The key creative issues in this implementation were the way in which existing technology was harnessed in conjunction with a new paradigm, to create a way of delivering a technology solution that was (and is) both elegant and cost effective.

The solution is targeted at wholesale banking in the custody sector where there are corporate action events that are created as a result of a corporate (issuer of shares) declaring an event (typically in this case, a dividend). As custodian banks manage the assets of their customers, they are significantly impacted by any dividend distribution where the recipient or 'beneficial owner' is resident in a country different from that in which the income was received. This is because both the issuing country and the receiving country will try to tax the income. Double tax treaties between pairs of countries allow for a recipient to be entitled to recover tax that is essentially over-withheld by the issuing country, but the procedures and processes by which the recipient's custodian is able to do this are both complex and expensive because they are essentially manual. So this case study looks at how GlobeTax, with a processing solution, SWIFT with standards and network routing and one of the largest custodians collaborated to create a new paradigm.

This new paradigm is important for two reasons. First, it is new and it is probably one of the most important technology management projects undertaken this century. Its ramifications flow well beyond the particular project which kicked it off. Many back-office financial services processes have a manual element which mitigates against the perfect solution of straight through processing (STP). The unique way in which GlobeTax collaborated with industry participants is a good benchmark for others interested in the latest model for technology management in financial services.

Case Study 2 V-STP – a lesson in corporate actions automation

Background

As of January 2008 there were over US$100 trillion of assets under custody worldwide. Of these US$30 trillion were held cross-border, that is, the beneficial owner of the asset was resident in a country different from the country where the asset was issued. The growth in cross-border asset values is currently growing at just over 16% a year. With over 500,000 dividend events each year, there is an extant tax amount that is, the amount of tax to which beneficial owners can claim an entitlement under Double Tax Treaties either as 'relief at source' or as a remedial claim of just over US$1 trillion. Of this, less than 7% ever reaches those who have the entitlement either because no claim is filed at all or because the claim is filed late. This establishes the scale of the need that customers of financial intermediaries have.

SWIFT has over 8,200 member institutions and processes around two billion messages a year. Only 2% of those messages relate to corporate action events, of which dividends form a part even though there are ISO15022 messages defined and designed to support corporate actions messaging.

Figure 6.1 graphically demonstrates the technology management issue. All the boxes which are shaded and all the lines which are dashed

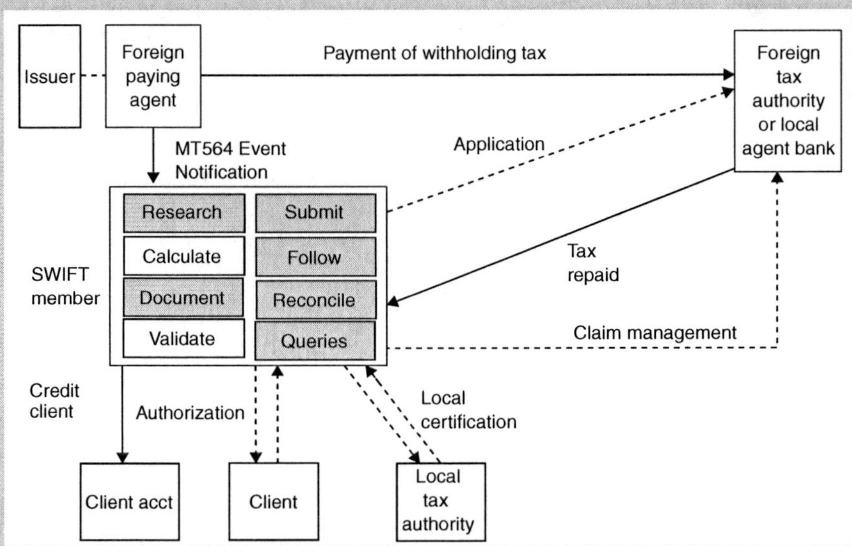

Figure 6.1 Current tax processing practice by financial firms

Source: GlobeTax.

represent parts of a process to optimise a customer's tax position and they are manual. As can be seen there are several different 'actors' in the process, but the custodian, represented here as a SWIFT member, has the responsibility as the custodian of its customer's assets to 'make things happen'.

So, two things collide here, the rock and the hard place. Most, if not all custodians would espouse the concept of straight through processing (STP). This would mean that all the elements of the process are reduced to data elements handled, validated and transmitted between the parties electronically. This is common among other corporate action events including proxy voting, stock splits, class actions and so on. So the problem is that while the financial institution wants STP, at the corporate action level it is simply not possible. In the case of withholding tax, apart from any given custodian's use of technology, there are others in the process chain that either cannot or will not accept STP, namely tax authorities either in their capacity as local certification authority or in their capacity as foreign tax authority receiving a claim.

In the current scenario this is a paradox. There would appear to be no way to achieve STP through the use of technology.

The solution

So, here we have it. Custodians can't use technology to automate this process. The solution actually lay in bringing together three concepts.

GlobeTax already provides withholding tax services to beneficial owners and custodians. So, in principle, if the custodian were prepared to outsource this process, it would remove the manual process. The problem is that while the processing solution exists, the custodian has a regulatory obligation to keep its client data safe. So any transmission of data must not only be secure, it must also be protected in transit. Finally, if the custodian is to truly automate the process on a consistent level, any transmissions must use a recognised standard. Enter SWIFT.

SWIFT worked with GlobeTax to identify the suite of ISO15022 standard messages that would be needed to encompass all the information movements needed to give the custodian a 'data out, data in' solution. GlobeTax applied for and was granted the ability to run a Service Bureau on the SWIFT network which would give it the ability to receive data to work on.

As in any technology management project, there were issues to resolve. Service Bureaux on the SWIFT network are not permitted to have their own nodes (or Bank Identifier Codes). These BICs are the addresses used to send and receive data on the network. Although GlobeTax is a service bureau, it didn't have its own BIC. So the problem was finding an address to which a custodian could send data, from where GlobeTax could pick it up. The solution was quite simple. SWIFT allowed the custodian, already a SWIFT member, to be granted an 'additional destination BIC' or 'ADBIC'. The management of that ADBIC was assigned by the custodian to GlobeTax. Now, essentially the custodian is sending data to itself, that is, from its primary BIC to its own ADBIC. Its just that the ADBIC is managed by GlobeTax, so it picks the data up.

The second problem was the nature of the messages. GlobeTax needed two types of data to do its job: Income data and Beneficial Owner data. The first could be delivered using a SWIFT message MT566. But there was no message type in the SWIFT corporate actions catalogue that allowed for a list of beneficial owners to be transmitted between the parties. At this stage, the methodology for standards development, discussed earlier, becomes important. Any institution can submit a request to SWIFT to modify the scale or scope of use for any given message. Two years earlier, GlobeTax had already submitted a request to modify the scope of use for a message MT574 in order to support its ability to help its customers meet the regulatory requirements of US Section 1441 NRA tax regulations. That modification allows beneficial owner data to be transmitted. So the circle was complete. This highlights one of the keys to technology management in financial services. Its not always obvious what the solution is going to be, at the time that you define the problem. In many cases, its necessary to 'posit' that a technology deployment would work if certain things could be done, even though they aren't possible at the time. In fact I would argue that many deployments are possible but never get designed simply because the business level always assumes that technology deployments will use existing techniques and not invent new ones or deploy them in a new way.

To return to the corporate actions solution. The third problem was multiple blocks in messages. Certain message types can allow for several repeated subsections within one message. This makes certain data transmissions very efficient. The lack of repeatable blocks conversely means more pain as each sub section has to be sent as a separate message. SWIFT's solution here was to suggest one of its other products, FileAct which could wrap multiple data sets together wherever the equivalent MT message did not have the appropriate functionality.

So, as you can see, like any technology management issue, there were difficulties to be overcome. But the essential element was thinking about the technology problem in a different way and not presuming that just because it hadn't been done it could not be done.

The solution, once the problems were ironed out created the potential for a process that, from the custodian's perspective, was STP. It wasn't real STP because all that had happened was that the manual parts of the process had been outsourced. But where outsourcing is usually seen as a business issue related to cost or risk reduction, in this case outsourcing was a tool designed to be a catalyst for a different model.

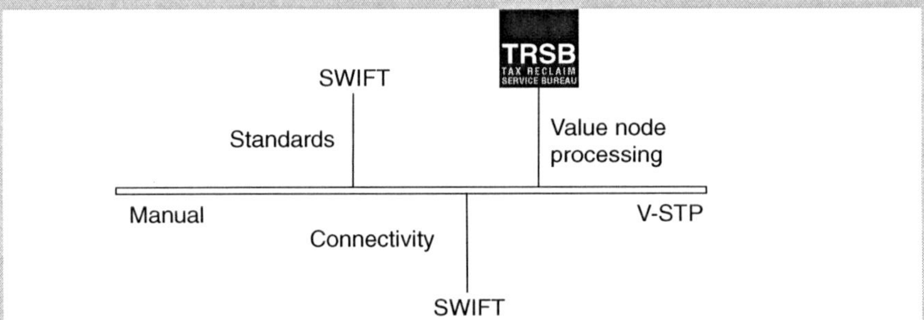

Figure 6.2 V-STP management model
Source: GlobeTax.

Figure 6.2 above shows the summation of the solution. Each party brings certain elements to the solution. As a technology management project this demonstrates many of the issues discussed in this book. SWIFT brought ISO standards as well as a secure network over which data could flow. GlobeTax brought its processing solution ('Value Node') so that the messages had a reason to flow and could be integrated into its proprietary systems. The custodian (SWIFT member) brought the manual problem it had to solve and ended up with something that wasn't STP, but wasn't manual either, and so the term was coined Virtual-STP or V-STP.

Referring back to Figure 6.1 earlier in this chapter, the reader should now compare that with Figure 6.3 which represents the process flow of the ultimate solution.

One has to ask the question why, beyond the need to process tax reclaims, would a custodian engage in such a potentially complex solution. The answer is that it fitted their global strategy to automate corporate actions; it was the only model that was capable of delivering automation in the circumstances and, as a paradigm, it clearly offered additional benefits for potential automation of other corporate actions processes.

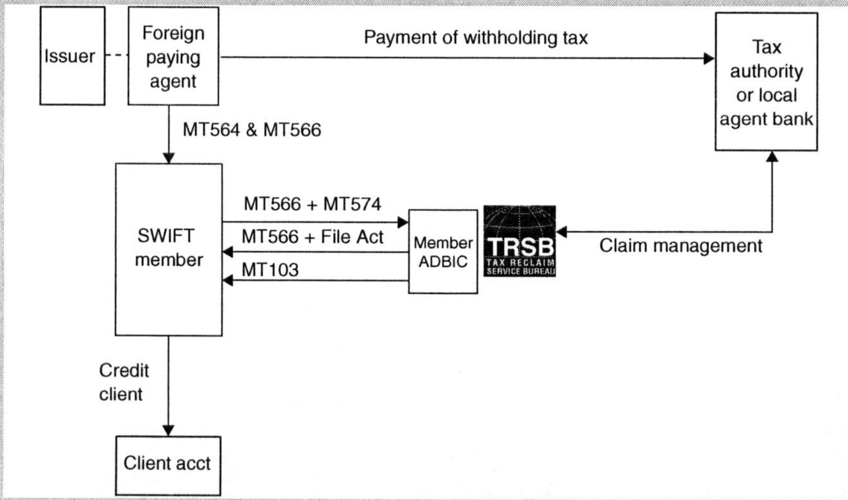

Figure 6.3 V-STP in practice
Source: GlobeTax.

The implementation

There were six stages to implementation:

1. Contractual – customer signs a service level agreement under which it obtains an ADBIC and assigns it to GlobeTax;
2. ADBIC Acquisition which is coordinated between the three parties;
3. Set-up in which the customer implements an exchange of electronic 'keys' to authenticate the routing of data. This makes sure that only the correct data arrives at the ADBIC;
4. Testing which is facilitated by SWIFT issuing a test ADBIC as well as a live ADBIC to the custodian;
5. Parallel production in which data is checked and validated for layout, format, receipt confirmation and so on and compared to a manual data set from the beneficial owner to make sure all the data is being picked up; and
6. Live production in which data is received and acted on by GlobeTax.

The model was tested using six branches of the custodian each located in a different European country. Twenty client accounts were used representing three types of beneficial owners resident in four countries.

In addition to new paradigm for processing corporate actions, this process also broke some new ground in managing the technology (Figure 6.4). It may look like a fairly normal phased introduction, but

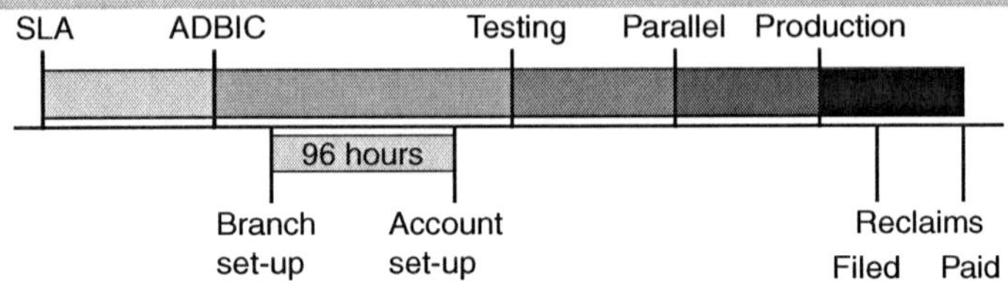

Figure 6.4 Implementation process
Source: GlobeTax.

the difference lies not in the phases themselves but how long they took to implement. Because the parties worked closely together to understand the reasons for the steps, the allocation of the ADBICs took only a couple of weeks. The set-up and exchange of keys took only 96 hours. Parallel production was left at two months as a safety net, but once into live production, results were being delivered within four weeks.

If you asked most technologists how long it would take to invent, set up, test and implement an entirely new processing paradigm in a backwater of corporate actions processing that is at least 60% manual, no-one would be surprised at development times of around two years. This solution was in place and delivering results within three months.

The results

Like any technology management issue, it has to deliver results. As we've already identified however, there can be results measured in the short term, medium term and long term. Some of these results can be quantified and some can only be qualified in terms of their potential. The custodian concerned cited the results as

1. Impressive – it works;
2. Has clear and identifiable benefits including
    a. control and presence in the process,
    b. delivery in good time with minimal cost,
    c. ability to provide a platinum level of service to customers, and
    d. the possibility of rolling out the service to their wider branch network

Of course the custodian was not the only beneficiary of the technology deployment. The account holders also benefited. GlobeTax used its much larger processing volumes and internal proprietary processes to add value. At the end of the day, the custodian's customer had only one interest, getting their tax recovered in the fastest possible time. So, not only did this paradigm provide a long-term methodology to automate corporate actions generally, it also provided a way for the custodian to mitigate risk and provide a better service to its customers.

In the test cases, within three months of live production, over US$104 million has been put back into the beneficial owners' accounts at the custodian. Of this figure, over US$44 million was recovered by GlobeTax in under four weeks from two markets against a market average expectation of 12 to 18 months. The beneficial owners estimated that the time value of having that money 11 months earlier than expected and available for reinvestment, was over US$2.5 million. So,

- Beneficial owners delighted – increased efficiency of service and faster money flow.
- Custodian delighted – automated a manual process and laid the groundwork for automating others.
- SWIFT delighted – created a paradigm that increases its value to its membership.
- GlobeTax delighted – essentially created a V-STP model so simple that it established the firm as a utility in the area.

Of course, it is not often that one can cite a technology management issue whose result directly puts money into someone's bank account. In such circumstances, the benefits and thus the driving force behind the project become very clear and easy to understand.

However, this remains, in my opinion, one of the guiding light projects this century to use a combination of communications, standards and messaging to manage a technology deployment efficiently.

I do have one afterthought. While this paradigm creates V-STP for the custodian, it doesn't remove the manual processing, it just shifts it somewhere else. As we approach the second decade of the twenty-first century, its not inconceivable that the ISO20022 modelling process plus changes in attitude by the actors in this process, may open the way for a complete front to back automation of the process.

CHAPTER 7

Open Source in Financial Services

Open source is software that can be accessed and used, free of license restrictions. The reputation of these products and solutions has increased over the last twenty years to the point that the end product of open source efforts are now accepted as deployable within major businesses throughout the globe. The financial sector is one among many that use these products. However, as with any software from whatever origin, care must be taken in selecting a suitable product to meet the needs of the business. This chapter looks at open source and the issues that surround its use.

At first glance, the fact that open source is 'free' software seems to make it an obvious choice for the organisation that is used to building its own solutions. But cost isn't the main reason for its increasing success in the financial sector. Open source has had a reputation for reliability for some time. Many coders have used open source at home or in an experimental capacity. This had led to a high degree of confidence in its efficacy. For the firm, an attraction is the way support can be addressed – open source enables a company to select among a number of providers, often minimising risk by mixing and matching support. This approach helps establish control of the supplier and the support base. It also alters the normal relationship with a software provider, by enabling the purchaser to select support as and when needed, rather than pay for it in advance and through a licensing agreement.

WHAT IS OPEN SOURCE SOFTWARE?

Often known as Free Open Source Software (FOSS), the Open Source Initiative (OSI) sees open source software as an idea whose time has come. After twenty years of building momentum it is breaking through into the commercial world, and changing the rules of software implementation. The OSI presents 'open source' as a simple proposition: by allowing programmers access to source code, this code can be improved; it evolves at a speed that would be impossible in the world of conventional software development. The assumption is that this environment produces better software than the traditional model.

OpenForum Europe, a not-for-profit organisation set up in 2002 to promote the use of Open Source Software (OSS) in business and government notes that the 'free' in Free Software refers to freedom, not price. But a fuller definition comes from GNU, in 1986, where four freedoms define Free Software:

- The freedom to run the program, for any purpose. Normal license and use options are not in place.
- The freedom to study how the program works, and adapt it to your needs. There are no legal or practical restrictions on the modification of a program. This releases the source code, the heart of the program, open to all.
- The freedom to redistribute copies so that you can help your neighbour. Software can be copied and distributed according to interest, with no restrictions, though you can charge for it if you choose.
- The freedom to improve the program, and release your improvements to the public, so that the whole community benefits. Modification can be carried out, for a charge if necessary, but it must be made available to the whole community.

For the open source community, these are rights, not obligations. It is also implicit that Free Software does not exclude commercial use. And significantly, Free Software makes it legal to provide help and assistance, although it does not make it mandatory.

USE IN THE FINANCIAL SECTOR

How far is open source being used by companies in the financial sector? A recent survey by Actuate, a business intelligence specialist, uncovered some interesting results. It surveyed 600 senior managers across the United States, Canada, United Kingdom and Germany. A summary of its results, in Table 7.1, presents a picture of widespread use of open source across the financial sector.

Table 7.1 Financial companies using OSS

Open source software	*Companies using open source (%)*
Tomcat	40
Linux	50
MySQL	9
PHP	30
Mozilla	24
Red Hat middleware	21

Source: Actuate.

Table 7.2 OSS Areas of use

Open source use	*Companies using open source (%)*
Operating systems	71
Application development	58
Database development	55

Source: Actuate.

Table 7.2 illustrates the way open source has drawn strength from its durability and reliability. The operating systems on which most business applications run, have to be as reliable as possible and well supported. Open source, through its widespread use of Linux and Linux operating system variants, has proved to be very popular. Given this base product, other solutions can operate with confidence as both stand-alone and as networked products. Operating systems here refer to server solutions as well as client platforms.

RISK MANAGEMENT AND OPEN SOURCE SOFTWARE

So what are the risks of using free and open source software (OSS) that financial services should be aware of? A key aspect of the use of OSS is easy access to the source code, generally the intellectual property of developer.

Well-known examples of this are Linux, the Apache web server, MySQL and associated utilities, such as network monitoring, diagnostic, and systems testing tools. This powerful combination has enabled many businesses to launch and maintain software services for major customers at very low cost. It has meant that instead of having to invest in expensive platforms because of proprietary operating systems, such as Unix, FOSS runs on cheaper machines. Sometimes the systems that sit at the back of the storage cupboard can be resurrected and made to run business applications because of the light use and robustness of Linux and its applications.

However, such an attractive proposition does not come risk free. The use of FOSS should mandate a careful scrutiny of the real costs involved, those over and above straight purchase. Procurement specialists would insist that the fuller costs are not simply capital expenses (capex), but a combination of capex and opex (operational expenses). So significant is the choice that it should be part of a strategic business decision making process. If mission-critical applications are to run on 'free' software, it should be considered as a longer-term risk and subject to a full risk analysis.

PROCURING SOFTWARE

Institutions evaluate the implementation of software in terms of its effectiveness, efficiency and support for growth. Generally, we might consider that software falls into three broad categories, all of which are found within firms and organisations across the financial sector:

- vendor supplied software, either directly or indirectly, as part of an 'integrated' solution;
- in-house or bespoke software; and
- open source software.

The acquisition of open source software should be subject to the same rigours as any proprietary, vendor-specific software. In its use are the major risks. These risks might be considered as analogous to those of in-house developed software. However, FOSS solutions sit astride these two common approaches; they generate the benefits of both and some of the disadvantages, as risks. The idea of future use is important when we consider the normal procurement life cycle. An important criterion is the way a software vendor supports its product. That is, a number of questions have to be satisfied and weighed as part of the selection process.

- Is the software vendor viable? That is, is it likely to be around for an estimated five years, the safety margin of most written-down software assets?

- Can the vendor support the software with sufficient resources?

- Is there a defined roadmap, with improvements and future developments clearly timelined?

- Is the software capable of being demonstrated with realistic loadings?

- How well does it integrate with other related software, allowing inputs and outputs to be exploited and bespoke refinements developed with low cost in terms of skills and resources.

The context of use is also important. Buying a piece of software often involves an investment in hardware, or other software for integration or networking purposes.

- Is the physical platform reasonable? That is, does it require a legacy system, such as a mainframe or vendor-specific operating system, with heavy support costs?

- Can it share a physical platform? Is it expected to?

- How well does it scale? Given large numbers of users, processes, transactions and so on, can it manage loading according to its specification?

- Are there accessible users who are happily using the software and can vouch for its stated capabilities?

There are many such questions that contribute to the selection process. Inevitably there are trade-offs, but all vendors will attempt to address the questions as best as they can and seek to make themselves as competitive as possible. At the end it often seems to be a question of money – how much does it all cost? But such costs are flexible and frequently only estimates. The purchase must also satisfy a range of very human responses – such as the look and feel of the solution, how user-friendly it is and so on, which are not quantifiable. These qualitative elements can be as important. But, overall, it is the risks of this purchase that this process of questioning and prioritising seeks to minimise.

It is a cliché within the context of this book that software requirements are determined by the institution's strategic business objectives. These are tightly linked to risk management. This includes issues such as

- code changes,
- platform architectures and
- product maturity,

and practical concepts such as

- forking,
- the integration of systems,
- support and
- the total cost of ownership.

What do these risk look like?

MANIPULATING CODE

Open source code is publicly available. This fundamental feature has enormous implications. It means

- The business has to have a clear idea of what it needs from the software, because a vendor has not carried out research on its behalf, tested and tried solutions in the unforgiving arena of competitive sales, to produce a durable and convincing product that meets a number of identified needs.
- The institution has to do this for itself, or at least with the context of industry best practice.
- The firm has to have the ability, in terms of skills and experience, to commit longer-term to the process of software development.

These demands present a series of risks that relate closely to those of in-house development. Such development offers a model or reference for dealing with open source solutions and platforms. Using this model the institution should

- follow accepted software development cycles;
- test and trial code thoroughly;
- ensure the code meets all the criteria of acceptability, common to user acceptance testing, such as confidentiality, integrity and availability of systems and data;
- be confident of its capabilities and ensure that controls are in place; and
- manage and protect its intellectual capital.

PLATFORM ARCHITECTURES

There are so many challenges in getting software from a variety of vendors to work together that frequently firms have to rely on the specialist arms of systems integrators to patch together a working framework. Apparent incompatibilities have to be overcome. Ensuring solutions can share information through a workflow or internal business process, ensuring their 'interoperability', is a primary objective for many procurement cycles. Along with this is the necessity to reveal hidden cost in platforms, where the apparent cost of purchase is inflated because of the need for specific platforms on which to run the solution. A proprietary software product from a vendor is generally certified to be compatible with its hardware platform. Beyond that, vendors will vary considerably in their commitment to the platforms available in the market. This is especially so for the smaller vendors with niche interests.

For some time, the call has been for players to produce products that are compatible with open standards. The exact nature of these standards and their acceptance, however, also varies. A particular advantage that open source can claim is its commitment to open standards. For this reason alone, it is often more interoperable than proprietary software. However, certain concerns and risks do quickly come into play. Everything depends on the market and the willingness of vendors to recognise and work to standards. Very often there is strong vendor self-interest in promoting a specific standard, especially when proto-standards are competing for control of the market. A dominant vendor can dictate what the standard will be – generally one which it has contributed to and to which its software most conforms. But supply and demand might force other vendors to adopt competing standards. To reach consensus is not always easy, nor is it timely.

Once agreement has been reached a standard can then go through a process of recognition and support, and develop a formal certification process. Simply stating a product conforms to open standards, which should greatly assist interoperability, is not enough. The product must be certified; it must undergo a process, often costly, of testing and approval. Generally when vendors agree on a standard some form of funding is forthcoming to set up a standards oversight body to support the certification process and maintain the standard. These costs are met from industry profits. Questions might arise over how such costs are met from something which is nominally 'free'.

Considering this, financial institutions using open source software should be careful to ensure it meets their needs for compatibility and interoperability and closely examine the context in which it will be used. There may be hidden costs in buying-in extra skills and experience to ensure the software works within its intended operating environment.

PRODUCT MATURITY

A question frequently raised is on the maturity of the product – how long has it been in use? This is really a way of asking, how do I know I can rely on this product? Based on experience, a new piece of software is

- more likely to have bugs,
- prone to a rapid series of updates to amend detected bugs and
- likely to have weaknesses which may not have been detected, even by the vendor, when operating in certain environments or at certain loading.

Any or all of these factors can reduce confidence in the product and be detrimental to a firm's business activity. Given that the software might be part of mission-critical activities the risks here are considerable.

For most vendors questions of maturity are fairly easy to address. Generally the software packaged for universal consumption has had a life as a bespoke product and evolved into a form that is deemed saleable in a wider market. It will be on an advanced version with clearly defined and well-known capabilities. However, the nature and economics of developing open source software is different. Questions on support in use are natural, but there are others that should be asked, more specific to open source.

All open source software is associated with a development community. This is very different for a single product developer. Whilst the developers of the code may be as professional as commercial coders, their binding interest is not monetary, and the drivers are not purely those of market demand. Their interests tend to be driven by curiosity and creative impulses. The degree of organisation and mutual cooperation within the community is open to question, as is their longer-term commitment. So we need to know more about the organisation or organisations behind the code. Along with a list of questions we need indications of where the answers might be found, as in Table 7.3.

For most open source groups, the communities are large and contain a high proportion of experienced coders with formal academic and business experience. The tendency is to control and manage development according to well-tried systems. A disparate community needs such discipline to produce something durable and worthwhile. It might be the case that the degree of change control and overall discipline in code development is stronger than some commercial software houses, which do have the same level of enthusiasm and have to respond quickly to commercial demands. These commercial drivers might not be suited to the realities of a truly bug-free and ideal code. Very often, development is seen as a project exercise with

Table 7.3 OSS FAQ

Question	*Information sources*
What is the nature of the community?	Related websites, conventions and trade events as well as specialist magazines.
Level of commitment?	Proceedings and discussion portals for special interest groups (SIGs).
Documented support for product and its development?	Derived from website sources.
Support from commercial players?	Certain open source software, such as Linux, is widely supported by vendors. The level of support and commitment can be checked through their websites.
Availability?	Downloadable, but available also from specialist vendors at low cost.
Versioning and track record?	The tendency to develop, within a community, is strong, so a decision may need to be taken on the significance of this.

Source: Author.

well-defined project leaders or managers overseeing the community. There is also a real interest in using and adapting code developed by commercial vendors, where possible, to incorporate the best of the best into the final released product. A principle at work for most of these communities is that the product is a living thing, and since it is not dependent on commercial sales, it is unlikely to die as a product set.

FORKING

The creative impulse is a strong one and should not be underestimated. A feature of open source software is that it offers coders an opportunity to take a copy of the code and manipulate it so that they produce a piece of software that can be operationally distinct from the original. Normally, access to source code is difficult and it is protected under copyright. This activity is not legally possible without the originator's permission. Open source recognises no such constraint. This process of transforming source code is known as 'forking'. From our perspective this is not an issue unless a major fork occurs, when the development community sees a group take the code in a very specific direction not mutually sanctioned. This can lead to internal disputes and should be addressed by curtailing further development on the forked code as a 'standard' version. Forks can present unexpected and unwelcome changes of direction in code for a firm or institution that has adopted and used the original. For this and other related reasons, the firm should ensure it has enough expertise in-house to manage any such change in circumstances.

A mitigating factor that can make a difference here is that once committed to using open source software, the firm becomes part of the community and contributes to it. This means, unlike with most commercial software, the firm can have a direct influence on the direction of the code. While, to an extent, commercial vendors allow customers to influence their product road-maps, the user is a licensee and not a stakeholder in the open source project.

PRACTICAL ISSUES

Licensing

In acquiring open source products, the firm's use of the product is potentially constrained by only a few principles which allow

- copying,
- distribution and
- modification.

However, licenses, although often quite thoroughly specified, do not contain any warranty or indemnification clauses. The Open Source Initiative lists a number of common licenses that can be used in the acquisition process. Sometimes these are supplied by the intellectual owner, sometimes they are negotiated. The OSI has a License Review Process to ensure that licenses and software labelled as open source conforms to existing community norms and expectations. The review process is public. The process has a specific remit, to

- ensure approved licenses conform to the Open Source Definition,
- help identify appropriate License Proliferation Category,
- discourage vanity and duplicative licenses,
- ensure a thorough, transparent and timely review, generally within 60 days and
- provide the current status of license review requests.

The OSI Board offers to help with the formulation of licenses before the formal review. The OSI Open Source addresses the sometimes vexed issue of license proliferation. Its response is a guideline based on a tiered approach; it places approved licenses into a list of recommendations such as

1. Preferred,
2. Recommended but not preferred and
3. Not recommended.

These licenses have been approved but reflect the OSI's own standards for OSS.

There is a license frequently referenced, the General Public License (GPL). Under this license anyone can use the software and change the program code, but the new code cannot be redistributed as a proprietary application. Another well-known license is the Berkley Software Distribution license (BSD). It has similar clauses but with restrictions, such as a copyright notice and a disclaimer which must be included. However, the BSD license does allow products created using BSD-licensed code to be used in proprietary software.

The structure and financial terms of many licensees include a base and a per-user license. This enables the number of users to be tracked against the licensed number to ensure additional licenses are taken out as the use of the software grows. OSS does not require license by user. But Value Added Resellers (VARs) of OSS might introduce a limitation on the number of servers accommodated by the license. These aspects of licensing will be scrutinised as part of the diligence process in procurement; it is especially important to determine the nature of licensing if an OSS is supplied as part of a bigger, integrated solution using proprietary software.

Very often the use of the code constitutes a readiness to recognise and abide by the OSS license, and an integrators general terms and conditions might or might not override these.

Financial institutions and firms should consider these licensing arrangements under legal advice.

Warranties and indemnities

The organisation will be used to buying software that has a warranty and an indemnity.

- Warranty – that the product will meet the performance and capabilities stated.
- Indemnity – that the vendor will support the user in the event of an infringement resulting from proper use of the product.

This level of security is absent from OSS. Open source is licensed without warranty or indemnity. However, as open source has been taken up by VARs and vendors, licenses have appeared which add these qualities, often extending them under the umbrella of proprietary software. Other vendors provide dual licensing – based on a BSD or GPL license. One is usually some form of the GPL, and the other might include performance warranties and indemnities. Firms should evaluate any indemnification offered by a VAR. It might be wise to consider third-party insurance as well.

Operational risks

Operational risks exist within any IT operating environment. A good source for risks, controls and prudent risk management practices are the FFIEC *IT Examination Handbook* issued by the Federal Financial Institutions Examination Council (FFIEC). The Council was established in 1979, to prescribe principles, standards and report forms for the federal examination of financial institutions. It was established by the Board of Governors of the Federal Reserve System in the United States. Some of the key operational risk considerations linked to using OSS include the integrity of source code, the management of documentation, contingency planning and product and software support.

Code

We have seen how there are risks associated with such code and its manipulation. Institutions are recommended to develop standards and procedures to ensure they acquire code from a trustworthy party. They are also encouraged to check the code for security risks such as malware. These standards should be applied to software updates and patches. There are a number of bodies that can provide assurance on the integrity of code, such as SourceForge and assist in this process, such as the CERT® Coordination Center.

Documentation

One aspect that sees a great variety in the quality of open source, is the documentation available. It may be less comprehensive than that of proprietary software, or very comprehensive indeed. Minimum standards should be established for documentation and a process dictated for making good any documentary discrepancies.

Contingency planning

A degree of contingency planning should be considered, especially for software that has forked and found to be by-passed by the development community. Good practice here is in line with assurances about the longevity of any software and coverage and access to code in the event of a software company failure. Generally software companies don't fail but are absorbed by larger competitors. OSS is not covered in this way.

External support

We have seen how support is also variable but increasingly provided by stable VARs or vendors. Certainly, in evaluating support from the OSS development community, institutions should be astute enough to cover a number of points.

- They should have enough expertise to be able to spot issues of support in the development community.
- The shortcomings of a community should be tracked, noted and weighed as part of the assessment.
- They should contribute to a support group. This can be very productive and enriching since many institutions such as public and government bodies and universities may be members and contributors.

Copyright infringement

In a litigious world more and more dependent on intellectual capital, copyright is jealously guarded. An institution that uses software runs some form of risk of infringing copyright or patents. While this may normally be low and protected by indemnities, OSS is developed in an open environment where code is shared and modified by numerous bodies and individuals. The appearance of proprietary code in a OSS offering is greater. Institutions should mitigate this risk by exploiting any VAR or vendor arrangement possible over licensing, as discussed earlier. Other prudent methods include

- seeking legal counsel to advise the institution on issues,
- define policies and business rules to ensure licenses are enforced,
- explore the consequences of combining OSS and proprietary software and
- exploit existing in-house standards over code development.

LINUX

A popular and good example of an open source software solution that illustrates a number of the points raised is Linux. Linux is a Unix-like operating system that provides the functionality of Unix across multiple platforms. It is a relatively easy transition for staff with Unix expertise to adopt Linux as an alternative or supplementary platform. It shares the stability of Unix without some of the platform complexities associated with a full Unix implementation. It is an example of open source software much affected by 'forking', but without any detrimental affect on the market. The varieties of Linux are seen to be complementary rather than competitive and exclusive of each other. SUSE and Red Hat are two well-known versions of Linux that are marketed by vendors.

One strength of Linux is the way it can be implemented on relatively simple and low-cost platforms for niche activities and to supplemental existing systems to get the most out of them. Interoperability is also simplified since open source is, by definition, catholic in its lack of preference for a given platform. This is recognised by major vendors and major customers. HSBC, RBS and LloydsTSB and Standard Life have used Linux supplied by Novell. Microsoft have bitten the bullet on open source and seeing the advantages of working with rather than against this trend now distribute certificates for redemption against SUSE Linux Enterprise Server upgrades. For customers who use open source this is seen as beneficial in that it improves interoperability with

Microsoft products. For many, the future is not in any form of exclusivity of sources, but in a mixed source computing world.

Front and back office

Linux can be used at the back and front end of business activity; it can host applications for acting as 'thin' client platforms for users. The use of Linux does vary. For HSBC Linux is primarily used as an operating system (OS) to support servers. Across the industry it is used for online banking to capital market transaction applications. This flexibility casts it in the role of the friendly, always-useful operating system in a fast changing and demanding IT environment.

Trading rooms see a wide range of IT solutions. Not surprisingly the ability to run a stripped down and highly functional environment on a Linux platform makes open source very popular. Buying cheap PC-based platforms with a fast and thin open source OS makes this a line of least resistance. In environments where speed matters, open source can have real advantages. The high availability and ease of use makes this a winner. In some instances trading floors have to go the whole way and decide to build integrated systems on open source.

Migration at the desktop, as well as back office upgrades, are simplified when open source is involved and the skills are available. As long as support is adequately addressed, the transformation is such that it can often be handled in-house. Although multi-tasking desktops are largely based on Microsoft, once established, open source single-task platforms are feasible, since the costs are low and functionality is good.

OPEN SOURCE – HURDLES FOR ACCEPTANCE

But adopting open source is still subject to suspicion and concerns. Three frequently expressed concerns have been largely overcome over the last five years:

- Support – how do we support the software?
- Legal uncertainty – there have been many law suits and disputes about copyright and patent misuse.
- Security – how do I know this software is secure?

Support has been addressed by the prevalence of open source solutions from standard vendors. It is claimed that support for Linux in the enterprise is comparable with that of HP-UX, AIX or Solaris, the major Unix brands. Legal uncertainty is perhaps more of a deterrent, since Red Hat Linux has seen some litigation. However, in buying open source from major providers a firm is normally guaranteed against legal issues. Yet, problems of identifying copyright and intellectual property rights, especially for extensions to open source software developed in-house, can be of concern to the risk-averse legal departments of major financial institutions. Policies governing the use of software have to take this into account and so too does risk analysis. When it comes to security, there has been a view that open source software is inherently more secure than many proprietary products, such as Microsoft Windows. Although this is debatable, security is a feature of the way the development of the software is researched and generated.

Levels of acceptance, as witnessed in the Actuate report, indicate that there is an increased use of open source by financial sector organisations. The attraction of downloading and trying out software without any restraints is very strong. Sun Systems' initiative with Java, although not open source, as a freely available product has further primed the market for experimenting in this way. Financial sector companies and firms have a long history of innovating with software to meet their specific needs. This alone is a strong driver for increased interest and use. There is now a body of open source solutions around regulatory compliance that is strengthening this tendency. Given the support proprietary vendors are now giving to the movement, especially for Linux and allied operating systems, this trend is likely to continue for the near future. The risks associated with the use of OSS by financial institutions are fundamentally different from those presented by the use of proprietary or self-developed software. However, this might see the adoption of some distinctive risk management practices with which institutions must be familiar.

PART II

Technology Acquisition and Management

There are typically four approaches to acquiring technology (see Figure PII. 1). There are two major factors which affect which of these is in the ascendant at any one time within a financial firm. The first is the 'corporate philosophy' usually expressed as 'what does the CEO want'. The second is at what stage in the macro-technology cycle is each of the options, expressed as 'what is the in-thing' to do. You'll notice that neither of these factors has much to do with what the best solution is for the business. There are usually too many political issues clouding judgement to make the efficacy of any one method over any other a real factor. Financial firms are, for the most part, extremely conservative with a small 'c'. Hence they do not like to be the first in the market with anything, particularly in the back office. This may seem unduly cynical, but it is just as well to be realistic.

Building a technology solution has for the last ten years at least been the least favoured of the technology solutions. This is partly due to the Y2K effect which was originally caused by the programmers responsible in the early seventies for the mainframe computing systems which banks have historically favoured because of their high transactional capabilities. With memory at that time being extremely expensive, the shortcut of using just two digits to represent the year was a logical one, but which was created because of their conservatism and lack of long-term planning capability. These two factors still persist in many financial firms and lead many of the new breed of IT director to focus on external solutions rather than an internal build.

There are however some changes which are making this an option for the future. Each of the solutions in the cycle has different characteristics, 'pros and cons'. The evolution of disruptive technologies makes it likely that the

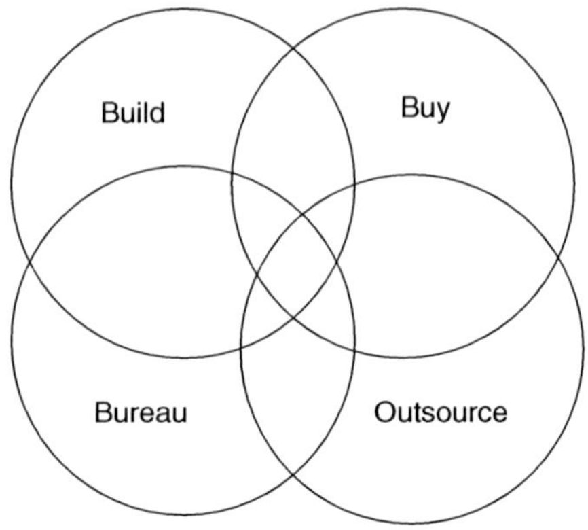

Figure PII. 1 Strategic options for delivery of technology projects

Source: Author.

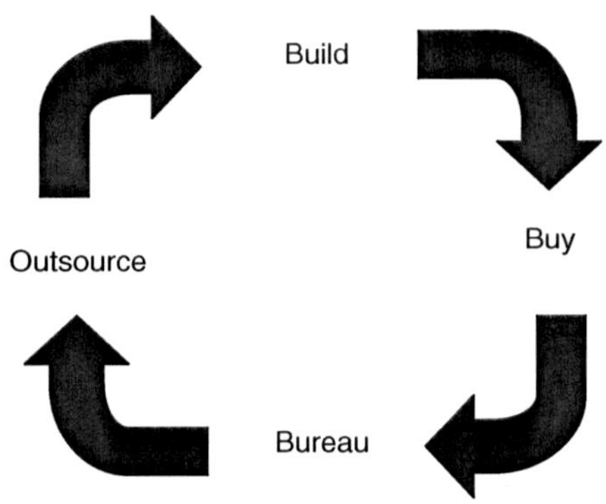

Figure PII. 2 The macro-technology cycle

Source: Author.

IPR gained by owning the solution in the twenty-first century will outweigh the costs of self-development.

Figure PII. 2 above shows how the cycle typically rotates. Building a solution is often favoured by older firms where there is great store placed on maintaining the entire value proposition in-house, even when this would dilute the company's core skills base. As competition increases in a market, third parties aggregate what they can learn of the dynamics of market and offer this as an off-the-shelf or customisable solution. As purchased solutions become more complex as markets mature and more difficult to maintain, niche or boutique providers crystallise in the market, automating particular process elements effectively and offering a unique solution combined with standardised connectivity. As the markets mature further and the number of process elements become greater, purchased solutions become too complex to maintain and multiple bureau providers too complex to manage. Either though aggregation or some other method, third parties come into the market effectively creating a build solution surrounded by a 'departmental' philosophy so that the offering is complete; that is, not a technological solution per se where internal staff use a 'built' product, but where the third-party provider brings all the benefits of multiple cross-market practices, niche-level specialist technology solutions and a knowledgeable team to implement – outsourcing. Eventually, outsourcing stimulates concerns in financial services that competitive advantage is being lost or that the core brand values are being diluted and the firm returns to a 'build-it-ourselves' philosophy. While the market generally can be at any one point in the cycle generally speaking, and currently it is at the outsource stage; individual firms in the industry can be at any one of the four stages depending on their history and management background.

CHAPTER 8

Build

There's a reason why most mainframe systems today are called 'legacy'. Distributed processing is now so in-built into our way of life that large number crunching mainframes are somewhat of an anachronism. Having said that, the retail financial services sector needs massive processing capability to deal with many millions of transactions per day.

DESIGN

I want to talk about design because I have strong views on the subject, influenced by my background in marketing. In my experience, design of user interfaces in any deployment has two limiting factors:

1. The limited availability of flexible solutions for interfaces and

2. The limited view and non-inclusion of marketing in the design process

Many believe that marketing has no place in most deployments because they are not usually customer-facing. The reality is that the marketing function is usually the only function that has any skill set that includes psychology. After all, their job is to create environments in which people will be manipulated to do things they either wouldn't normally do or to do things they would do, only quicker and in a particular way. To achieve this they have to have, even at only a practical level, an understanding of why people do things. To this extent they are best placed to provide a semi-independent view for most technology deployments that will help people use systems more effectively. Some examples of questions rarely asked in a technology deployment but which can have material effect on their success and/or useability:

Proportion of females in the user population. This has an effect because females have a different approach to technology than males in a number of ways. First, females approach technology, successfully, when it is designed in a more rounded, emotive form. They also have very different visual cortex processing – they react differently to colours than men do. If the population of users has a large female element, it is incumbent on the management function to recognise this and adapt the system design accordingly. This might either be a deployment designed for the majority *or* a deployment where the interface can be adjusted to suit the psychological profile of the user on a gender basis. Women also navigate systems differently. The old cliché abut women and map reading is a good example. Brains are 'wired' differently. Any competent manager of a technology deployment should have user acceptance testing (UAT) groups that represent the different elements of the full user population *and* should include sufficient psychological knowledge to understand why a particular sub-group within the UAT group takes a particular viewpoint and associate that with the appropriate weighting.

Age profile of the user population. In a way similar to the gender-based approach, age is a differentiator in how people successfully use technology. Younger users tend to be able to deal with a much greater number of variables at once, whereas older people can deal with a much smaller number of data elements on a screen.

Of course, if the operating system, for example Windows or OSX, allows it users can to a limited extent, vary their own experience of any given interface, but this, in a build environment is a 'cop out'. The operating system's ability to provide flexibility is severely limited because it has to average out the population. Most users given the opportunity, do not change visual settings from those established as default settings.

Yet, in many, many technology deployments, I have seen attention to such details rarely. The build scenario is particularly relevant here because there is a better opportunity to affect change. In bought systems, the user interface is most often (i) designed by men and (ii) had no real analysis performed on it for useability. The opportunity to get a 5% improvement in employee loyalty and productivity by including such subtle design activities, and communicating the process to users, has a disproportionate effect on the ultimate delivery success and user response.

Localisation. This is the term usually used for creating a technology deployment that is to be used or accessed across different national or cultural boundaries. It is strange that technology managers do think about localisation, but rarely take the concept to its logical conclusion. Localisation is most obvious in the availability of a technology deployment in multiple languages. Often, especially in the back offices of banks, staff have English as a second language – if you're lucky – and many will have no English at all. The difficulty for technology managers is the degree to which localisation is 'paralleled'. In other words, if the only users of a system are, let us say Italian, then clearly an Italian language system is fine. However if users are global, then every screen implementation must be localised to its user audience. This creates additional cost, opportunity for errors in translation and added maintenance and upgrade headaches as every localised version will need to be checked every time code or user interface changes.

Language also has impact on screen design The length of words varies depending on language. German for example is 33% longer than English. So what might fit nicely on one screen inEnglish will not on a German langauge screen leading to fundamental screen view differences. As people are more and more mobile, the time taken by people to adapt to the same system when implemented in different countries using a localisation methodology can cause productivity drops, if not basic errors. These differences are summarised in Table 8.1.

Similarly syntax and grammar can have an effect. Typically in Europe, the decimal differentiator is the comma (,) whereas in the United Kingdom and United States it is the period (.).

These are only a few of the factors involved. They are not intended to be an exhaustive list of factors. They are intended to highlight the fact that in

Table 8.1 Summary of factors for management in technology deployment

Gender	■ Visual cortex processes colours differently
	■ Screen complexity navigated differently
	■ Help system navigation approached differently
Age	■ Increasing age means slower response time to changes and need to 'flag' changes on complex screens
Nationality	■ Length of average words can cause screen design variance
	■ Syntax and grammar variances can cause translation errors
	■ Translation

Source: Author.

managing technology in financial services and elsewhere, it is all too easy to focus on the general issues and miss out the issues which are more subtle, but which actually differentiate a good technology deployment from a great one. In my experience, best practice within the design phase of managing technology should

1. include a statistically relevant sample of the user population in the specification and UAT teams;

2. provide for sub-groups comprising the major types (gender, age etc.) and then allow for cross-disciplinary groups to conduct peer reviews.

If you're going to spend potentially millions of dollars on a deployment, the least you can do is spend some on the ergonomics and have some method of knowing whether what you are doing is having an effect.

Ergonomic Fit (Ef) measures the degree to which the different variables in the deployment have been factored in. Since there is a degree of judgement involved here, the measure uses the results of sub-group pre- and post-deployment analyses to provide an indication of both absolute fit and relative fit, that is in the latter case, the degree to which the spend on ergonomics has delivered value.

$$\mathrm{EF} = \sum_{1}^{n} (p - q)$$

where p is a result score generated from a questionnaire given to a focus group post-deployment, q is the result score generated from a questionnaire to the same focus group pre-deployment and n is the number of groups (i.e., if age and gender only are grouped then $n = 2$)

SCALE

As can be seen, one of the biggest issues is that the sheer scale of build solutions combined with the long development and test cycles involved mean that firms choosing to build their own solutions are faced with a fast moving competitive environment and tools that are not suited to it.

Even smaller-scale builds suffer from the same disadvantages. Build-your-own solutions are rapidly falling out of favour simply because the firms involved, although they have the size and resources to accomplish a build, fail to understand that the sheer scale of such projects distracts the organisation from its core purpose. In other words, in anyone else's book, the scale of a build-your-own project would make the project bigger than most businesses in their own right.

INTEGRATION

Businesses are not consistent entities. Not only do they fluctuate as their skill base fluctuates, they do not necessarily integrate as well as the theorists would hope. In one of my fields of expertise, cross-border tax, this is very common. The skill base within a custodian bank for instance can fluctuate widely because the internal departmental structure is top heavy that is, the real skills and knowledge are focused in a few people and the real intellectual property of the business model of the firm has not been integrated into its systems. So what one custodian bank does very well today in terms of market performance, can change very quickly to a much lower level of service tomorrow when key staff move on or when management decides on cost cutting measures in a particular point in the economic cycle.

When technology deployments are planned and discussed, one of the common problems is that in order to plan, one key assumption is made – that the business is homogenous and well integrated.

In build-your-own solutions, this issue can rapidly cause overruns on budgets and deliverables simply because key staff needed to make a project work either leave or are deployed elsewhere.

So, in a similar vein, managing integration should contain a few of the more focus analyses to help sustainability and ultimately enable delivery of value.

Integration coefficient is an important measure. It assumes that each group involved in deploying a technology project can be mapped in terms of its employment characteristics. So for example, in one sub-group (n) for example back office clerks, we can presume that staff turnover is high and that employment time is relatively low. This can be graphed. Taking similar graphs for other groups will produce different results. When overlaid, as indicated by the integral sign of the benchmark, it is possible to derive patters of integration. For example, projecting typical average employment period for different types of staff may highlight a particular period in the future, say 18 months, where it is likely that staff will change. If the management graph and the lower-level staff graph coincides on this point, it is likely that not only will there be a major change in the user community, it is also likely that there will be a significant reduction in the number of people qualified to use the system and indeed train others on it. So from a technology management perspective it is important to be able to predict such patterns in order to plan for them.

$$\text{Ic} = \int_1^n f(x)$$

where f(x) is the function that describes for each group involved in the project the historic and future trend of resource availability.

IPR

One clear advantage of a build methodology is that there is a clear opportunity to deploy technology in a new and unique way that can stay proprietary within its own constraints. As we've seen in an earlier chapter, many technology deployments require connectivity to other systems often at third-party sites and counterparties. Where this happens, standards and messaging are useful as a layer between the core function of the deployment and the proprietary nature of the project. This doesn't have to be an application, although it very often is. It could just as easily be a new way of configuring hardware to be more cost efficient. Either way, building a solution allows the organisation to protect and enhance its value in the market, particularly to shareholders while delivering some benefit to its customers.

Of course one of the problems with any proprietary build is assuring the continued security of that IPR. Given a benefit delivered in the market and some intelligent people with industry knowledge, it is often not difficult to reverse engineer what must have been built. So, in any proposition to management, protection of IPR through a self-build methodology must be mitigated by the likelihood that the protection will not last as long as the solution will.

Building also poses some other IPR problems. In larger-scale projects, the employees who design and deliver these solution are vulnerable. They cost a great deal of money to employ and maintain. This creates the 'self-fulfilling prophecy' department where new projects must be invented and self-justify themselves as 'build' opportunities simply to support the continuing cost of staff employment. These equally represent a risk. The IPR of any build design must be rigorously protected in contract with employees who could otherwise easily take those ideas elsewhere. The legal costs of such protection are increasing as the Internet is now often used as a backbone in many projects with multiple hubs for unique code. In such a landscape, the jurisdiction of IPR is not always clear.

BUDGET CONTROL

I have never come across a build project that came in under budget. Nor, it has to be said, have I ever seen one that was adequately and extensively costed before it was approved. Some of the issues raised above never see the budgetary light of day, even in a risk assessment.

The reader can assume that I'm not a great fan of building solutions in financial services. There are far more ways for such projects to go wrong than there are for them to go well. The speed with which firms now have to act in the market is too fast to really follow for a properly designed system ever to hit the ground before it is entirely or substantively obsolete. Even the build projects which are collaborative between large players, more often than not, fail spectacularly or simply never get enough traction in the market to succeed.

PROCESS

Everyone has a different model to work to and there are certainly as many development methodologies as there are consultancies to dream them up. Apart from the technical development methodology however, such as Rational Rose or SSADM, I believe that a simple yet stringent approach is vital. These elements, described below, have almost the same relationship to each other as aims do to objectives and objectives have to activities. Each is a nested element that relates both upwards and downwards and is iterative in any good deployment.

1. Business Specification – defines the needs of the business and the top level objectives that the deployment must satisfy. These would usually be categorised as (i) mandatory and (ii) optional;

2. Functional Specification – defines the specific function sub-set that, in aggregate, allows the business level objectives to be met. This may include both technical and non-technical aspects. This is where the issues raised earlier, for example age and gender, are incorporated through user group analysis. Technical aspects may include things such as acceptable response speeds as well as the fundamental processes the deployment must achieve;

3. Technical Specification – defines the technical architecture that will be delivered to meet the needs and parameters of the functional specification of the project. This may include adherence to general policies in the business that are not elucidated in the business specification, regulatory requirements (although these are likely to also be in the business specification). Typically, most deployments will technically follow the layered approach discussed earlier – communications, systems and application levels;

4. Technical Development – represents the build itself;

5. Testing – represents several issues, some of which are often forgotten or left out. First, the final project must be tested against the technical and functional and business specifications to make sure that all the required constraints have been met. This is usually an iterative process. Second, the project must be tested in its environment with user groups, who will, in a high-grade deployment, also be tasked with simultaneously testing against required deliverables, and also developing the embryonic training schedule, help systems and other peripherals that users will want, and that users are best placed to design. It is a mistake to leave help systems to technicians. They are neither qualified nor best placed to present information to users about the use of the system. This also provides a robust counter-balance to the technical development and an additional layer of fit testing to the basic functionality;

6. Training – would seem to be obvious, but is rarely so. The user groups that were part of the specification stage should be the core of development of training together with the professional training department, if there is one. The development of training schemas should also involve a third group, if resources allow. This is a control group, essentially a group that has no knowledge of the system and can provide a relatively naïve response to the training schema without the pre-judgement of the content;

7. Roll-out – again a critical issue where communication is paramount. Many deployments fail to achieve their full potential simply because the staff that built and tested the system are so close to it that they fail to communicate effectively. A degree of complacency through association is common. The answer is to find a deployment champion who has been peripheral to the project but is senior enough to reinvigorate the project at this critical time and essentially stimulate and excite people about the upcoming launch;

8. Version control – Any deployment of any size will have version control. This has two meanings here. The technical meaning is not our concern here, but the iterative process of identifying, classifying, developing and integrating new ideas or fixes to an existing deployment is of concern to us from a technology management perspective. The success of a deployment is linked to the way in which users interact with it. Unless it is managed well, users fall quickly into a failure approach. The fact that the deployment does mainly what it is supposed to do becomes secondary to the little niggles and bugs that always exist. Other improvements

are often market driven and so beyond the remit of many users. And so, the need exists to keep users enthused, to highlight the good things and the savings and efficiencies that are being made. Management version control (MVC) may or may not be contemporaneous with technical version control (TVC). Clearly, many 'fixes' will be used as a reason to fly the flag, but this would be a false message. MVC needs to reward users directly for their part in the continued existence of the deployment, not just make them aware of the problems with it.

DELIVERY AND ROLL-OUT

If you've managed to design and build your own system, the chances are that you are an extremely large organisation. These are really the only ones that can afford it. So, by inference, one of the largest issues, given that the solution designed does what it is theoretically supposed to do, is how it is delivered to its intended audience.

I have been struck in recent times, by the degree to which even large organisations have very little sense of self other than at brand level. I see this as a major failure of senior management. There are firms spread over the globe that share the same brand name yet don't have a clue about who or where their co-workers are, what they do and what business units are involved in the same business. I know of firms with global reach who have data on different platforms where the data is not held in a consistent way, where the platforms have no way to communicate with each other and even simple data mining exercise would take months. I see firms which, even though they have a regulatory requirement to keep records for several years, could not produce client transactional data older than six months. These things are not only common, they are endemic to an industry, which along with everyone else thought that two digits to represent the year in a date field would be sufficient. Problem in that case was that the financial services industry, of all the industries on the planet, have the highest reliance on date-based information. So, before we get too far into the discussion based on a view of the world that uses rose-tinted glasses, let us be honest with ourselves. Our technology management currently sits in the context of constantly papering over the cracks faster than the cracks start to show.

So, presuming a build has been effected, its roll-out needs to be considered in some detail. Most obviously, who are the intended recipients? What is their knowledge level? Less obviously – whats their turnover rate? What language do they speak? What documentation is needed and in what forms (note the plural)? What training needs to be given and at what frequency and by whom? How will the trainers be trained? How will the new system's training be integrated into new hire's itineraries? Many of these questions have commonality with any technology deployment of course, but where the solution is 'owned' by the business, there's no-one else, like a supplier, to turn to. You have to write it yourself and deliver it yourself.

One of the most difficult areas of roll-out is integration to existing systems. In any new deployment, integration will need to take place in the context of

1. Legacy systems that the new deployment replaces

2. Other in-house systems which either
   a. Needed to communicate but could not
   b. Could communicate but the new system requires a reengineering of interfaces

3. Other in-house systems that the new system will need to communicate with that the old legacy system did not or could not communicate with

4. Third-party systems that
   a. could not communicate with the legacy systems but a need existed
   b. existed and could communicate with legacy systems but did not
   c. are contemporaneously implemented or implemented after the new system where communications are required

As you can see, even within this rather limited context, what any new deployment does in and of itself is, in the context of modern financial services, by no means the only consideration as to its ultimate efficacy.

The most common scenario is that a firm's 'built' systems consist of two or three core elements that form the basis of its business. Other systems, more peripheral to the core, are open to potential buy or outsourcing as there is a clearer business case to access third-party skills. The core systems, however, are usually a much more ethos-based issue and represent, at least in the minds of the board of directors, the intellectual property of the firm and are listed as such on the balance sheet. To outsource these is a much more painful process, hence core systems in most banks continue to be built rather than bought. That's not to say that outsourcing doesn't have a place. Many firms for example, outsource the hardware portion of a deployment while retaining the integrity of their IPR in software systems and knowledgebases.

The one major benefit of a built system is of course that it does encapsulate the skills and knowledge of the employees and the firm's unique propositions in the market. This represented a key value element in the last century. In this century however, the degree of inter-connectivity of systems, and the degree to which otherwise competitive companies must collaborate to survive, means that built systems have far less value in the long run. The cost of keeping up with the outside world using merely internal resources is just too great.

Built systems do share some common elements as I have pointed out. Some of these in terms of roll-out and delivery, are the issues of training, maintenance and support.

TRAINING

Hopefully the reader will by now be getting some idea that the concept of a built system is one which has many more facets than might originally be thought. Training is a critical issue. Often, the people who helped develop the concept and tested the deployment will also be the people using it, so training might be deemed to be of little importance. However, in the larger organisations, particularly those with multi-country operations or at least multiple language personnel (as opposed to multi-lingual personnel), those who helped in the design and testing phase will usually be a small part of the overall user universe. For the rest, the provision of training is vital if the deployment is to be successful.

Some of the more common management mistakes are

1. the belief that all users will be enthusiastic about the deployment,

2. assuming that everyone will understand English and

3. assuming that having an intranet site will suffice.

There are many more. Essentially, one of the most visible activities associated with technology management in financial services is the communication with users that takes place after the deployment is implemented. Yet most planners, while acknowledging the 'importance' of training, almost without exception, fail to allocate sufficient resource or attention. Often training actually has two jobs to do. The first is actually 'buy-in'. It is not actually training that staff need to know about first of all, but what the new deployment is, what it is supposed to do and what benefits over the old system it brings. This may sound obvious but in twelve years in financial services I have come across more people who 'have new systems' that they 'don't understand' than I can count. The net result is that the real user base fails to understand new deployments, see them as a way for the IT department to keep its jobs and feel excluded because they were never involved in any of the preceding decision making.

Training needs to start well before any new deployment gets past the technical specification stage. One of the biggest mistakes I see is the appointment of small committees, typically 'UAT' groups which 'represent' the community within the company that the deployment will service. Since most of these people have day jobs, they have no training in and of themselves to know how to act within such a committee nor how to interact with the user base whom they represent. The result is often a deployment that suits the needs of the UAT group rather than the total user base.

ACCOUNTABILITY

Of course with a 'built' solution there is complete accountability, although there are those that would hold that to be a two-edged sword. The difficulty, as the reader may by now be realising, is that accountability is usually determined with regard to very few benchmarks – delivery on time, to budget and to specification. In most large financial firms, politics plays an important role and we should not underestimate the political pressure on projects to be 'under-defined' in order to give leeway for cost overruns and such like.

Case study 3 – Lessons of a retail pensions build project

I was commissioned by a pensions provider in the retail space to review a new deployment for its usefulness in the market. The pension company operated using a diverse sales force, arranged in branches with the sales force segregated by level based on their income producing performance. Not an uncommon model. At the top level were sales people capable of earning over £250,000 a year in commission income alone. As is also common, the company concerned wanted to try to both streamline the sales process and reduce costs at the same time. The problem at the time was that the sale could only be confirmed using the client's signature on the pension application form and the sales methodology was based on a fairly long cycle time to sale with assessments of risk and several meetings between first meeting and closing the business. The firm was finding an unacceptably high level of NPW (business that was quoted and even signed, but where the client, during the cool-off period, changed their mind – so the business is called NPW or 'Not Proceeded With'). Overall, management therefore had little real control over the sales process and more importantly could not help management to improve productivity.

Their response to these market conditions was to provide their sales force with a new laptop-based computer application designed to make the process of selling pensions more efficient. Pension sales in the retail sector are typically based on fear, so the usual model is to provide several 'illustrations' based on a client's perceived priorities, to create a raft of products, among which is almost certain to be a pension, which ultimately meets the financial needs of the client. The illustrations must conform to a model of risk provided by the Financial Services Authority (FSA) in terms of expected growth in asset or fund value.

The net result was an application suite, to be used by a range of salespeople to speed up the process. As I analysed the application, it was clear that, in theory, this application would be revolutionary. In order to make the senior management's information more clear and supposedly to help the salesperson manage multiple contemporaneous sales, the application had the ability to note any and all sales activity by either the client or the salesperson. The application had communications technology so that inbound and outbound business-related calls were routed via the laptop. So, once a client's details were entered, an inbound call could be related to a client and the length of the call automatically monitored. The salesperson would then have to allocate the call to a type of activity. Conversely, all calls made by a salesperson would be recorded as to time and duration so that the salesperson could later allocate the call to an activity. Finally, once a month all these data would be uploaded centrally to be analysed by management with a view to improving performance. As far as selling was concerned, if the client wanted to sign up, the data collected could be used to populate the relevant form at head office and subsequently sent to the client for signature. At the time of sale, using a portable mini printer, the salesperson could get a commitment by having the client sign a print out that confirmed that they wanted to proceed.

My observation was that there were several things wrong with this implementation, which hopefully the reader has already spotted. First, the psychology of this deployment is completely wrong. While a successful implementation would undoubtedly deliver excellent results, it was never going to be a successful implementation because it doesn't reflect the psychology of sales. I later fund out that the IT department had designed this application without consultation with any sales person. It showed. A good sales person has only one interest – selling. Anything, including administrative work, that detracts from time spent with a client won't work because there's an inbuilt antipathy towards it. Second, having the system effectively do a time and motion study on the salesperson was counterproductive. The designers had designed the system to a level of granularity that would not be supported in practice, nor had they considered the cost involved in having senior managers analysing the mountain of data that would be delivered as a result. They had also not considered that sales people would be highly unlikely to use the level of consistency in data entry (e.g., all calls in and out must be logged) necessary to make the mountain of data valid at the analysis stage. The clients in all this also had a problem. No-one had asked them what they thought of automating this process. The vast majority of people in the United Kingdom do not have a pension, but the majority of those who start looking for one, do so in middle age. It is rare for the young to plan ahead that far. At this age, most are married with the male as the main financial decision maker. So, the constituency of potential clients have an age and gender profile that mitigates against this technology. The generation after them would think nothing of buying a pension completely on-line with no human intervention at all. The generation before them would be highly untrusting of a sales process that included any technology. The generation concerned however, did not fit nicely into the gap. Because the regulatory structures required (and still do) a hard signature, all the technology benefits grind to a halt as separate processes have to be built to parallel a technology process with the manual one required in law. It is also true that the market perception of financial sales was not enhanced by this technology because it devalued the personal relationship between client and salesman and devalued the product. If it is just a case of crunching numbers, anybody can do that and clients are quick to realise this. Attempts to build in a sort of pseudo-skill by having a 'risk analysis' questionnaire which defines the allocation of assets for a given portfoloio simply did not work in psychological terms.

So, all in all, the company spent £2 million developing a solution without reference to its user base, client base and the broader aspects of market morphology.

The lesson is twofold. First, in a build project, the greatest danger lies in presuming that because you work in the industry means you know how the industry works. The second danger is that you fail to create an independent review body which can slow or stop activities that may be logical, but which don't add value (at best) and actively detract from value (at worst).

CHAPTER 9

Buy

Buying solutions is increasingly a viable option. It has many advantages over building your own solution and not many of the disadvantages. That said, there are disadvantages and, in the same way as building a solution requires an honest assessment of the risks, so too does buying a solution.

SPREAD

With a build solution, while you are able to leverage the ideas of your own workforce to deliver a unique solution, you are at the same time constrained in that you do not have open access to the ideas of others (without paying exorbitant consultancy and research fees). Purchased solutions have some merit because, as part of a third party's business model, it must aggregate market practice and innovation into a package that has attraction to a wide variety of customers with an equally wide variety of needs. In other words they have to be flexible. So any solution that is put forward in a 'Buy-it' model would naturally be expected (i) to have a high degree of fit to your existing business model and (ii) offer potential improvements to your business model that you would not have otherwise thought of. This is called spread.

RISK

This is rather a broad term in this context and really it encompasses all the potential downsides of a buy solution.

Over 60% of all the software companies in the United Kingdom, for instance, have less than 15 employees. This is because, particularly in financial services, many of the supplier companies are either deliberate or accidental spin-offs from the IT departments and almost without exception single-product companies. Someone there saw an opportunity and figured that there was more money to be made selling it as an outsider or the firm itself spun off part of the department either because it saw it as non-core, a distraction or because it simply wanted to reduce costs. In any event, the technological innovation in most countries does not come from large, slow-moving, conservative firms and financial services is no exception. Equally small-technology companies are at once financially more risky and less able to meet the global needs of financial institutions. If they have good ideas, they will grow too quickly and overextend themselves and be bought out by larger players thus losing their innovative style. If they grow too slowly their solutions will not be viewed as providing enough benefit – that is, not enough aggregation of market practice because not enough clients.

There are some excellent third-party providers out there and certainly for most of the late 1990s applications providers were experiencing their hay-day.

Following are things to watch out for when bringing in a third-party solution:

Financial stability. Will they still be there to support you in a year? Insist on strong due diligence and analysis of their financials. In many countries including the United Kingdom, you can get published records of a supplier's financial history. Analysis of these records can tell you a great deal. Particularly in the United Kingdom, where lists of the shareholders can also be obtained as well as details of all the officers of the business, most technology purchasers limit their analysis to either the current profit and loss account and/or the balance sheet. In much the same way as financial institutions vary in their performance over time, so do technology suppliers. It is therefore important not just to analyse this year's performance but also previous years to see if there is any pattern that could warrant further investigation. As an implementer or project leader, you aren't going to look very good if you miss the fact that your software supplier has a set of reasonable current financials but a balance sheet that shows it is paying off massive debts from mistakes.

History and references. It is important not only to know who some existing clients are but also their rate of replacement. You must obtain a good picture of their historical development in terms of both customers gained and also customers lost.

Business model. The norm is a licensing model formed of a one-time up-front license followed by annual 'maintenance' fees which are usually around 10%–12% of the up-front license fee. There are other models and if the opportunity is right, some suppliers will engage in a transactional model, particularly if the project has income possibility for the purchaser in which the supplier can share. While this is a lower up-front cost option than licensing, this can cause cash flow problems for some companies.

I often come across this model and technology managers need to be aware that there is no basis of science in the fact that maintenance fees are 10%–12% of license fees, just as there is no real science, other than what the market will bear, for the level of any given license fee. On the retail side of banking this model is falling out of favour in preference to the 'pay per click' methodology. Managers beware that this method may sound very reasonable as it relates to a payment for actual use rather than a notional use; but unless you have very good modelling for usage, this could easily backfire and cost the business a great deal of money.

Updates and upgrades. An update is usually either a small change in the code of an application or an update of some market data that is managed by the supplier as part of the solution deployment. An upgrade is usually either a major change in functionality or a change in supported operating system. Corollaries exist for communications and systems-level projects. Either way, these cost money that must be budgeted for as part of the 'cost of ownership'

RFPs. Small companies hate RFPs and rightly so. 'Requests For Proposal' fall into two categories from a financial services perspective. Either they are the result of lazy technologists who come out of the woodwork every couple of years to find out what the best and most current ideas are, by getting small innovative companies to do their work for them or they are real projects. The problem is that most application providers cannot tell the difference and have to assume the latter.

This is a technology management book, so RFPs deserve some comment in detail here. The biggest issue is that most RFPs are taken as templates (see Appendix 1) by those implementing them. While it is true that any half competent manager should be able to construct the obvious elements of a general RFP, most of the RFPs I have seen have been well short of a quality that would tell the recipient anything substantive about the vendor's actual capabilities. In a build scenario, there are clear stages to a deployment, business specifications, functional specification, technical specification, gap and integration analysis, testing, integration, roll-out etc. However, in a buy scenario, most of these excellent concepts are dispensed with. A business need is identified, potential suppliers are identified and essentially a top-level gap analysis decides the winner. The gaps can also be extremely 'loose' both in definition and interpretation. For example, more weight might be allowed for a vendor with local time zone support than for another whose solution actually has more technical merit. So decisions are made on no rigorous absolute basis, but more on a relative and 'look and feel basis' with the presumption that if they have other clients that have a similar profile, then their solution will probably work.

Of course, these are only the most important examples. When buying a solution there are a range of other issues that need to be considered. The difficulty is that by the time these concepts are being weighed, at least one of the key decisions has already been made – whether to buy at all. It is rare for a financial firm to structure an RFP that would allow for more than one top-level operating model. Most of the templates for RFPs assume in the nature of their language, that the objective is to buy a solution rather than outsource it.

REVERSION

This is a dark place to be. Reversion occurs when one model fails and another has to be adopted. For senior management, lower levels of management often disguise reversion as something else. In a recent case of reversion a software supplier was encountering some serious financial problems and effectively had had a significant negative balance sheet for several years after an abortive attempt at product development. For small software firms, product development is a knife-edge as they often don't have the financial strength either to develop more than one product at a time or to suffer a failure of a product to sell. So, what starts out as a positive in an RFP, that the firm is awarded a contract partially on the basis of its seeming strength in product development (which would of course benefit the vendor), the end result can be very different. The absolute value of a software vendor lies in its source code. So, the signs of a failing vendor are clear, as shown below. The end result is often the acquisition of the source code by the financial institution. This is almost the reverse of how most financial services-focused software firms come into existence. Usually either the software company is so strapped for cash due to plateauing or declining sales and failure to invest or it manages finances well or through competitive pressure, that it is forced to first lower its license fees. This is a signal that cash flow is more important than the product. Apart from the signal that this sends to earlier purchasers of the product, an intelligent project manager will analyse a prospective vendor's pricing history to look for such tell-tale signs. Other signs include a change in the structure and level of maintenance fees and/or a more frequent update and upgrade program. All tell a similar tale – cash flow is tight and taking over management decision making. Typically this means that purchasers are faced with an increased frequency of updating or upgrading the software in the vendor's efforts to generate cash flow to support its operations. The end result, if all the above fail, will be loss of source code. This will happen in one of two ways. If the purchasing financial institution recognises the signs in time, it may 'require' the source code from the vendor in order to protect its own operations and mitigate risk. Alternatively, and much the worse scenario, the vendor may be in such a difficult position that it has to 'offer' the source code to its client. In the first instance, the lower levels of management in the financial institution may see the risk and disguise the source code acquisition as a necessary move because of the vendor's inability to keep up with the needs of the institution. Effectively 'we need to get the source code because they can't meet our needs and we have more resources to manage the code'. Much of this obviously depends on the criticality of the application to the institutions day-to-day operations. So, for financial institutions the control issues of purchasing technology are both external and internal. Reversion describes the process of starting off with one model – buy, in this example, and being forced into a different model, in this case build.

CHAPTER 10

Bureau

Bureau is the middle ground in the technology acquisition stakes. Building a solution gives you complete control over your business process. The problem is you may be out of date with your competitors and your build may not be very good and it will be expensive to maintain. Buying a solution gives you the opportunity to get the best of breed but you may be spending money on things you don't need in the vendor's solution, you are always subject to changes in the vendor's product that may have no relevance to your needs, notwithstanding their financial stability. Bureau is often seen as the perfect solution. Define a business process. Select those elements that you are good at and implement them internally. Identify what you are not good at or cannot do and bring in expertise to fill the gap.

One of the most successful of these in recent times in the wholesale sector is SEI which has built a 'backbone' technology solution to which members of the financial intermediary and funds communities can connect to obtain services. One of the values brought to this model by SEI is the provision of 'best-of-breed' service providers so that a purchasing institution can opt for those elements of the back office service that it either has not already built or bought solutions.

This seems to be a best-fits-all scenario and it is certainly true that if you presume that there is a plethora of solutions available in the market, it is much more likely that you'll find the benefits of those solutions outweigh the build option. The problem is that each of those other options will probably have elements for which you have no need and as such they are overspecified. On the other hand, a best-of-breed bureau solution effectively takes away the time-consuming portion of the project by reducing the available option to those which some trusted entity deems to have the right combination of skills and products.

We must beware here of the bureau solution being taken to its logical conclusion and that is not just the segregation of functions for example, a corporate actions function or even a sub-element for example, proxy voting, class actions or tax processing; but the segregation down within a function. Bureau operations work best when the functional element they address can be easily sectioned off and its inputs and outputs easily codified and controlled. A good example in tax processing would be the segregation of form filling from calculation at one end and filing at the other end. At this level, the requirement to know which forms to fill in for any given combination of recipient type, year of income, country of investment and income type would seem to be (i) relatively simple and (ii) easily configured into a bureau system.

In reality this is a good example of when not to bureau. A second-level analysis would show that while the type of form required is dependent on a data set that could easily be input, and while the output would have some value, the rest of the process is so manual and requires so much effort that the cost saving accruing to having someone else find and fill the form out is minimal. So, it is important when selecting a solution type that attention is given to the analysis of the whole process and to the relative values of each segment within it.

Case study 4 Lessons in managing bureau providers

Most providers of bureau services are small software companies that have a buy solution that contains several elements, some of which can be fragmented into sub-elements and it is these that are often found in bureau form. I make the distinction here, particularly in financial services between a bureau, as described, and the more common 'service bureau' concept found on such networks as SWIFT. The latter take complete business processes as value propositions and effectively create 'value nodes'. Where SWIFT is essentially a network administrator, the value nodes are third parties that help SWIFT add value to its membership by creating connectivity to allow members to access services. The services described by this model are (i) usually complete business processes for example, tax recovery, and not sub-elements of a business process and (ii) they are true services as opposed to applications.

In this case study, the vendor is a small software company which was created, as is often the case, by a group of back-office workers who spotted an opportunity. The software created was specialist and very niche. As with many such firms, the resource base was very small, essentially one or two people per function – sales, management, development. Each has originally been working in one firm. The firm concerned saw an opportunity to reduce costs while maintaining control by 'spinning off' the development portion of the company into a separate firm. In this new capacity the original financial firm still represented the largest single customer for the new entity, which gave it the illusion of control (as it did not have a shareholding stake). The new firm had the illusion of guaranteed revenue from its largest client with the freedom to go and find new clients in non-competitive areas.

The net result is a model that is all too frequent in financial services vendors and must be reviewed carefully for sustainability by larger financial institutions. The company concerned had a management that wanted to prove itself – no point in just keeping one large client that you used to work for; but without significant investment they made the mistake of micro-managing cash flow, that is, the best way to increase customer base when your product is very expensive and the cycle time to sale is very long, is to unbundle the functionality and sell it separately. And so, their software got fragmented into a 'bureau' offering.

For the vendor here that was fairly simple and gave them an apparent immediate increase in product breadth without significant expenditure. The firms approaching this bureau provider were lulled into a false sense of security, mainly by the apparent breadth of offering, that the vendor was very efficient on a cost per employee basis and return on capital employed (ROCE) and that therefore this must be a very good vendor to deal with. The reality was that the firm had overstretched itself by selling what it could not support. It had not structured its initial spin-off at all well, as none of the team had any real management experience. The approach is called 'fishing' or 'vapourware' – creating an apparent product based on an existing technology and seeing who decides to buy it before deploying any investment in its real development. Many of these facts were not apparent to the larger financial institutions looking at this company's products. Not only was their due diligence easily subverted by clever responses in Requests For Proposals (RFPs), but no real qualitative analysis was performed on the company, as opposed to the product. Neither was any time-based sensitivity analysis performed to see what the likelihood was that the company would be able to sustain its operations.

The lesson here does apply to the broader categorisation of technology management, but is more appropriate in buy and bureau models. In outsourcing, these concerns are not so relevant because the nature of outsourcing requires as a fundamental a level of trust gained through test (TTT), a methodology that would normally catch such inconsistencies as those described in this case study.

The original company spinning off this smaller business unit is not exempt from problems in managing future technology projects. For a time, especially if there's a contract in place, the spin-off may have guaranteed pride of place or most-favoured provider status with its parent. This may not lead to the best solution being deployed and certainly mitigates against any competitive offering. The parent's needs 'appear' to be best met by the new spin-off, but actually, the new spin-off is spending so much of its effort in figuring out new markets so that it can become truly stand-alone, that the needs of the parent are often reduced.

A bureau service offered by a small company is high risk. The benefits of 'leading-edge' thinking created by smaller business units, particularly spin-offs are often eradicated by the lack of management expertise that is fundamental to the success of deployment.

CHAPTER 11

Outsource

Outsourcing is one of the most misunderstood terms or rather misused terms in modern business practice, merely because no-one really defines what they mean by it nor why they think they may or may not need it. Commonly, outsourcing is used where the process to be outsourced is 'not core to the business'. If this was a true statement then there would never have been buy or build solutions in the first place. The fact is that this reason is completely spurious. Whatever is required to understand what a customer wants and get it to them for a profit is, by definition, core to the business. The reality is that outsourcing is more often applied to an activity or process that no-one can be bothered to spend much time on, isn't seen as 'exciting' or that the firm is just so inefficient at that some third party can do it cheaper. This may seem like I'm not a fan of outsourcing – quite the contrary. It is just that I see more outsourcing deals done for the wrong reasons with the wrong set of benchmarks than I do almost any other business activity.

While there are two broad categories of outsourcing, IT and Business Process, there are usually only three reasons given for outsourcing in financial services. There are actually six:

- Competency
- Complexity
- Cost Reduction
- Compliance
- Corporate governance and
- Competitive advantage

The best way to exemplify each of these six is by case study.

Case study 5 Lessons in outsourcing

We will take the example of international withholding tax, the bane of many custodian banks and one bank's thought process in coming to its decision to outsource, based on the six principles.

Competency

There are some areas of bank operations which, while they may be core by our previous definitions, are nonetheless extremely complex and expensive to undertake. These are also the ones which an FI finds it most onerous to be competent in. To take a wholesale banking back office example, making sure that the net results of corporate actions such as dividend distribution are dealt with effectively includes attention to international taxation of such instruments. This is an extremely manual, but expertise-intensive process. The effects of lack of competency (as opposed to incompetency), are loss of investor return, potential liability and risk because clients who are entitled to be taxed on income at treaty rates (typically 15%) are very often taxed at statutory rates (sometimes as high as 35%). Best practice requires *relief at source*, where available, to be obtained for the benefit of the client so that he has maximum funds from day one. Some *countries* have 'accelerated' recovery processes and failing to meet the deadline can result in a ten-year wait for client money. Some *security types*, such as American depository Receipts (ADRs) have no direct reclaim possibility, only indirectly on the underlying shares and through the sponsoring bank. Some *investment vehicles* are transparent to tax authorities and reclaims may be missed if confidentiality keeps broker income streams and client identities separate. Some *methodologies* are transparent to tax authorities, so brokers who claim title to securities may think they are entitled to apply treaty rates, when foreign tax authorities will disagree and penetrate title to beneficial ownership. All this demonstrates the need for extreme competency and deep knowledge. Outsourcing becomes logical because it is the primary focus of the partner and *all* its expenditure is aimed at this one objective.

Complexity

There are around 200 countries in the world, each may or may not have a treaty with other countries for the avoidance of double taxation. For each of these country pairs there are a number of types of investor and a number of types of income, any combination of which can result in a different rate of withheld tax and treaty entitlement. The date on which the income is distributed also affects the entitlement, and other factors increase the complexity further. The number of permutations is over 40 million. The in-house cost of recovery, for any fund with multi-residence members or custodians with broad client bases, will be prohibitive compared to the number of likely reclaims that will be generated. A good outsourcing firm succeeds because its business model leverages economies of scale across the whole process. In the last twelve months the largest outsourcing firm in this area processed nearly two million tax reclaims. At that level, the focus of research and investment buys a greater assurance of success compared to what they could deliver on their own.

Cost reduction

This is the number one reason that firms consider outsourcing. However, while important, it is not usually the number one concern of firms that understand the value of withholding tax. The big benefit that delivers cost reductions is in the removal of hidden internal processes. Even if you have a software system, some significant proportion of the process is manual, and, for financial services as we all know, manual is bad. Outsourcing allows firms to convert a costly, semi-manual error prone process into an STP, Straight Through Processing function. In a well-benchmarked STP environment, clients send a file one way and receive funds and reports electronically in the other direction. And from their viewpoint, that's pretty much all there is to it. All the manual elements of the process, indeed, all the elements of the process, are opaque. Information flows one way, money flows the other way and that's exactly what fund managers, custodians and investors like.

Outsourcing also usually brings up issues relating to the degree of cost comparison. Because an outsource solution is 'packaged' to make the purchaser's life easy, its often compared to an incomplete internal cost comparison. So, essentially, the people doing the cost comparisons fail to include everything and therefore the benefit is not as great as it should be. It is also common at the other end of the scale to miss out on issues relating to integration of outsource servicing and replication of effort.

A full cost comparison for example would include

- Employment – Cost of Full Time Employees (FTE) and their equivalents (part time);

- Space – costs of space for the function itself and proportional cost of space allocations for management, cost control and so on;

- Technology – costs of IT, software development and so on (see buy, build, bureau etc.), integration;
- Training and development – costs of maintaining knowledge base to use system;
- Maintenance – costs associated with maintaining systems, connectivity, command and control systems, retraining and so on;
- Cost of money – the deduction made at balance sheet and P&L for the investment made in the above that is, inter alia, not available for investment elsewhere.

Typically firms will have to engage the above costs in advance of seeing the return (which may or may not be financially visible) whereas outsourcing can usually be achieved by being billed for a service in arrears.

Replication of effort in this scenario comes from the fact that the bank concerned had obligations under regulation to hold certain documents about their clients and keep information, both of which are needed by an outsource provider to do its job. So there will be a level of replication where the tax provider uses documents and data locally to do its job and those documents and data are needed at the outsourcing institution to meet its general regulatory requirements. This doesn't mean that outsourcing is the wrong way to go, quite the reverse. It does mean that you have to be clear about areas of overlap and how they will be handled to maintain integrity on both sides.

Compliance

If you can't produce an accurate assessment of a client's recoverable tax or eligibility for relief at source correctly the first time and every time, you stand a good chance of falling foul of regulatory compliance. How many headlines have you seen in the last few years of heavy fines being issued for failure to keep and maintain accurate client records? It's these very records that underpin the assessment of eligibility.

The idea of outsourcing a function to minimise compliance risk may seem paradoxical. However, the number of regulations now in force that evidence some sort of extraterritorial jurisdiction gives corporate actions departments and compliance officers, nightmares. Outsourcing, in a functionally selective way, can actually reduce the burden on compliance and operations departments by releasing them from some proportion of concern over whether they have their structures integrated and monitored. It then becomes the job of the outsource partner. The benefit is that the accuracy of the underlying data is critical to the outsourcer's business, because it is its only focus.

Corporate governance

Financial services firms face two corporate governance issues, not one. Their own governance, usually overlooked by regulatory authorities, and the corporate governance of their clients. Investors are becoming increasingly activist and holding their investments long as the balance in yield strategies changes. The result is that more are receiving dividends and being overtaxed. Typically, two institutional investors with different residencies may be taxed, and therefore overtaxed differently. If the CFO of the invested company does not take action, his investors lose money. Similarly, if the custodian fails to act, the investors may lose money. The publication in 2003 of proxy voting policies on probity in withholding tax evidences the pressure on the investment management chain to demonstrate that everything possible has been done. Investor concerns should make custodians and fund managers consider outsourcing more strongly to demonstrate best efforts on behalf of their client's underlying shareholders.

Competitive advantage

Most relationship managers would happily enter a pact with the devil if they could get a legitimate and clear service advantage in the market and withholding tax is one such. Unfortunately, when taken at the fund management or even custodian level the internal costs are so high that profitability is difficult to achieve; so many either don't address withholding tax at all, or do so inconsistently, or have policies which disenfranchise some clients. Outsourcing allows the creation of a profitable withholding tax service which is complete and inclusive for all clients and converts a fixed internal cost into an external, variable and contingent one. This is an area I come across frequently. So many front office relationship management staff do not appreciate what goes on in the back office that they do not identify key advantages for their business. Similarly functional managers in the back office are usually so focused on the complexities of their own functions that they fail to communicate these advantages effectively through the chain. From a technology management viewpoint, one of the key tasks should be to identify those aspects of an outsource supplier that are benefits to the market. In this case, the outsource supplier's own benchmarks far outstripped

> the bank's simply because the vendor had the benefit of much greater volumes and could therefore deliver faster recovery of taxes with more certainty of time frame. This placed them, even though they outsourced the function, at the top of the rankings for tax processing within their market vertical – a clear market advantage.

HOW TO OUTSOURCE?

Spend your time finding out whether you can trust your potential partner and not whether you think his process is better or worse than yours. Trust is built up in a number of ways. What's the financial position of your partner? Who uses them? Take up references and pay attention to the tone as well as the words used in references. That's all 'head'. Now add 'heart'. What does your partner put back into the industry and into your business in particular? Is he looking after your interests and your clients' or just processing data? How does he go the extra mile? Trust is the key that opens the door to successful outsourcing.

Make sure your end result is as STP as possible by making it all about file transfer from your viewpoint. This can be achieved in less than half an hour with good client IT support. It is because if your partner is processing over a million reclaims a year, they have to be able to do that, it is their business to make the transition smooth and efficient. The result the client sees is electronic files out and money and electronic reports in.

These are lessons at the granular level and are repeated at several points during this book, because they are fundamentals of technology management when dealing with third-party suppliers of any kind. In my view contracts are important but trust is more important. Contracts are after all, essentially a codification of what happens when things go wrong in a relationship. I've very rarely found the need to use contracts in this way because if you develop a good relationship with a supplier you can usually pick up the phone or meet to resolve issues without recourse to the contract.

WHEN TO OUTSOURCE?

While withholding tax is a seasonal business, outsourcing takes only a few weeks to implement. Full transition (the big bang) can of course be done between dividend seasons to allow the same stabilising process, but given that the result is essentially a data feed out and account credits in, there is actually no reason why big bang cannot occur at any time. This is because of Statutes of Limitations. If initial analysis shows significant sums about to

fall out of Statute, big bang is not only feasible, it is also preferable to avoid potential liabilities later on. Whether big bang or phased introduction is selected, the Statutes typically give several years in which reclaims can be filed so that whatever is handed over is not usually mission-critical. Having said that, best practice benchmarks this activity at less than two weeks from notification of income to filing of tax reclaim.
In summary:

1. Outsourcing is something everyone is already doing and has been doing for years. Outsourcing withholding tax is about a change of degree, not kind;

2. Outsource for *several* good and solid reasons;

3. Choose someone you can trust, that knows the difference between a partner and a supplier and can prove it;

4. Choose someone whose business volumes demonstrate the basic principle of outsourcing efficiency;

5. Choose someone whose reputation in the market stands testament to the fact they'll still be there in ten years.

6. Check benchmarks. International benchmarks for withholding tax processing were published by Euromoney Institutional Investor in 2003;

7. Make it STP from *your* viewpoint;

8. There is no real timing sensitivity or seasonality to outsourcing withholding tax – how fast do you and your clients want to realise the benefits?

PART III

Delivering Value from Technology

It is one thing to have a strategic view. It is another thing to really deliver value from the implementation of that strategic view. In this part of the book we will focus more on strategic and tactical issues and find out how they actually deliver value. At the strategic level we must consider the impact of disruptive technologies as these are becoming far more common than in the last century. Similarly, at the tactical level we will look at the value that can be leveraged from proper testing methodologies and the need for adequate levels of documentation. Finally, we will look at ways to benchmark value.

CHAPTER 12

Disruptive Innovation – Threat or Opportunity

One of the problems associated with delivering value from any technology is the environment in which it exists, the speed with which it is deployed and the effect it has on pre-existing technologies. In this latter case, the environment of speed of deployment or innovation, can be, respectively, so sensitive and so quick as to create a shock or disruptive effect. The effect is felt negatively for those firms on the receiving end and (usually) positively for those creating the disruption. This, it has to be said, is a generalization. It is by no means certain that any given disruptor will successfully manage a new technology's emergence. For every successful social network, there have been many failures. As I said at the very beginning of this book, several marketing and business issues must be present at the same time for a new principle to succeed. Equally, sleeping giants can easily be awoken by the advent of an unforeseen threat and if the threat is not robust enough, the larger firm can be reinvigorated either to kill the technology as was the case in the video tape format wars, or, from greater resources, take over the disruptive technology to its own advantage.

Either way, we live in a world where invention seems to be increasing apace and financial services is not immune to its effects. Therefore, it is important to take some cognizance of what disruptive innovations are, how they develop and what threats they pose.

John Maynard Keynes once said 'It is dangerous … to apply to the future inductive arguments based on past experience, unless one can distinguish the broad reasons why past experience was what it was'.

WHAT IS DISRUPTIVE INNOVATION?

A disruptive innovation is an innovative product or service that eventually overturns the existing dominant businesses in the market. The concept of business disruption comes from Harvard Professor of Business Studies Clayton Christensen, whose research into what caused huge businesses with enormous resources and high-performing managers to completely miss market changes that badly damaged the incumbents, forced them out of lines of business and, in some cases, resulted in their eventual demise. The most recent example of course in the United Kingdom is Northern Rock, whose managers adopted a high-risk business model and then failed to anticipate or recognize changes in the market that made their model unsustainable. There was nothing wrong with a high-risk model. It worked perfectly and gave Northern Rock an excellent competitive position in the market – as long as the conditions on which the business model was based were in effect. Their failure was not the risk level inherent in their model. Many other parts of financial services have equal if not higher levels of risk, for example derivatives trading. No, the failure was not seeing the effects of change of liquidity in the credit.

Christensen's first book, *The Innovator's Dilemma: When New Technologies Cause Great Firms to Fail*, created intense interest and caused a number of major businesses to reevaluate their strategies. For instance, Intel introduced the low-end Celeron processor within a separate business division in direct response to *The Innovators Dilemma*; e-Bay, itself a disruptor, not surprisingly, has a senior director of Platform and Disruptive Innovation.

The theory of disruptive innovation is one of the few business theories in which scientific deduction has been used to identify the causal mechanism underpinning success. Most business theories take the examples of a few successful businesses, identify a few common traits and then recommend that all businesses adopt those traits – without identifying the circumstances in which, or the reasons why, those traits were associated with success. Only by determining the circumstances in which particular strategies are successful is it possible to predict when and how adopting those strategies will create success for others.

The financial industry has historically not been seen as being particularly vulnerable to disruption. In 2006 *Business Week* ran a cover story about the world's most innovative companies. Not one financial services company made it into the top 25, only one was in the top 50 and just two more struggled into the top 75. This suggests that either there is something about the structure of financial services that protects it from disruptive innovation, that few disruptive innovations succeed in financial services or that, to date, no disruptive innovations have been tried in this market.

The lack of historical experience here is partly due to the breadth of scope of many financial sector businesses. Disruption affects individual markets and the larger financial institutions operate across many markets, so we have not seen the same failures of incumbents among large financial institutions that we have seen in other industries. However, large institutions have been, and will continue to be, chased out of significant global markets by disruptive businesses. This will change – innovative companies such as specialist funds and the monoline insurers will be more vulnerable to disruption because they have no other markets to retreat into.

Disruption is important to understand because disruption is often stealthy. The capabilities of a disruptor will often initially be far inferior to those of the incumbents, leading to dismissal as a competitive threat. Within financial services for example, this is evidenced by the growing trend for one type of intermediary to encroach on the activity of another type, for example brokers and custodians. Although in the period upto 2006 this occurred in a gradual, therefore non-disruptive way, the increasing development of utility style business models will, from 2008 onwards, allow for the explosive development of competitive business strategies. Disrupted companies tend to adopt visible stances:

- Disruption cannot be adopted within the incumbents' business model, and attempts to do so only destroy what makes it disruptive. Only when it is too late to recover its position will the incumbent recognise its mistake.
- The disrupted tend to flee from the markets being disrupted rather than fight.
- Disrupted businesses may be absorbed by the disruptor to service the high-end of the markets it serves, may find a way to survive as a niche player or disappear entirely. Either way, the powerhouse that was a household name has been overthrown.

This chapter will explain the characteristics of a disruptive innovation, show how to separate new non-disruptive businesses (to which the word 'disruptive' has been wrongly tagged) from truly disruptive businesses, explain how to recognise vulnerability to disruption and explore what developments could lead in time to disruption in key financial markets.

'DISRUPTIVE' IS OVERUSED

Almost every time a radical new product or service is announced the word 'disruptive' appears, frequently in the commentary from industry pundits but also occasionally in the PR from the businesses themselves. In almost every case the word has been misapplied.

Clayton Christensen himself noted this phenomenon when he changed the use of the term from 'disruptive technology' to 'disruptive innovation'. There really is no such thing as a disruptive technology. Instead, most new technology can be applied in a disruptive or non-disruptive, or sustaining, way. It is the business model that the technology is employed in that is disruptive. This is why low-cost airlines like EasyJet and discount shops like Wal-Mart are disruptive – they employ exactly the same technology as the incumbents, but within the context of a different business model. Similarly, an incumbent can often adopt a new low-cost technology in its own business model, such as the incumbent telecommunications operators are doing with Voice over IP. Disrupting mobile commerce infrastructure technologies, like the Internet, are themselves neither sustaining nor disruptive. Each can be used in either a sustaining or disruptive way. Equally, in financial services, GlobeTax's development of V-STP is a business model founded on a unique combination of standards, outsourcing, networks and messaging. It is a disruptive innovation inasmuch as it removes the need for any financial services firm to engage directly in the costly area of tax reclamation. Some financial firms are/will be disruptors by using this innovation to radically reduce costs and improve service levels, giving them an unchallengable market position. Others will be subject to the disruption and eventually suffer loss of client base and market reputation and probably leave this market segment to those who have effectively created the utility for the industry rather than the less than palatable 'do-it-yourself' business model.

ISSUES OF DISRUPTIVE INNOVATION

Disruptive innovation is really three separate but related issues. The first issue is the concept of disruption itself. To be disruptive an innovation must target either non-users – which is a new market disruption – or must be a low-end innovation which provides existing customers in the market who are increasingly overserved by the functionality of the mainstream product, with sufficient functionality to meet their needs at a much lower price.

The second issue is centred on Resources, Processes and Values. This deals with why incumbents fail to recognise and respond to disruptive threats. The incumbents' resources – the assets it controls and the people that work for it, its processes, how it transforms its inputs into outputs of greater market value and its values – the criteria that the company uses to allocate its scarce resources, all determine the opportunities that the incumbent sees as attractive in terms of return on investment.

The final issue is Value Chain Evolution. This exposes another type of disruption, which is an inevitable shift of the highest profits within the value chain as products change from *Not Good Enough* to *Good Enough*. Essentially, firms should seek to control the activities in the value chain that affect the attributes of the product that are important to customers.

The theory of disruption

For the finance industry, a new automated trading exchange technology could be used to sustain an existing exchange business or to create a low-end disruptive model. To be disruptive the low-cost model must either underperform the incumbent, attracting only the low-volume exchange users not willing to pay premium rates for a bells-and-whistles service, or must find a new market among the unserved, perhaps introducing them to the attractions of trading for the first time. New market disruptions will tend to become low-end disruptors over time. This approach creates an asymmetry of motivation – the incumbents are motivated to flee in the face of the disruption towards the more profitable, underserved customers.

New entrants will almost always fail if they target the mainstream customers of the market incumbents. The incumbents will be motivated to fight and will have better processes, products and resources to do so.

An example of a low-end disruptor is Dollar Financial which is targeting underbanked, low-waged customers that are largely ignored as unprofitable by the larger banks such as Bank of America. Bank of America is motivated by its profitability and growth strategies to innovate with new high-margin products for its most demanding customers. Dollar Financial instead sees the low-waged as a market that can be profitably served by a low-cost, no frills model which is completely unattractive to Bank of America's mainstream customers. The incentive for Dollar Financial is to improve its profit margin by innovating within its low-cost business model to attract the next tier of overserved customers. By removing the low-profitability customer base from Bank of America, Dollar Financial is actually helping Bank of America to reduce its costs and improve its profitability – for a while.

An example of an innovation that started as a new market disruptor is Grameen Bank, a microcredit provider. Grameen originally provided small loans with no fixed repayment scheme, delivered to villages by mobile bankers on foot or bike and enforced by a communal structure that limits loan amounts within groups based on the group's repayment status. With a Grameen loan a poor villager may be able drill a new well or buy a goat while building a credit history without getting trapped in a cycle of spiralling debt. Most of Grameens' loans are from pennies to a few hundred dollars, but they free poor communities from poverty, for which Grameen's founder, Muhammed Yunus, was awarded the 2006 Nobel Peace Prize. By the start of 2007 his bank has served over five million borrowers and lent over $6.5bn, with a 98% recovery rate. It has financed the building of over 650,000 houses and deployed almost 300,000 village phones. Before Grameen these communities could not obtain credit from normal institutions – all they could get were high-interest rate loans from loan sharks.

Resources, processes and values

The second issue of disruption is concerned with resources, process and values. This explains why incumbents cannot respond effectively to disruptive innovators.

Every company that becomes good at what it does develops a collection of assets and capabilities that makes it more efficient and/or more effective than its competitors. Its resources, including its people, its technologies, its information and its brand are the basis on which its capabilities are built. Business processes are how the business encapsulates its knowledge into repeatable structures that confer competitive advantage. Values are much more than just the beliefs of the company – they are the decision criteria that the business and everyone in it uses to make decisions about which products to create, which opportunities to pursue and which customers to target. These values depend on the size of the company and its asset base – innovations that appear to have a small market are unattractive to a large business looking for growth opportunities, while opportunities must cover the financing cost of the companies assets.

Targets for return on capital, return on investment and similar key performance indicators (KPIs) are the yardsticks by which opportunities are measured. These values are why large companies completely miss disruptions – because the potential for an entirely new market cannot be known in advance.

Value chain evolution

As incremental innovations eventually make the performance of any product exceed the needs of the majority of the market, value chain evolution describes how the majority of the profits move elsewhere in the value chain. Companies choose whether to be vertically integrated or to specialise, with suppliers and distributors providing the remainder of the value chain. Whether vertical integration or 'componentisation' works best depends on whether the performance of the product underperforms or outperforms the needs of the majority of customers.

One example of this in action is the case of the IBM PC. IBM's skills are as an integrator, taking components and using its engineering skills to integrate them into a better computer than their rivals. In this market IBM's engineering skills allowed them to create better, more powerful computers at a time when this is what customers valued highly. This was how IBM became the masters of the mainframe computer world. However, they were subsequently blindsided by the disruptive departmental minicomputers of Sun and Digital Equipment. IBM then saw an opportunity to create a small computer that businesses could use for stand-alone tasks. This computer was the IBM PC.

The way IBM did this sowed the seeds of its own exit from the biggest market for computers that ever existed. IBM decided to use components from elsewhere as it always had done. However, to reduce the cost of manufacture of the PC, IBM defined a set of standard interfaces with the idea of buying standard components from multiple sources at lower cost. The interfaces were good enough to allow anyone to make an equivalent computer – what weren't good enough were the components such as the processor, memories, disk storage and operating system. This meant that the best components commanded a premium.

Unfortunately for IBM, the standardised design meant that computer manufacture became an assembly task, something that IBM was not good at. IBM's processes and values were not designed for pile-it-high, sell-it-cheap mass manufacture and it struggled. IBM had to compete at the margin with other assemblers for whom assembly was a core skill. IBM succeeded for some time by developing improved interfaces, but eventually Compaq, then HP and finally Dell forced IBM out of the desktop and subsequently the more complex laptop markets. If Thomas Watson walked back into IBM today he would see a company he recognised, with largely the same resources, processes and values as in his day and doing roughly the same type of things – making the biggest and best computers, developing complex software and providing IT consultancy.

WHAT DOES IT TAKE TO BE DISRUPTIVE?

The key to disruptive innovation is to identify unserved or overserved markets and find ways to service them. An unserved market is one in which a large population lacks the skills or finance to participate; an overserved market is one in which the trajectory of product improvement, driven by the most demanding customers, has left the mainstream of the market open to a cheaper but good-enough innovation.

Figure 12.1 illustrates a low-end disruption. The mainstream product, through continuous sustaining innovation, seeks to take more revenues from the most demanding, least-satisfied tier of customers who are willing to pay more for a better product.

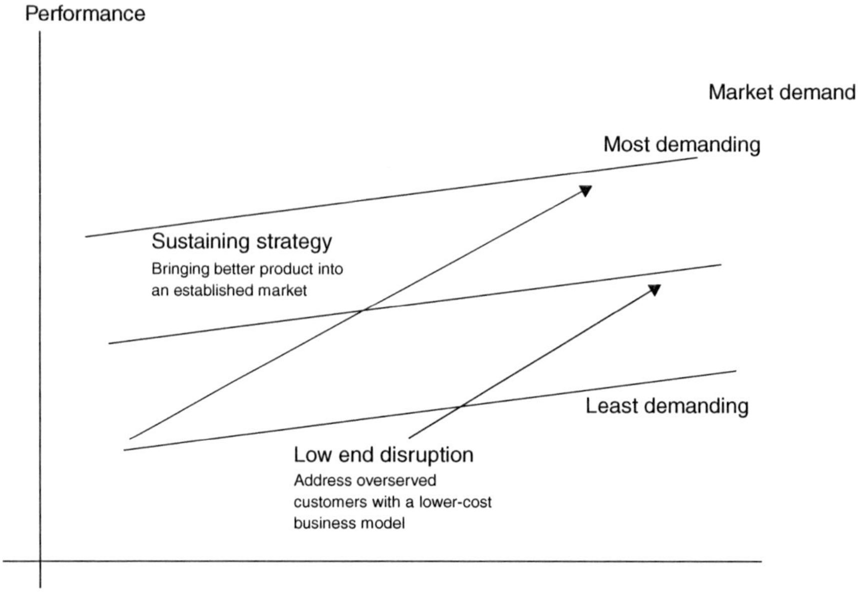

Figure 12.1 Low-end disruption: the innovators' dilemma

Source: Tom Foale.

Meanwhile a disruptive product that appears later does not appeal to the great majority of the mainstream customers. The disruptive product costs less than the mainstream product and so is attractive to the most overserved users of the mainstream product. Its creator is initially satisfied with making lower levels of profitable income from the lowest tiers of the incumbent's user base.

Over time the disruptor is incentivised to improve the performance of its product to attract more and more customers away from the mainstream product. The incumbent is not motivated to defend these marginally profitable customers by providing a competing product because its limited resources are fully focused on serving its higher-margin customers and developing new products to satisfy its most demanding customers.

Once it recognises the threat that the disruptor poses, the only defence that the incumbent has is to create a disruptive innovation of its own, sacrificing its low-end customer base. However, if that response is created within the existing business it will inevitably fail because the mechanisms the mainstream business uses to allocate resources will not favour the new innovation.

Many disruptive innovations start in unserved markets, where the incumbents do not see any need to respond, and subsequently move into the overserved market where they start to remove the less-profitable customers from the incumbent. In fact, to be disruptive a product relying on new innovation must be capable of improving so that it gradually takes more and more of the incumbent's market. The disruptor will again be motivated by increased profitability and growth, to create the improvements and innovations needed in their technology to sell to, what will be for them, the much more profitable customers.

The key requirements for an innovation to be disruptive are that

- The industry incumbents cannot incorporate the disruptive business model within their own business;

- The incumbents are motivated to flee rather than fight. This presupposes that they have an attractive growth area to flee into.

The reason that incumbents cannot adopt such business models are that their resources, processes and values prevent an innovation being proposed as an attractive use of the shareholders' money. In other words, the economics of the disruption are deeply unattractive to the incumbent. To be disruptive the technology must also be unattractive to the incumbents' main customers, otherwise it is just a threat to be dealt with. Returning to the corporate actions example, V-STP is a disruptive innovation because the combination of resources cannot be used by custodians to automate corporate actions internally. This is because many parts of the corporate actions process (more than 60% in the case of withholding tax) are fundamentally manual. Equally V-STP is unattractive to a custodian's customers (i) because they lack the resources to deal with the issue effectively and (ii) that's why they employ their custodian. The difference in this case is that the disruption is being offered as a competitive advantage to custodians in the market. Its inventor, GlobeTax, can't use V-STP directly because it doesn't compete with custodians, they are its customers. So, what is a complex, manual and difficult area for custodians becomes a clear differentiator for them, if they are able to adopt the innovation to put them a step ahead of their in-market competition.

If a new business attacks an incumbent's main market then the incumbent is motivated to defend its territory. A disruption has to attack either the overserved – those who don't need all of the features of the incumbent's service that are designed for the more demanding end of its market – or service the unserved, those who cannot afford the incumbent's services. Once the disruptor has established a foothold it can then go on to improve its services to attract the next tier of overserved customers away from the incumbent.

Sometimes legislation unlocks the potential for a disruption. For instance, MiFID changes the rules governing financial exchanges and has allowed the major UK banks to create their own share exchange, Turquoise, which is disruptive to the Stock Exchange. V-STP as we have already discussed is disruptive to the corporate actions processing of custodial banks. Many other new exchanges are in development.

Network effects can sometimes protect the incumbents' position for some time. In the financial services industry access to liquidity may play a significant part in protecting incumbents from attack. However, network effects may also accelerate the progress of the disruption, as has happened with Skype in the telecoms arena.

TRAJECTORIES OF DISRUPTION

Wave after wave of disruptions can be caused by the gradual development of a technology. The transistor is an excellent example. The original transistor was expensive and very low power, only suitable for very limited roles where its robustness and resistance to vibration were valued, such as in aerospace and the military. The development of the transistor then led to the basic integrated circuit and ultimately to the microprocessor. The ongoing upscaling, scale economics and diversity of function of the integrated circuit now means it is used in a huge range of applications including very low cost RFID (Radio-frequency ID) devices used to tag millions of products, is hidden in household items and children's toys, and at the high-performance end is the workhorse of the revolution in electronic trading and on-line banking.

While technologies themselves are not inherently disruptive, it is the trajectory of improvement of technologies that creates many of the opportunities for disruption. Most new technologies have inferior performance in many of the critical areas required for existing products, compared to existing technologies, when they first appear. For instance, the first transistors were small and rugged, but lacked the power-handling of the vacuum tube used in most products at the time – home radio units and television sets.

It is this lack of performance in most areas that allows disruptions to develop. By creating products that use the areas of performance in which the infant technologies do perform well, entirely new markets are created. This allows the company creating the product to make profits while developing the expertise to make the best use of the new technology. As the new technology continues to improve it eventually invades the territory of the incumbent, which by now lacks the resources and expertise in the new technology to compete.

Christensen uses the example of Sony to illustrate this point. While the television manufacturers set about trying to develop the transistor to the point where it could be used in their large sets, Sony used the transistor for what it was good for at the time and created a small, low-cost low-power radio. This radio's performance was in turn far inferior to the large household valve radio sets of the day – its sound reproduction was tinny and it could only power an earpiece, not a loudspeaker. However, the new radio created a new market of teenagers for whom the alternative was not listening to music at all, and who were now able to listen to their own choice of music with their friends wherever they chose.

Sony went on to create more and more new products, eventually moving into low-cost portable black-and-white TV sets while the mainstream TV manufacturers like RCA and Rediffusion were developing large colour sets that still required the capabilities of the vacuum tube. As the technology developed still further Sony and others were able to use the transistor to meet the demands of the market for colour televisions. RCA and Rediffusion were gradually displaced from the TV market partly because they lacked the skills in the new technology to create competitive transistorised products – we will look at other reasons later.

The exponential rate of increase in processing power of microchips, a prediction known as Moore's law that the industry has followed now for over 40 years, is the basis of a sequence of disruptive developments – the mainframe computer, the minicomputer, the desktop PC, the hand-held computer, the datacentre, distributed computing and so on.

Gordon Moore, one of the founders of Intel, predicted in a 1965 paper that that the number of transistors that can be inexpensively placed on an integrated circuit will increase exponentially, doubling approximately every two years. Moore's law, shown in Figure 12.2, has proved true for 40 years and is predicted to follow the same trajectory for at least another 10 years.

The development of hand-held electronics, including the personal digital assistant (PDA) or high-functionality mobile phone, has been the result of the continuing development of many different technologies which have been combined to create new and exciting products. The iPod is a good example – the battery, screen, processor, touch-sensitive controls, the iTunes music management system and digital copy protection all combined

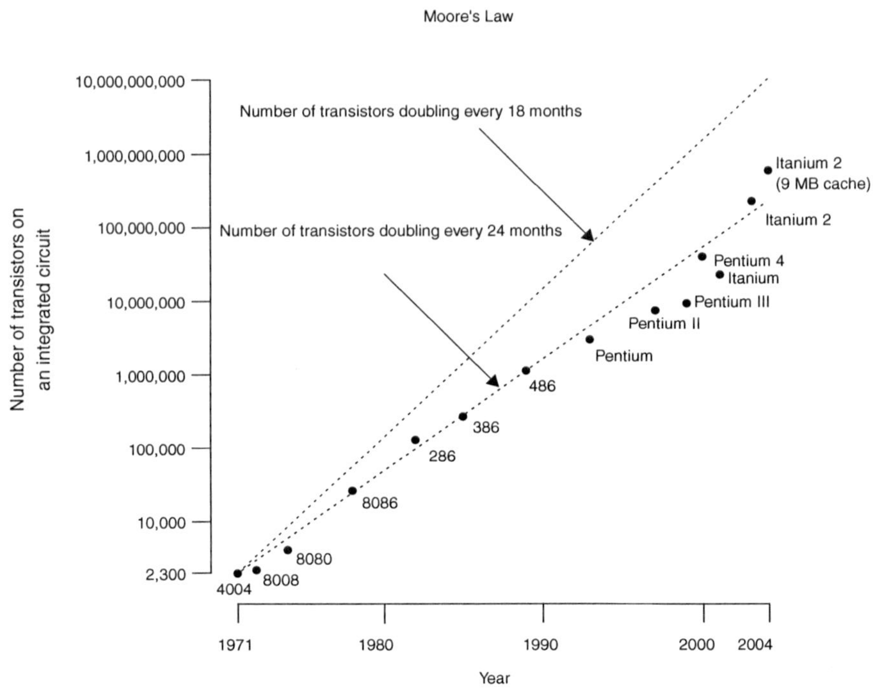

Figure 12.2 Moore's Law

Source: Wikipedia.

with Apple's funky magic to create a ground-breaking innovation that has had as big an impact as Sony's original transistor radio. Much of this would have seemed irrelevant to the financial services industry even as little as two years ago. However it is already clear that mobile banking at the retail level is set to roll-out into the markets over the next 18 months. The iPhone and many other hand-held devices already have good enough Internet connections to provide access to on-line banking sites for customers. What is less clear is what innovations will flow through to back office processing from these technologies.

Parallel developments in various technologies including memory, disk drives, batteries, display technologies and so on have allowed the continual introduction of new and innovative electronic products. Peer-to-peer technologies combined with open source may perform a similar feat in the financial industry.

Progressive developments of technologies have the tendency to make industry pundits look extremely foolish. They successfully predict the use of the developing trajectory to make sustaining innovations while invariably completely missing the opportunities where the innovation has finally become good enough to form the basis of a product that creates a whole new market.

DISRUPTION AND THE VALUE SYSTEM

Disruptive innovations often have to create their own value chain. Suppliers to the incumbents are often not attracted by the early low volumes and need for low-cost components for the new product. Their components may well not have the right characteristics for the disruptive product.

Early investigations into disruption looked at the computer hard disk drive industry, where successive waves of disruption were caused by different sized discs (form factor). Each form factor had a different customer base in the computer industry, which were themselves successive disruptors of each other. This caused a parallel disruption in the disc industry, where the incumbents in each form factor were unable to profitably adopt the next form factor.

Similarly, the cheaper disruptive products are not attractive to the existing distribution mechanisms who cannot make the profits they need at the margins available. The disruptor has to find new, lower-cost ways to get their product to market.

Earlier in the chapter we looked at Sony and the demise of the vacuum tube-based TV set manufacturers. One of the key reasons that RCA and others failed to successfully adopt the transistorised TV set is that their distribution network was the no longer suitable.

As vacuum tube sets required regular tube replacement they required a network of electronics specialist repair shops who both sold the sets and maintained them. These specialist shops could not make sufficient profits from selling TV sets that didn't break down. In contrast the more robust transistorised set could be sold by department stores and, later, consumer electronics shops. By the time RCA wanted to distribute its sets via the new channel it was fully occupied with the disruptive manufacturer's TV sets.

Many new disruptors must create their own value chain, particularly in the highly integrated financial industry. Many of the new disruptors have little recourse to the existing high-cost financial value chain as they have to keep costs pared to the bone (for a summary of these see Table 12.1).

Table 12.1 Characteristics of a disruptive innovation

	Sustaining innovations	*Low-end disruptions*	*New market disruptions*
Performance	Performance improvement in attributes most valued by the industry's most demanding customers.	Performance that is good enough at the low end of the mainstream market.	Lower performance in 'traditional' attributes, but improved performance in new attributes.
Customers	The most attractive customers in the mainstream market who are willing to pay for improved performance.	Overserved customers in the low end of the mainstream market.	Customers who historically lacked the money or skill to buy or use the product.
Impact	Improves or maintains profit margins by exploiting the existing processes and cost structure and making better use of current competitive advantages. .	Uses a new operating and/or financial approach.	Business model must make money at lower price per unit sold and at unit production volumes that initially will be small. Gross margin dollars per unit sold will be significantly lower.
Affects	Incumbent businesses.	New businesses.	New businesses.

Source: Author.

DISRUPTION IN THE FINANCIAL SERVICES INDUSTRY

The financial services industry has proved remarkably resilient to change. Major innovations, including the introduction of credit cards, ATMs, on-line banking, hedging, new financial markets and so on have been adopted by the larger and older institutions with few problems. New entrants such as Paypal and Egg have been accommodated. The finance industry has been protected because the capabilities that are the bedrock of the industry – trust, economic knowledge, capital management, risk management, capital distribution etc. – have until now been better incarnated in large, integrated organisations like banks. However, this could be about to change as IT technologies become good enough to allow some of these capabilities to be disconnected and redistributed in ways that the industry could find it very difficult to defend against.

To understand where vulnerabilities might exist it is necessary to look at where the financial service delivers value, its cost structures and its value system. New business models and new technologies that could form the basis of new business models must be evaluated to see if they can meet the criteria for disruption. For managers in technology and business units, this is a key issue. The rest of this book is rightly focused on best practice and methodology for the deployment of technology. This chapter serves as a warning shot across the bows that insufficient attention and lateral thinking about new innovations could lead to disaster whereas historically such innovations have led only to minor annoyance.

The underlying value proposition for the financial services industry is to manage, distribute and lend assets and to redistribute risk. Banks create wealth through capital lending to consumers and wealth-creators. Other financial companies act as intermediaries in what is often a zero-sum game.

Some clues to where technology-based disruption may come from are given by Betfair, which has provided a platform where, for a small fee, gamblers may bet against each other and the odds are set by matching of bets. In traditional gaming the gamblers bet against the bookmaker and the bookmaker carries the risk of losing heavily in some events. The bookmakers set odds that allow them, on average, to make sufficient money to carry on the complex operation of betting. Betfair, on the other hand, does not get involved in the risks of gaming and makes a very good living from merely providing the platform. This means that more attractive odds can be found on Betfair, and the platform is causing considerable disruption to the traditional bookmakers' livelihood. Betfair and others are now moving into the spread-betting part of the financial market where they may cause a similar disruption.

Zecco.com is an online financial portal and community where investors trade stocks for free. Zecco has attracted executives from Brown and Co. and E-Trade with its zero-cost concept. Zecco is a lot more than a trading platform, it is a community for the exchange of ideas and information about shares between the shareholders. Zecco makes its money from interest on margin balances, the interest on deposits placed by traders (a minimum balance of $2500 is required to get free trading) and from commissions on premium brokerage products like options trading.

Like a lot of disruptive startups Zecco does little marketing, preferring word-of-mouth to acquire new customers. This is using the power of networks to create its market, and provides something of a natural limit on competitors because word-of-mouth marketing favours the largest.

Low-end unsecured lending will also be a target for entrepreneurs. Person to person lending is a new development in lending that takes investments from individuals of any size and provides small unsecured loans. In one example, Zopa (http://www.zopa.com), the business model is a marketplace with Zopa taking a fixed fee for arranging a loan. It takes deposits from lenders, with interest rates being set by the lenders and with no level of return being guaranteed. Borrowers are credit checked. The service distributes the risk of each loan across many lenders and pays interest to the lenders based on the overall income. Defaulters are chased by a collections agency whose cost is borne by Zopa. Lenders' money, when not lent, is retained in an escrow account.

As these systems are markets, not banks, this is a potentially disruptive model. The reasons are

- by cutting out the middleman the system promises lower interest rates to borrowers and higher returns to lenders if they actively manage their lending;
- the lender, not the service, carries the risk of bad debt;
- the agent is not required to maintain any liquidity;
- the agents' returns are volume-based rather than risk-based.

Zopa is a product that redistributes risk. Entirely in line with the rest of the financial system, the lender accepts a higher risk in return for higher returns. A Zopa lender runs the risk of individual defaults, even if these are low, and is also exposed to systemic risks which could, in the worst case, see the loss of their entire stake. A bank depositor is only exposed to systemic risks affecting the rate of return on their deposit, with the deposit itself largely protected by the banking systems. Zopa itself assumes no risks except the cost of chasing defaulters, whereas the financial system owns the entire risk of its loans.

It remains to be seen whether Zopa and its peers are able to step up towards collateral-backed or mortgage lending. There are no technical obstacles to Zopa offering an increasingly sophisticated range of lending products using the same mechanism, offering a wide range of different lending opportunities to those looking for higher returns.

Betfair, Zecco and Zopa and their peers are all disintermediators. They replace a financial intermediary with an automated matching system and are happy to accept much lower fees in exchange for higher volumes and, most importantly, no share of the risk. As the rewards are volume-dependent, as these businesses scale well and as the platforms are essentially interchangeable these new players are likely to consolidate quickly with the most successful operator buying other successful operators and the weakest failing.

In 2007, Capital One, a consumer credit company, launched a 'decoupled debit' card. The new co-brand debit card offered merchants new payment solutions that drive incremental sales and customer loyalty. The card enabled a consumer to have both credit and debit cards from the same retailer and to pool rewards across the two products – with a consumer being rewarded for purchase activity on both cards in a single loyalty account. The rewards from using this card were estimated to be 2 to 5 times superior to the rewards from using a debit card from a bank issuer. There was no need for the consumer to change their cheque account because Capital One used the Automated Clearing Houses (ACH) and the Barclaycard. Capital One dealt with all of the risk management associated with ensuring that funds were available for debit purchases on these cards. This card threatened the debit card business model of the deposit-taking institutions, which are based on high fees and interchange income.

eBay's success and near-monopoly of the on-line auction market stems from its reputation management system. After every trade the buyer and seller are asked to rate each other and this rating both contributes to a points system and is visible to everyone else that might wish to trade with either party. These ratings are jealously protected and are essential to the trust between traders – who often refuse to trade with those with low trading exposure or a few recent negative ratings.

eBay itself is vulnerable to disruption through this very mechanism. eBay's reputations may be spread across thousands of individual transactions of widely differing value, so a few acts that might damage that reputation can get lost in the noise but might disproportionately reward the transgressor. Reputation is also contextual – someone with a good reputation in one transactional environment may have a much worse reputation in another. If some way could be found to create contextually based reputation mechanisms then eBay may find that individuals prefer to trade in smaller groups in which the nature of the transaction is taken into account and any transgression is more visible.

Reputation is vitally important in the financial world, where creditworthiness is the rock on which transactions are built. The reputation of players in the financial world regularly takes a beating, with public perceptions of poor customer care, 'obscene' bonuses and greed playing a large part in this. This potentially allows large organisations with a consumer-friendly brand image into the market, at least in a financial intermediary role. The UK supermarket retailer Tesco now offers savings, loans, insurance and credit cards, using its consumer-friendly and value-for-money image along with its massive customer base to make big inroads into household banking. This is a joint venture with the Royal Bank of Scotland as Tesco does not hold a banking licence – yet. However, as a retailer Tesco has a huge cash pile which is due to the timing difference between its customers paying cash for goods and it having to pay its suppliers. It cannot be long before Tesco starts using that cash to earn higher returns from its banking businesses than it can earn on the money markets.

Peer-to-peer messaging may also be a threat to the finance industry. Peer-to-peer software started with Napster as a means of sharing files. It does this by exchanging messages on a peer-to-peer basis between software clients on users' computers, running in the background while the user gets on with other tasks. As the peer-to-peer software uses the Internet as its transport mechanism the network costs are very low – just the cost of a broadband connection. Currently peer-to-peer software is more closely associated with music piracy than financial transactions, but commercial uses (like Skype) are starting to appear.

The finance industry exchanges a huge number of messages on a daily basis, which need to be securely transmitted, verified as received and with non-repudiation. These messages are transmitted over secure private messaging systems such as SWIFT using carefully defined message protocols. The high cost of SWIFT membership and the cost of creating and ratifying the message protocols prevents some categories of financial transaction being carried out in this way.

Peer-to-peer software does not have the capabilities necessary to carry the vast bulk of the SWIFT traffic and quite possibly never will have. However, there is no reason why peer-to-peer software could not improve to the point where it could be entrusted with traffic that requires encrypted transmission, verification and non-repudiation but is more concerned with cost than the transport of those messages over a secure private network. This type of network could be used to carry less well-structured messages as well – effectively at zero cost. Whether peer-to-peer could step up to the point where it could carry the highest-sensitivity transactions is not clear.

So the disruptive risks to the finance sector come from disintermediation, loss of reputation relative to other non-financial organisations, decentralisation of risk management, decentralisation of trust and decentralisation of transactions.

HOW TO TAKE ADVANTAGE OF DISRUPTION

The best business model to adopt in the face of a disruption is that of a conglomerate. Many of these successfully create and grow disruptive businesses within their portfolio. However, the disruptions need to be managed as separate entities – because the resources, processes and values they need to do well will be very different from those of the incumbent. Even the value system they exist in will be different. An example of this is Hewlett Packard, which created its ink-jet printer division at the same time as having a healthy and growing laser-printer division. As the quality of ink-jet printing has improved, the ink-jet printer division has gradually taken over personal printing from the higher-quality laser printer division, which has moved up to serve the departmental printer market.

In financial services the small exchanges, electronic spread-betting and trading platforms that merely support transactions rather than provide liquidity, credit unions, community banks for the un-banked and all of the other innovations may appear unattractive – small, low-margin businesses nibbling at the margins of the real money movers – but the incentive for these innovators is to move up, to gradually provide more and more services to those with poor credit histories or those who want to manage their own risks and thereby take them away from the mainstream financial system. And there is very little these institutions can do about it. The only question that remains is how far they can go.

CHAPTER 13

Documentation

Documentation is not often cited as a method of delivering value in and of itself. I disagree. While documentation is normally reserved for the process control, its effective use can materially improve the speed with which any given deployment delivers value into the business. From a longer-term perspective it can also reduce costs because audit trails of activity and reasoning are clear for management.

If all goes well, the management of a technology deployment can be an exciting even exhilarating time. For many however this is not the case. Projects mostly overrun in cost and/or in time – usually the result of a failure to plan effectively. Most don't get the buy-in of the users at an early enough time. Most have things go wrong at some stage causing extra work. One of the key elements of the planning process is of course documentation. Documentation is most often viewed as a necessary evil – the administrative workload is often misplaced and mismanaged. Where appropriate, explanatory notes to documentation steps below will use outsourcing of corporate actions processing – tax processing as an example as this particular corporate action is highly complex and evidences most, if not all, of the issues that need to be discussed from a documentary perspective.

Documentation falls into several categories:

- Pre-business case analysis document
- Strategic business case
- Business specification
- Functional specification
- Technical specification

- Project control document
- Compliance specification document
- Risk profile
- Contract
- Maintenance control document

There are different methodologies available to control projects but most have the same elements in one form or another. Beware however of rapid application development methodologies that attempt to provide a 'quick route' to deployment. Many of these methodologies attempt to shorten the process by missing out documentation steps. This is all very well until something goes wrong, particularly in small software companies.

PRE-BUSINESS CASE ANALYSIS DOCUMENT

This document is usually a set of smaller research projects which together help business managers scale and scope the key issues and benefits that any given deployment will have. It is used primarily to help business managers create a template for a strategic business case document. Typically this is where the 'what we have now' scenario is spelled out in terms of what the deployment will address. For example, it may identify a particular department or function (tax reclamation or corporate actions would be good examples). The pre-business case analysis would then identify the key metrics – how many staff are employed in the function, total FTE equivalent cost, location. This document would also identify any existing benchmarks of performance. If there are no benchmarks (which does happen), this document would also note this fact, as perhaps one of the benefits of the proposed deployment would be a set of benchmarks that could be used to make the business more efficient or competitive. Finally, it is equally important in this pre-business case phase, to identify what is not happening. In other words, while there may be benefits derived from doing something more efficiently, there may also be benefits from doing something that is not currently being addressed at all. At this stage, there is no real definition of the project or deployment itself. The analysis seeks only to codify, whether quantitatively or qualitatively, the current business scenario, then posit a 'what if' in terms of output. For example, to use the withholding tax case, the following may be the basis of a pre-business case analysis.

- Number of staff (FTE equivalent) employed
- Number of reclaims processed per year
- Average recovery time by market versus market benchmarks
- Fail rate
- Cost per reclaim
- Fit (degree to which services match client structure)
- Age debt performance (effectively cash flow forecasting)
- Process efficiency
- Statute risk (measure the risk that you will run out of time to file)
- Backlog index (measures the size of backlog which in turn identifies potential bottleneck areas that can increase cost and risk and reduce efficiency)
- Threshhold index (measures the level below which reclaims are not filed)

For a full set of benchmark definitions see *International Withholding Tax – A Practical Guide to Best Practice and Benchmarking* by McGill, R. published by Euromoney.

Taking the above data set for example, 'Fit' may identify (as is actually often the case) that a proportion of clients are structured in omnibus accounts but that the internal processes cannot cope with reclaims for this kind of entity. So, what may be thought of as an all inclusive service is actually, on analysis a more limited service. So, a project to improve efficiency in tax processing would either have to build a more complex system to deal with layered accounts, buy a solution or more likely outsource it to a provider that already deals with such structures.

For each of the key analysis points (KAP), this document will identify what the business currently achieves and also what is available or potentially available through one of the four operational models (build, buy, bureau, outsource).

Clearly, the degree to which the initial pre-business case analysis is completed is a driver for the strength of the business case itself.

STRATEGIC BUSINESS CASE

This is usually a relatively brief overview of the proposed technology deployment addressing the market or internal need; the window of opportunity, if there is one, that the deployment must be delivered in in order to maximise its value; the expected output in terms of market advantage, cost saving, efficiency improvements and so on; any major top-level constraints on the project, for example restrictions on the deployment related to company policy and/or regulatory issues. This document also usually has some top level cost associated with it from a pre-business case analysis. Typical sections in a strategic business case would include

- Synopsis of case (aka executive summary),
- Background (market conditions),
- Current operations (pre-business case analysis),
- Proposed change (main description of the project from a business perspective),
- Reason for change (e.g. competitive pressure, regulatory etc.),
- Constraints (regulatory, compliance, risk, technical, policy etc.),
- Expected output,
- Associated activity (marketing sales etc.),
- Measurement,
- Project time frame and
- Outline budget.

BUSINESS SPECIFICATION

This document is the real first stage in the project itself. The strategic business case review at board level will have approved the project and given time frames for each of the subsequent stages. In many cases, the board will want to review each stage before proceeding to the next. While the technologists will usually work to lower-level documents, this will usually be the highest-level document to which they have access. The business specification has many elements of the strategic business case repeated in a somewhat different form but also contains more detail in terms of constraints and deliverables. For example a strategic business analysis may identify key performance objectives that could be improved as a result of the project, for example speeding up of tax recoveries, better competitive stance from having a higher threshold of recovery through lower per transaction costs, business acquisition and retention improvements through better quality of service and so on. At the business specification level each of these areas would be expanded upon so that at the management level it is clear what the priorities of each element are, how they fit together and which are mandatory and which are optional.

FUNCTIONAL SPECIFICATION

This document takes as its base the business specification and looks into more detail at each area. Most technologists come across these documents in the context of a software deployment, but essentially, these documents and processes lend themselves to any kind of project among the four types available. There is additional advantage to this consistent approach. It means that for any given project there will always be a consistent set of documents on file that will allow quick and easy comparison for value delivery. The functional specification would typically include:

- Identification of the key functional areas of the project. For example in tax processing this would be:
  - Process related
    - Data acquisition (upstream income announcements)
    - Research (availability of tax rate data for any given client and investment data set)
    - Document acquisition (beneficial owner documentation – must this be done manually or can it be done electronically?)
    - Calculation (of entitlements to relief at source (RAS) or reclaim)
    - Validation and certification
    - Forms completion (manual acquisition, auto generation)

  - Submission (electronic vs manual)
  - Tracking
  - Reporting
  - Payments
- Solution related
  - Response speeds (screen response time for software, connectivity up-time for outsource etc.)
  - Training requirements
  - Help availability

- Restatement of the constraints on the project at functional level, if any; for example
  - Risk management (targets for number of acceptable fails and/or clients where services are not economically viable)
  - Platform and operating environment for example Windows, Linux, .net
  - Compliance (e.g. must meet terms of MiFiD, double tax agreements, data protection etc.)
- Project related
  - Delivery schedule
  - Budget

In summary the functional specification must answer the question, 'What should the solution do?'

One issue I will raise here is that of fees in the wholesale market. Most custodians in the wholesale banking sector offer their services on a bundled fee basis, usually in the range of 3–5 basis points. Currently, major projects are having their functional (and by definition business case) specifications altered to include an unbundling of such fees. The reason is that, particularly in areas of corporate actions processing, the cost of the service is rarely calculated as a proportion of the bundled fee. Whenever it is calculated it is seen that actually the fee range is not high enough to cover the costs of the service overall. So, value added services are being identified as a business methodology to create more profit opportunities. Seen in context to the tightening of credit in 2007/08 and significant losses posted by many banks and brokerages, many projects are only being successful if they can either cut costs and/or create justifiable profit.

TECHNICAL SPECIFICATION

This document takes the functional specification as its starting point and breaks down each area into technical detail including

- Programming language,
- Operating system requirements,
- Connectivity specifications,
- Database descriptions and
- Hardware and software requirements

The technical specification is written by a group different from the one that wrote the functional specification, and before any technical specification is signed off it will usually go through a review process to ensure that the technical platform meets all the constraints of the functional specification. So, for example, there would be no point in the retail sector, to specifying a mobile banking technology solution unless the available hardware and connectivity could deliver response speeds that were consistent with the functional specification, which in turn would be based on market research included in the pre-business case analysis.

PROJECT CONTROL DOCUMENT

This document is needed to codify how the project proceeds. Most often this will be in the form of a project plan, for which several software applications are available to assist. However, most project control documents in my experience fall short of delivering on their true potential. Certainly the key elements described in this chapter, as serial or parallel 'events' would be expected in any project control document. But a project control document should be so much more. Most project control documents contain risk analyses based on the progress of a project so that if any element of the project is likely to overrun in time or budget, this is clearly available for management to review. But project control should also include a continuous process of evaluation against market movements. After all, the business does not operate in a vacuum. Many outside elements are known. For example, it may be that a constraint in the project is related to a particular regulatory issue, for example MiFiD, SEPA, Sarbanes–Oxley and so on. But there will also be changes in market perception driven by uncontrolled events. Generally speaking, once a project is started in a financial institution, it acquires a momentum of its own and is essentially segregated from the world around it. This is clearly not the true state of affairs although it has to be said that if there is a market change which makes the project completely irrelevant, then projects can be cancelled. What is missing is a more continuous review process of the project in context to its environment. A project that establishes a base of specification at the start and then measures effectiveness only when deployed (with an on-off switch in between) is a fundamentally flawed process. Unfortunately in classical project management there is no document which acts as a repository for ongoing comparison to the original precepts on which the project is based. This is one of the key functions of a project control document. In other words, in addition to answering the question 'how are we doing against plan?', it must also be answering the question 'how relevant are the original assumptions we made to the current state of the market'. The project control document therefore acts as a storage medium for continuous research out in the market about changing conditions that are relevant to the project's success or viability. These factors would be identified originally in the strategic business case. The document therefore allows for reviews of the project in terms of objectives, deliverables, time, budget and a number of other factors in a more fluid way, which means that, even in a changing environment, the resources being deployed by the board are less likely to be wasted if the environment changes.

COMPLIANCE SPECIFICATION DOCUMENT

This document identifies the key regulatory and compliance issues that impact the project. This is important because most technology deployments fail to grasp the issue of regulatory overlap. In my book *The New Global Regulatory Landscape*, published by Palgrave. I identify 24 regulatory structures on a global basis and classify them in terms of their overlap, the issue being that some overlaps of regulation are 'constructive', that is, if addressed intelligently, expenditure on compliance can be optimised – spend once, comply with multiple regulation requirements. Other overlaps are 'destructive' that is, expenditure cannot be optimised. The problem for most technology managers is that they fail to see the overlap at all. The compliance specification document is therefore mandatory, in today's regulatory world, and by definition must be an interdisciplinary authorship.

Compliance functions, in and of themselves, are unlikely to spot deep functional areas that can be affected. Similarly, each functional area may only spot that regulation structure which most affects them. This is very clear for example in data protection which affects many technology managers both in retail and wholesale financial services. It is useful to know for example that

- The EU Data Protection Commissioner has examples of what are acceptable terms for clients to agree to allow their data to be sent outside the EU. Yet most institutions do not comply with this requirement seeking instead to use small print to give them freedom with our data.

- While many institutions try to outsource customer service to India and other low-cost environments for purely cost reasons, they don't take account of the fact that India, in this example, has no data protection regulation at all. So, apart from the simple commercial issue, outsourcing to India creates unnecessary risk and liability and is at odds with generally accepted conduct under EU Data Protection Principle 8.

RISK PROFILE

This document seeks to document the risks and consequent liabilities that flow from the concept of the project and from each stage of its development. If the project control document is being managed in the way I suggest, risk profiling can be a continuous process. Clearly if there was a risk X inherent in the project at inception and market conditions change during the course of the project, the risk assessment created from the project control document when the change is identified might be X+Y or X−Y. Either way, it is important to maintain a constant review of risk.

In the tax example we're using throughout this book, risk is indeed inherent in many parts of the process. The key risk is loss of recoverable, the secondary risk is failure to file for a recoverable. In both cases the associated liability is that a client finds out that their positions have not been optimised and require to be made whole. While that might take place behind closed doors, in an increasingly activist shareholder environment and with cross-border investments up by 16% a year, there is a risk that a major client may pursue the matter through the courts rather than through the back door. In that case the consequential risk is loss of reputation and credibility, both of which may spark a corporate governance regulatory issue such as a Sarbanes–Oxley event. The loss of recoverable in a project, as an example, could take place because insufficient resources are applied to the issue resulting in a backlog which extends to the point where a statute of limitations is exceeded. It may also exist because a filing is made incorrectly and is rejected. Similarly, if a filing is not made at all, for example if the recoverable is below a certain value level, unless a client is made clearly aware of the rules of the game, their position would be that the recoverable is their entitlement and the custodian or broker has no rights to disenfranchise them from their entitlement. This example can be modelled across both wholesale and retail projects very easily, the essential message being that risk profile documentation must be continuously reviewed for changes.

CONTRACT

This document is usually used only where the technology is to be supplied in whole or part by a third party. In my opinion this is quite wrong. The following contractual principles are just as valid in the form of an internal contract as they would be with an external supplier. In my opinion, internal contracts establish good management controls in addition to those already identified in this chapter. One of the key weaknesses of a built solution is that the control documentation does not include a contract. While some may say that the other documents adequately cover functionality and technical design, therefore equating to a contract, in today's world many projects are global in scope and therefore require the collaboration and cooperation of many different business units. It therefore makes sense to hold those units and personnel accountable for the delivery of the project beyond a mere statement of objectives.

A typical contract would have the following elements. I have annotated this template based on an internal style of contract. Readers would be familiar with the external form and reason for such contracts so an explanation of the internal context would be of more value here. What is also valuable to note is that most managers in the technology space act in a siloed manner. In other words, looking at the list below, many will discount areas as being of no relevance to them because they dealt with, for example, contract control or the legal team. This is a major flaw in management. The legal team may not have any conception of the implications of any given contractual clause and may be implementing 'blindly' or from policy. It is the role of the management to cover the gap between what the legal team thinks and what the business needs.

1. Parties

- This establishes the parties to the agreement. In an internal contract this may be between two departments of two independent business units. It may also be more generically defined as the parties delivering the services and the parties commissioning them. For an external contract of course this would be the commissioning form and the vendor. It is important to identify the correct legal form of both parties as well as their registered office address so that, for tax and other purposes, this is clearly defined.

2. Scope

- In US agreements this section is often termed 'Recitals'. It establishes the nature of each of the parties and their respective skill sets, business activities and desire to enter into an agreement. For an internal contract one party would usually be the IT function while the other, the commissioning business unit, may be marketing and/or sales; or an operational back office function.

3. Definitions

- This section defines key terms. This is important because technology is renowned for using abbreviations, as is the business community. As can be seen from the length of the list of abbreviations in the preliminary pages of this book, it is important to establish a common language or dictionary so that everyone is clear on the various technical and busiuness issues involved.

- An example of this could be the definition of 'cutover' from test phase to production phase. Precisely when this occurs may be a technical issue or a business issue. Defining it here makes a clear identification of what event must take place for one phase to be completed and another to start. Examples of typical definitions would include:

  - Agreement – this document;

  - Charges – the fees charged by one party to the other (or in the case of an internal contract, the budget deductions made in the following year);

  - Commencement date – could be either the execution of the agreement or a specific date or the date of approval by the board;

  - Cutover date – could mean the date on which users are capable of using or accessing the technology according to its specification;

- Initial term – in an internal contract it may be reasonable to limit the application of this type of agreement to a specific period after which a review of the applicability of its terms and conditions becomes relevant. This is particularly relevant for long gestation period projects where market conditions may have changed;

- Infrastructure – depending on whether there is a hardware or systems connectivity component, this definition should clearly identify what is meant by infrastructure so that subsequent clauses can define what is included and not included within the terms of the project;

- Specifications – should be defined in terms of the business, functional and technical specifications and the levels of the project that they address. This is important because if there are any failures in delivery, the first port of call will be the specifications;

- User/Subscriber – must be clearly defined both in terms of who is authorised to use the output of the project, which should be related to the level of expertise expected as well as the seniority of the person accessing the output for its purpose;

- Separate definitions should also be included to clarify:

  - That words importing singular meaning are automatically to include the plural. This avoids complex sentences where legal teams want to cover the firm's position with respect to users etc.;

  - That words referring to 'persons' may, if relevant also by definition include corporate bodies;

  - That where figures are referred to in words and numerals, which is to take precedence in any dispute;

  - That any regulation referenced should probably mean that regulation as at the date that the agreement is signed with a caveat that the agreement automatically includes any new regulations related to the original as updates;

- Many of these may seem irrelevant to day-to-day management but when things go wrong, this degree of work and planning pays off enormously in shortening the cycle time to recovery.

4. Appointment and Commencement

   - Many departments, particularly IT, have several projects running contemporaneously. One of the most aggravating issues for business managers is that while a start date may be defined within one project, IT has a habit of scheduling projects according to a different agenda. So, it is not unheard of, in the absence of an internal contract, for a department to believe that its project is scheduled to start on a given date and to find that other projects have been moved up in priority or that resources are unavailable on the intended start date. In terms of an internal contract the use of a commencement date, as with many clauses, is dependent on the 'teeth' that the contract has to enforce a particular clause.

5. Services

   - This is the section where the product or service itself is defined. In most cases this can be shortened to a reference to the various specifications, which are appended to the agreement and form part of it, together with a brief description of the service itself for context.

6. Core components

   - If there are core components required, these may be either internal to the project or external to it. For example, if a project requires an operating system at a certain level, this must be specified here since, without that level of operating system, any other development work would be wasted.

   - If there are elements of the deliverable that have sublevel activities or deliverables associated with them, these should be identified here as a description. So, for example, in a SWIFT connectivity project, the department may be responsible for delivering connectivity to users; the core component of the term 'connectivity' at the SWIFT Alliance Gateway would include:

     - Subscription to SWIFT;
     - Capability of concurrent multi-user access;
     - A number of concurrent connections;
     - A specified number of printer connections;

- □ Support hours;
- □ Configuration.

7. Market infrastructures

- It is highly likely that major projects will require access to market infrastructures. On the retail side this may be to telephony networks, ISPs. On the wholesale side, market infrastructures would include such organisations as The Depository Trust and Clearing Corporation (DTCC) in the United States, Euroclear in Europe and other Central Securities Depositories (CSDs) and International Central Securities Depositories (ICSDs). Market infrastructures would also include trading platforms, stock exchanges and STP and V-STP enablers for particular areas of market practice. These market infrastructures are often vital to the success of any project and they also often have very restrictive or standardised requirements which must be included in the agreement so that the project is not considered in isolation, thus causing a potential breakdown in connectivity at a later date. Each market infrastructure must be identified together with the impacts that it will have on the project, for example messaging.

8. Connectivity and Standards

- Closely related to market infrastructures, but definitely separate, any connectivity of standards issues related to the project must be clearly identified and scope, for clarity is different from a technical specification or functional specification. In those documents the granular detail will be defined. Their purpose in being defined in this type of agreement is to ensure that at the top level, cognisance is taken of the reality of the infrastructures and the terminology associated with them, as well as the top-level requirement that the project must meet any infrastructural requirements as a term of the agreement.

9. Responsibilities

- This section defines the project personnel, entities involved and their respective responsibilities with the project. Some of these are often covered in other specification documents but they are rarely, because of the level they are written at, exhaustive. So for example, this agreement would codify the name, title, address, telephone number and email of everyone involved in the project including legal counsel, senior management, marketing, compliance, risk management and sales, as well as project-specific personnel such as project director, manager and implementation personnel.

- This section should also contain alternative contacts, should the primary contacts not be available, as well as any constraints on action (COA). An example of a COA might be:
  - If there is a functional variation in output in a certain area, no change may be implemented without legal review and sign-off.

10. Disaster recovery and resilience

- This is a regular item in third-party contracts and is usually the subject of due diligence at some point. At the third-party level, from hard learned experience, I now use as due diligence a methodology called Defence in Depth (DiD). DiD presumes as a starting point that the reason for Disaster recovery and Resilience, two sides of the same coin, is the protection of the organisation against untoward events. Those may be force majeure events or they may be simple failures in service provision. We must take the position that any third-party firm involved in trying to win a piece of business will (i) not always provide an absolutely truthful and extensive description of its DR, (ii) if it is extensive, we must presume that its resilience and DR procedures may vary in effectiveness over time for example through changes in staff or training or policies and (iii) most firms will not want their DR or resilience procedures to be included verbatim into contractual arrangements. The DiD methodology requires such procedures (i) to be included in the contract and (ii) to provide for the firm to be required to notify the commissioning body if changes in their firm result in a certain deviation from an accepted norm. For instance, some factors might be (i) a change in the company's staffing that results in an increase or decrease in the absolute number of support staff by more than 10% or (ii) a change in C-level staff and in particular any change in CIO or CTO.
- For in-house projects, this issue is often left out completely and is an example where project management assumes that the output from a project will automatically fall within the normal remit of others and that therefore they need pay little or no attention to it. Its inclusion here therefore is deliberate and intended to offer some level of DiD to business management to make sure that proper

attention is given to the issue. After all, there is no guarantee that a new project delivery will naturally be protected or will naturally assume some level of resilience already enjoyed by other systems. Indeed, if there is connectivity or integration between systems, it is possible that a newly developed project may impact on an existing system's resilience and that if DR is activated, significant proportions of more than one system will be unavailable.

11. Support

- Support includes definitions of the different types of assistance available throughout the tenure of the project. This may include
    - Help desk,
    - Telephone support line,
    - On-line chat support and
    - Intranet pages

12. Service level reporting

- Service level reporting is important both during and after a deployment. Typically agreements of this kind define only what is delivered after the deployment has gone live. So, for example there may service level reports covering the proportion of time the service is available for use (if the service is for example, supposed to be 24×365). But if the deployment is more complex, for example in our withholding tax case, it may be a service level defined by the length of time between becoming aware of a client entitlement and the act of filing a claim to recover it.
- The issue is also important because in a typical deployment there will be more than one person or group responsible for delivering service level support. There will be system level support, connectivity level service support and process and application level support. Someone in the organisation must be responsible for coordinating this support in a consistent manner.

13. Price and payment

- In a classical buy, bureau or outsource contract, this section defines the price to be paid for the services or products deployed. Clearly it is one of the most sensitive areas of any contract and one of the most fundamental. It is common to find core pricing for the deployment up to a certain level, but, in the same way that physical building projects have contingencies and unknowns technology deployments also have areas where, due to lack of information, there is no definable cost. In this area, third parties generally tend either to overestimate and take the risk or put in place a consultancy fee rate for any ad hoc problems that may occur. Both are fraught with dangers. As I outlined elsewhere, there are benchmarks which are based on a presumption of being able to accurately and precisely calculate costs. An underrun is just as telling of an inability to manage effectively as is an overrun. Its important to identify in this section where any 'amorphous' costs are and what model is being used to assess them. Consultancy rates are (i) usually exorbitantly high and (ii) are open ended. Once a project starts to eat into its contingency in order to cover amorphous costs from consultancy fees, this is a downward slope with a steep incline.

- From an internal build perspective, the contract should be better costed since most if not all the costs should be under more direct control. The usual issue is how to hold the business accountable in a way that motivates (i) the project staff to work together effectively and (ii) gives them clear guidelines as to the effect of any failure. Any sanction for failure at a departmental level is likely to be counter-productive. In other words, if the price calculation for a project is X and there is a 20% overrun, it makes no sense, unless the overrun is from some gross misconduct, to penalise staff financially or via their future development budgets. It makes more sense to positively motivate them through rewards for delivering project elements on target. However, while the use of this clause in an internal contract is of dubious value, it does have a relative value in that senior management and board can use the review of delivered cost versus budget for ongoing resource planning so that, over time, the skill set gets better.

14. Warranties

- This part of the contract is often problematic. Third-party suppliers will often include caveats in this section depending on how they are regulated and governed in their country of incorporation. For example, a UK-based company may provide a warranty exemption that is, they will disclaim that the product is fit for any purpose since that is a key legal differentiator in UK sales law. This may seem obtuse, but it is worth keeping an eye on such matters.

- From an internal contractual perspective, warranties should be sought from team leaders in the project. This is where they put their reputation on the line within the firm to deliver what has been asked for. It is often said that these are either not relevant or meaningless. However, in my experience, wherever they have been used, they have been successful. This is a non-monetary commitment that, within certain agreed parameters, the delivery group will meet the objectives. Some firms I know of also connect these warranties with retention strategies by linking the warranty with a successful deployment through certification. As a team or member is awarded certification that they have achieved warranty status (i.e. what they promise, they deliver), these can be used effectively to retain staff and motivate them.

15. Remedies and limitations of liability

- This is about what happens if it goes wrong. It is more relevant for third-party vendors than internal contracts. Most contracts, thankfully, are never taken out of the filing cabinet once executed. In a perfect world, even when things go wrong, it is more effective to pick up the phone, discuss a resolution and implement it rather than crack open the contract. Nevertheless, both internal and external contracts should pay particular attention to this section/clause. Often, where a vendor is small and the buyer large, remedies and liability put in place by a purchaser make no commercial sense. It is very easy to browbeat vendors, but it does not work in the long term. If your contractual partner has been weighed down with punitive contractual obligations, simply because you can impose them, you will find that the vendor (i) will always be looking over their shoulder to cover their position – which translates into a defensive even aggressive relationship and (ii) if you put your vendor out of business by imposing punitive liabilities or not providing a reasonable recourse to a remedy, no-one wins.

- Remedies should be reasonable and in proportion to the likely disfunction. If the problem is minor, you would expect a swift resolution at a low level. If the problem is major, you would expect that its escalation would be quick and well controlled and that ultimately it may take more time to fix. Ultimately if a remedy is unacceptable, this may automatically trip into dispute resolution (see below).

16. Equipment

- If the deployment requires hardware of any kind it should be noted here. Usually, technical specifications will identify the minimum configuration of hardware that will meet the need. It should be best practice also however to identify the optimum configuration and also a higher still resilient configuration. A resilient configuration will provide an extended period during which other processing parameters might change without affecting performance. For example, processor power can be overspecified so that there is a margin of safety for growth in the business.

- Hardware can be specified in both internal and external contracts. There may be policies on supplier which should also be noted here.

17. Confidential information

- Especially for an internal contract, employees must be made aware that it is likely that a project will include an amount of confidential information to be shared either across departmental divides or outside to third-party suppliers. A separate non-disclosure or confidentiality agreement is a good idea.

- It is also worth reminding employees in this section about the powers the employer has to monitor communications such as email.

18. Intellectual property rights

- Closely related to confidential information is the issue of intellectual property rights (IPR). In an internal contract this is a reminder to and constraint on project staff that the deployment belongs to the firm that pays their salaries. It is not unheard of for some personnel to leave a firm shortly after a successful deployment and the employer suddenly finding either that the employee has set up a competitive operation, or that the deployment is being replicated at a competitive institution. As far as the law permits in each jurisdiction, the organisation must protect its IPR firmly, and through clear messages to project staff.

- On an external contract, this clause is usually designed to protect one of the two parties with respect to any IPR created as a result of the project. This sword has two edges depending on how each firm views the strategic importance of the IPR created. For example, if the IPR is deemed by the purchaser to be non-threatening to its business, it may choose to offer its vendor partial or complete ownership of the IPR (with a consequential free reverse license so that it can use the IPR unencumbered) in return for a reduction in price. The vendor gets the benefit that it can use the IPR in other projects and so make money and the purchaser gets a lower-cost implementation. If the purchaser has any plans to 'spin off' its development department or outsource development, the IPR issue is also relevant and must be controlled.

19. Term and termination

- On both internal and external contracts, term and termination must be treated carefully. Term should reflect the time taken to deliver the project as well as any ongoing maintenance and support, although many firms will have a separate maintenance contract for this. Termination should define in particular, those elements of the agreement that will survive termination. This would typically include IPR, confidential information and so on.

- Termination should also be subject to dispute resolution procedures as termination may not be a natural event.

20. Invalidity and severability

- A common element for both internal and external contracts. This clause sets the rules on what can be used as a measurement of success in conjunction with any other factor.

- Invalidity means that any clause which is deemed to be invalid cannot be used as a general excuse to invalidate the whole contract or any other part of it. It is just as important for internal staff to know this as it is for external vendors to be subject to it.

- Severability means that any one clause can be taken on its own for measurement without necessarily having to connect it to any other. The contract can determine the level of acceptable or reasonable severability, but it is useful to know that legal teams usually put these clauses as general 'boiler plate' text at the end of a contract and try to render them non-negotiable. This is often unreasonable in the circumstances and it is an important role of business and project managers to 'role play' the contract to see if the invalidity and severability clause makes sense. Run a series of 'what if?' scenarios to determine what would theoretically happen and worst-case scenario, if these clauses were implemented generically and in full.

21. Relationship of the parties

- Some deployments require an extremely close working relationship between vendors and purchasers. In some cases, especially where services are being provided to third parties as part of the contract, it is important to know the difference between being a supplier and an agent. There is a legal differentiation and it must be made very clear in this clause.

- Where consultants or third-party programmers are to be used for example, there is often law that decides whether the consultant is actually, for all intents and purposes, an employee of the purchaser or whether the vendor is actually a recruitment agency with respect to project staff. These issues must be researched and clarified. In the United Kingdom, if this is not attended to, the purchaser may find that the HM Revenue and Customs has a case for collection of income taxes and national insurance contributions from the purported employer whereas this firm had thought it was merely purchasing project services. Different rules apply in different countries.

22. Notices

- Not a major section in any agreement. This merely makes sure that if there is a need to communicate at the contractual level, the relevant contact points are identified and the acceptable methods of giving notices are clear and agreed.

23. Force Majeure

- 9/11 was a force majeure event. Essentially this clause relieves one or both parties from their obligations in the contract, according to certain guidelines such as time, if any of certain types of events occurs. It is important to review these carefully rather than accept a generalisation. What may be force majeur to one party may not be viewed as such by the other. Force Majeure essentially means an event which has major consequences and was effectively unforeseen and unforeseeable. The technical definition is an unexpected event that crucially affects somebody's ability to do something and can be put forward in law as an excuse for not having carried out the terms of an agreement.

24. Dispute resolution

- Dispute resolution is critical for both internal and external contracts.

- In an external contract there may legal issues if vendor and purchaser are in different jurisdictions and subject to different governing laws (see below). Fixing problems is not defined here as dispute resolution. Problems at lower levels would be resolved though an agreed, but nonetheless important, procedure. Dispute resolution would typically arise if some aspect of the deployment could not be delivered for some reason or if some aspect of one party's obligations in the contract had been breached. Clearly, the detail to which the contract goes, defines the probability that dispute resolution may be required. In some jurisdictions there are dispute resolution mechanisms; for example, the United States has quite well-defined dispute resolution mechanisms including at the top end, arbitration and ultimately the courts. It is clear that cost will be an issue and certainly in some US states it is actually cheaper to go to court than it is to engage in dispute resolution.

- In an internal contract, dispute resolution will be closely associated with human resources and senior management. However, it is just as important for an internal contract to define for each of the major groupings of personnel just what tools are available to help them resolve major differences.

25. Entire agreement

- This clause is usually included to make sure that there are no documents or agreements that can come out of the woodwork later in a project as a defence for a particular issue being implemented in any given way. It is therefore important in both internal contracts and external (i) to have this clause and include any relevant documentation, certainly including all specifications and (ii) to assure everyone that, if it isn't in the contract, it isn't relevant to the mission. It is also important to cite here that, as a control document, any subsequent iterations of key documents, for example specifications, are by default, deemed to be included in the contract. This results in the need for high-quality document control and revisioning procedures to be included in the appendices to the contract.

26. Assignment and delegation

- This clause describes any limitations on one of the parties to be able to take its obligations and have them delivered by a third party.

- Assignment means that if one party, usually the vendor, goes out of business or has some need to do so, it can assign the benefit of a contract to a third party. This usually occurs if the vendor is actively seeking to sell its business as the perceived value of the contract may be included, if there is assignment capability, in any sale price. This connects to the opening clause on parties which defines the legal form of the contracting parties.
- Delegation means that, if during a contract, one party wants to have someone else do part of the work, they can delegate it, if empowered to do so.
- Typically assignment and delegation are only permissible or acceptable with the written consent of both the parties.

27. Tax

- Applicable really only to external contracts where a sales tax may be applied, this clause will deal with how that sales tax is to be treated and (i) whether any figures used within the contract are subject to tax and (ii) whether the figure used is inclusive or exclusive of such tax.
- In some cases, if the deployment is subject to a royalty payment for use of IPR, there may also be a withholding tax payable to the tax authority of the country in which the IPR is used. So if a German company licenses a UK application, the license fee will most likely be viewed as a one-off royalty payment by the German tax authorities and be taxed at the statutory tax rate for that country. So, in paying the license fee to the UK company, the German Tax Authority would expect a payment because that is where the IPR was used (as opposed to the UK where it was created). Many companies fall foul of this issue.

28. Governing law and jurisdiction

- With financial technology management now being a global industry it is not surprising that many contracts are executed where the two parties do not share a common basis of law to adjudicate differences or breaches. Needless to say, at negotiation stage both parties will try to assert their own governing law and jurisdiction. Governing law relates to the country which is agreed to have control over any issues. Jurisdiction relates to the specific courts which would have control within that country for any breach resolution purpose.

There are other issues that can be influential. For example, if the vendor is small and the purchaser large the vendor may feel under pressure to agree to foreign control of the agreement as otherwise it may have to walk away from the deal. To that extent, the vendor's influence will depend on the degree to which it has competition in the market. If it has little or none or is the clear market leader, even a major difference in size might not stop the vendor from asserting his local jurisdiction. In such circumstance, vendors are often also able to argue that a larger partner is more likely to have multi-country legal support as opposed to the vendor with a narrower legal experience base. So, it is fairer for the larger firm to submit to a different country of control since they are more likely to be able to afford and deploy an understanding of the vendor's market than the vendor is of the foreign firm's.

As you can see, while there is some latitude in the interpretation of a standard third-party contract, the form works well to motivate internal management especially if used in conjunction with the other documents in the series. It should also be clear that the use of this document significantly enhances the likely quality of an internal build.

MAINTENANCE CONTROL DOCUMENT

Once a deployment has gone into a production environment, it is usual to have a separate maintenance contract. As a descriptor for both internal and external documentation this is referred to as a maintenance control document or MCD.

The MCD covers such issues as

- Version control and release of patches and fixes;
- Updates of data;
- Upgrades of platforms and interoperability with market infrastructures' own maintenance programmes;
- Reviews of connectivity and hardware;
- Adherence to standards if appropriate such as ISO.

It is essentially the document that establishes and controls the ongoing operation of the deployment once it is developed and in place.

Documentation is vital and cannot be underestimated. Irrespective of whether technology deployment is internal or external or a mixture of the two, the degree to which the project is planned and documented is directly proportional to its likely success.

CHAPTER 14

Testing and Quality Control

There are those that would place testing and quality control at the top of the technology management agenda and there is no doubt that these two issues do take up a disproportionate amount of time and money in financial services. What is so surprising therefore is that so many financial services firms get it so wrong in placing the issues in context, understanding the difference between them and usually in implementation.

WHAT IS TESTING?

Most people are familiar with the concept of testing. You may think of testing the brakes on a car. But what would be a good definition for testing? Is there a definition that covers everything or is there a specific definition for testing technology?

There is a reason for carrying out testing. Testing gives us the confidence we need to use the product. 'Here are the keys to your new car. Oh, and we should tell you that the brakes haven't been tested.'

We carry out testing to see if a product does what it says it would do and to see if the product does what we need it to do. These are two different things. The first is about whether the product meets its specifications. If the specification for our car states that it must have four seats then we can test against that specification. If however the seats are too low and you cannot see out to drive, then the product is not useable as a car and will fail because it doesn't do what we need.

So testing is about evaluating a system and measuring aspects that relate to quality and suitability. Testing may be a static exercise where a document or a section of developer's code is reviewed or it can be a dynamic exercise where the system is exercised and the tester takes the role of a user.

Testing is carried out objectively. To be objective, testing must have something to compare the system to and as such testing should be driven by requirements and specifications. Requirements are about what we need the product to do. Specifications are about how the product does it.

Testing will reveal defects in products. With the complexity of modern financial systems this is always true. Knowing what the defects are and how they affect the system is crucial when deciding whether to accept a product or reject it. By implication we will accept defects in most products provided that they are not of major importance. In the context of financial services this may sound wrong. The reality is that all systems have defects. Modern code is so complex that testing can only go so far in finding out the impact of new inputs and outputs to any given piece of code.

So we can now define testing as 'the process of objectively evaluating a system to verify that it meets its specifications and that it satisfies the user's requirements'.

WHEN TO TEST

Traditionally testing takes place after the product is developed and before the product is deployed. This fits in to the philosophy of 'design, develop, test and deploy', often referred to as the Waterfall Model. Leaving all of the testing until after the development stage has been completed is no longer seen as the best way of carrying out testing. Before considering the question any further let's look at the typical development cycle for a product (Figure 14.1).

- Every new system, or any change to an existing system, begins with an idea. The idea is usually discussed for some time and eventually a business case is developed. At this point the business is keen to know if the idea will generate a return on the investment required to put the idea into production. Will there be a benefit to the organisation if the change is made?

- If the idea is accepted then detailed requirements are drawn up. The requirements define what the system has to do, how it interfaces with the business and how if will deliver benefit.

- Once the requirements are understood and agreed the functional specification can be written. The functional specification describes how the system will deliver the expected requirements and may contain details of screens, calculations, required fields and so on.

- A technical specification will be created by the development team. This document describes how the system will be built in order to satisfy the functional specification. It describes the architecture and approach to be used during development.

- The build phase is when the code is written and the system constructed.

- Deployment is the process of taking the completed system and putting it into the live environment. The live environment could be a business (as in the case of a share trading system) or a car (as in the case of the brake system). The level to which the process is followed and documented depends very much on the scale of the project and the maturity of the organisation.

- The final stage is the realisation of the benefits.

So when should testing take place?

The answer is 'continuously, from the idea through to the realisation of the benefits'. It is important that the ideas are 'tested' before going forward to the business case. An objective review by representatives of technical and business experts can help to reject poorly thought out ideas and shape others into practical solutions. Further reviews should take place when the requirements documentation is produced to ensure that the requirements properly represent the principles of the original idea, that the contents are not ambiguous or misleading, and that the requirements are 'testable' and not vague. A similar exercise will take place with the functional specifications. During the development of the system, completed components will be tested before the system is assembled onto the finished product. Testing will then take place before it is deployed into the live environment.

Not all of the test stages are appropriate for everyone. If you are receiving a system from a third-party supplier you would not expect to be responsible for the component testing or their system testing. A development organisation will not be responsible for the final stage, user acceptance testing. So although testing will take place throughout the system life cycle different teams will take responsibility for different areas of testing.

As a customer accepting code from a third-party supplier the natural tendency is to assume that testing does not need to be involved until the system has been completed by the developers and is delivered ready for testing. As

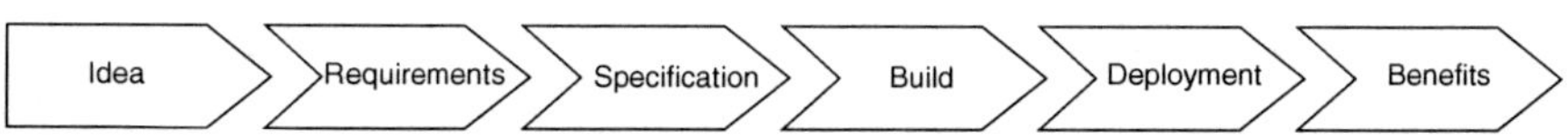

Figure 14.1 Testing phases

Source: T. Durham.

you will see in the test approach section below this is only half the story. Before we go on to consider the approach, let's look at the types of testing and who carries each out.

TYPES OF TESTING

As we have already mentioned there are several different ways we can carry out testing. Document reviews and code walk-throughs are examples of static testing. Exercising an application is an example of functional testing. There are also types of non-functional testing including performance and fail-over testing. We'll discuss these in more detail later.

Functional testing

For functional testing there are five main stages.

Component testing. A component is a section of code that will form part of the final deliverable. The code can be in any area. For a main system it may be written in COBOL, C++or Java. Middle tier code can be JBOS, Corba or Active-X. Components may exist in databases and may be PL-SQL, Abinitio, or MS-SQL-Stored procedures. Each component will be just one part of the final system and can be tested in isolation. This testing is normally carried out by the development team but it may also be carried out by a test team from within development.

Component integration testing. This is sometimes referred to as integration testing in the small. Component integration testing proves that the individual components created by developers work together correctly when built as a system (or part of a system). Component integration testing may take place at any stage during development as each new component becomes available. This stage is designed to expose defects in the interfaces and interaction between the software components and is normally carried out by the development team. It verifies the technical specifications and the software architecture.

System testing. Once the components have been assembled into the system and component integration testing has been completed successfully the functionality of the completed system can be tested. System testing is the process of testing the integrated system to verify that it meets the functional specification. The system is exercised and the results compared to the functional specifications. The previous integration test was only run to prove that the components worked together as a system but not whether the system functioned correctly. This testing is normally carried out by a test team within the developer's organisation that has access to the development team.

System integration testing. Large, complex solutions are usually made up from more than one system. Once the individual systems have passed their system tests they can be deployed together into the test environment. When deployment is finished the integration of the individual systems into the solution (or part of the solution) can be tested to expose defects in the way the systems work together. This is normally carried out by the customer's test team. Integration testing is not concerned with the functionality or value delivery of a system. It focuses on the interfaces between parts of the system to ensure that they work together. The parts of the system could be a database, an application, a web server and an email server. System integration testing verifies the business processes and the technical architecture of the system.

Acceptance testing. The final stage of testing is acceptance testing. This is formal testing conducted to enable a user, client, or other authorised entity to determine whether to accept the delivered solution. It will provide the user with the confidence they need to deploy the solution into their live environment or reject it. This testing is normally carried out by the customer's test team. Acceptance testing compares the features of the solution with the original requirements documentation to ensure that there are no mismatches or deviations and that the original business benefits can be realised.

Non-functional testing

Non-functional testing is testing carried out on the system (or solution) that does not look at the functionality. Functional testing will show whether exchange rate calculations return the correct results; non-functional testing will tell you if the results are returned to the user quickly enough. There are several areas of non-functional testing applicable to most projects.

Document reviews

We discussed document review earlier in this chapter. The purpose of the document review is to ensure that the documentation for any system is free from errors and ambiguities, and that the statements made within the documents are testable. For an exchange rate calculation the document might state 'the results of all calculations must be rounded'. This statement should be rejected because it does not contain enough information for the developer to know the exact requirements or for testers to know whether the delivered code functions correctly. In this case more information is needed and the final version of the document might be changed to 'the results of all exchange rate calculations will be rounded to two decimal places in the currency used. Where subsequent decimal values are 5 or less the amount will be rounded down. Where they are more than 5 the amount will be rounded up. For example 4.445 is rounded to 4.44 and 4.446 is rounded to 4.45.' An example of an untestable statement would be 'when the user clicks the Calculate button the exchange rate calculation must be returned quickly'. To make this a testable item the wording could be changed to 'returned in less than six seconds when running in the production environment'. The level of detail, the clarity and the accuracy of the documentation used to specify requirements and functionality is key to successful testing and deployment.

Code reviews

Code reviews and design reviews should take place within the development team throughout the development process. The code reviews ensure that the developer is adhering to the standards laid down by their organisation (for example 'the code contains comments explaining the functionality of each section, who wrote it and when it was updated') and that the code being written will deliver the functionality specified in the functional and technical specifications. Code reviews also help developers working in a team to write code in a similar style. Code reviews are normally carried out by one developer reviewing another developer's code s on a peer reviews basis.

Fail-over/resilience testing

What happens if one of your servers fails? What happens if you lose power? What happens if half the network goes down? How long can you allow the system to be off-line? As the architecture of our solutions becomes more complex there are more and more parts that can fail. This type of testing is focused on the hardware and is concerned with how it behaves when things go wrong. Applications will be run on the environment and testers will remove or shut down parts of the system according to a formal test plan. Some systems have redundancy built in so that if one server is shut down the system will fail-over to a second server without the user being affected. Other systems have spare components that can be used to swap out faulty ones. In this arrangement there will be only a short interruption to the service. This type of testing can be applied to power, networks, databases, servers, firewalls; in fact almost any aspect of the solution can be tested.

Load and performance testing

There are several different flavours of testing to be considered here. They are all based on simulating a large number of users working on a system simultaneously. Performance testing will measure how well the system performs under a normal load. Screen response times and database update times are typical examples of performance measurements. How long does it take for the results of a calculation to be displayed? What is the 0–60 mph time? How long does it take to stop when travelling at 30 mph? Load testing takes this further and provides data on the change in performance as the number of users is increased. The ultimate load test is the load-to-break test where the number of users is increased until the system stops working. Finally there is soak testing where a load is applied to the system for a long duration. The load may be constant or stepped up and down but the main difference between load and soak testing is the time the load is applied for. Soak testing is designed to find issues that may accumulate over a period of time. Small memory leaks (a memory leak is a defect where an application uses more and more memory over time until all available memory is used up and the system is no longer performing) may not cause a problem in a test run for 10 hours but may prove to be a problem when the system has been running for 7 days.

Disaster recovery

What happens if your server room floods or is destroyed by fire? Many businesses have a disaster recovery plan that allows them to continue their operations from a second site or, at least, to gather off-site backups and set their systems upon new hardware. Disaster recovery testing takes a business through the process to ensure that it is viable and to identify any shortfalls.

Operational acceptance testing

Our last non-functional test example is operational acceptance testing (OAT). When new systems are deployed it is easy to focus on the functionality and the hardware and easy to overlook the people and processes required to support the system. In areas such as service delivery, call centres and support desks OAT is particularly important. It will show whether the necessary procedures have been written, whether those procedures are fit for purpose and whether the staff have been trained and can operate the procedures. It will look at supporting systems such as alerting and logging systems that report on the health of servers and networks. Successful OAT gives the business confidence in the support staff and support infrastructure.

TEST PRINCIPLES

Now that we have described the various types of testing it is time to consider some specific aspects of test planning. We start with the test principles. The test principles provide the framework for planning.

Engage testing early

As mentioned earlier, testing used to be the next stage after development. Leaving testing until this stage in the development process is a high-risk approach on large projects. The longer you wait to discover defects in the solution the more it will cost you to fix them. This is illustrated in Figure 14.2 below.

It is estimated that the cost of fixing defects increases by orders of magnitude as the development cycle progresses. Defects found in documentation cost 100 times less to resolve than those detected in production. The most cost effective testing takes place earlier in the development process at the design and documentation stage. Errors or ambiguity in documents results in many man hours of work in developing systems that will not meet the customer's requirements.

Figure 14.2 shows how delays in testing move the detection of defects to later stages in the project where resolution is much more costly. This can be summarised as

- High proportion of defects reported by the customer – customer incurs losses because of poor quality system, further development and test costs due to rework of solution.

- High proportion of defects detected in testing – customer protected from losses but may incur costs as system is delayed, further development and test costs due to rework of solution.

- Maximise defect detection during reviews – defects are resolved before any development or functional test costs are incurred, in which case repeated development and test cycles are reduced.

Testing costs are incurred at the beginning of the plan to ensure that defects are detected as early as possible. Although this appears on the plan as an up-front cost, potentially reaching as much as 15% of the development budget, those costs will always be small when compared to the cost or fixing defects found late in test or in production.

Fail-fast principle

The Fail-fast principle means finding the most significant defects as quickly as possible during any test cycle or test phase. The fail-fast principle is achieved by prioritising the tests to be run based on the likelihood of failure, the impact on the system and the development effort that may be required to resolve the issues found. Test plans will be reviewed and updated before each test phase begins to reflect the fail-fast requirements of each release.

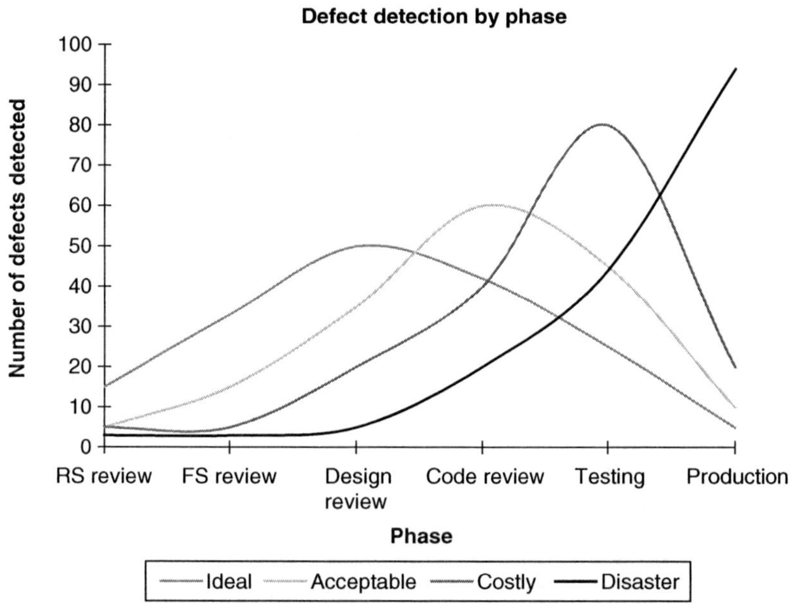

Figure 14.2 Defect detection by phase

Source: T. Durham.

Risk-based testing

You cannot test everything. Asking for 100% test coverage is not a reasonable request and any test manager that agrees to 100% testing puts himself in an impossible situation. Consider testing a pocket calculator. Assuming each test takes just 10 seconds to run – how long will it take to carry out 100% testing? One estimate, although it may understate the actual figure, is 3.5 million man years. The question therefore is what testing do I have to do to give you the confidence to buy the calculators I am selling? If we carry out less than 100% testing we introduce some risk that something may fail in an area we haven't tested. This is the risk-based approach that must be adopted for testing. Testing must be prioritised and focused on things that are more likely to fail and that will have a high impact on the business if they fail. This should be in preference to testing functionality that is more likely to work or has little impact on a user's business needs if it were to fail. For example, the figures displayed on a customer's bank statement are much more important than the spelling of the bank's address at the top. There is a section on risk analysis later in this chapter. There are also standard techniques used in testing to reduce the number of tests that are required. One technique, equivalence partitioning, will make a major impact on our calculator tests. Equivalence partitioning is primarily used where functionality is based on rules such as age ranges. Premiums charged for a pension policy may depend upon the client's age. Ages between 17 and 30 have a premium different from that for clients aged between 31 and 49. Six tests are required to confirm calculations using the following ages: 17/25/30/31/42/49.

We do not need to test that every age gives the correct result. We take the risk that if these six tests pass then any age in the range will also pass. Applying this test to the calculator we may test 3 × 3, 16 × 37, 128 × 7 and 7853 × 6291 and then assume that all simple calculation for integers with less than five digits will be correct.

The approach to risk is not dictated by the testers, it must be shared and agreed with the customer. If the customer is not happy with the level of risk then more testing can be undertaken but at a higher cost.

Data driven testing

Where possible the tests carried out should be simple and the test scripts should be reuseable. This reduces the number of documents required and also reduces the cost of script maintenance when applications change. One way of achieving this is to separate the data from the test scripts. This enables scripts to be used many times with different data to satisfy different test cases, conditions and scenarios. In the calculator test we can design our test as follows:

1. For each row in spreadsheet 0024
2. Press Clear twice
3. Enter the value from spreadsheet column A into the calculator
4. Press × (multiply)
5. Enter the value from spreadsheet column B into the calculator
6. Press = (equals)
7. The displayed results matches the value shown in column C

This simple script can then be used for any number of tests just by changing the data supplied to the tester.

No duplication of testing effort

There should be minimal duplication of unnecessary testing activities. Within each test phase, there must be full transparency of who is testing what, and the testing roles and responsibilities for suppliers and the business must be clear.

Where appropriate test plans and test scripts will be reused either in their entirety or as the basis for the next iteration of test documentation. This will reduce errors and costs, and ensure consistency throughout testing.

Timely and predictable arbitration

Where there are many participants in a system development programme there will be defects caused by differing opinions and understandings of the requirements. This is often the case when issues are raised by testing and debate ensues as to whether something is a defect or a feature. A process must be put in place for arbitrating between differing opinions in a timely and consistent manner. This is the defect management process and is described in more detail below.

Collaborative working

To enable the fulfilment of many of these principles (especially 'fail-fast', 'no duplication of testing effort', and 'timely arbitration') it is essential that the test team collaborates with all the other teams and suppliers. Collaboration will extend from the tester/developer level up to the management level and across all activities. Communication lines must be established to support cooperation between testers and developers so that software of the highest quality is delivered to the client.

Test management

In a typical testing project almost all aspects of the process are in continual change. In order for testing to give a reliable indication of quality these changes have to be controlled. The test process requires managing, as does the test infrastructure and test deliverables.

Success in testing requires:

- Clearly defined processes;
- Assurance that the agreed processes are followed;
- Management of the test assets and test environments;
- Monitoring of test progress to ensure that it is consistent with project objectives and plans;

- Effective change management;
- Effective defect management.

THE TEST PROCESS

The fundamental test process consists of seven distinct areas:

1. Establishing the business case
2. Planning
3. Analysis – the requirements to be included, business risks and prioritisation
4. Design – the test cases, scripts and data required
5. Execution
6. Recording
7. Checking

Establishing the business case

Testing should only be carried out if there is a reason for doing so. A new release of code that is never going to be deployed into the live environment may not need to be tested and the cost of testing it may not provide any benefit to the organisation. In this case there is no business case to support testing.

As both test preparation and test execution are resource-intensive and costly activities it makes sense to carefully consider what is tested and what isn't. As a rule no preparation work or testing should be carried out without a clear benefit.

Test planning

The first testing activity to take place is the production of a high-level, project test plan. This plan lists all the known activities that impact on the test team including code drops, testing cycles and environment availability. The project plan is the responsibility of the test manager and is put together in conjunction with the project or business delivery team. This test plan will be reviewed and agreed for each phase of testing before test analysis and design are carried out. This test plan is used to control the budget, manage the resources and schedule the test activities.

Test analysis

During the test analysis stage, the business requirements are read by the test analysts. This may take place during workshops with the development team and/or the business/system analysts. The output of this stage is the test specification document which contains a list of test requirements, shows how they relate to the business requirements and indicate the test priorities. The document contains a description of the work carried out by the analyst and gives a high-level view of the data required.

Test design

During the test design stage the test analyst defines the test cases needed to test each test requirement. For each test case the analyst will describe the event or item to be tested along with the circumstances that will be examined. The test cases are steps through the system that will be exercised with the test scripts. For example, printing a report may be covered by the following test cases:

1. Log-in to the system
2. Select the print report option from the menu
3. Print a report
4. Return to the menu screen
5. Log out

The test case doesn't contain any details or describe the steps required to perform these actions – there is no user name or password defined for log-in for example. Having defined the test cases the next step is to specify the test scripts – to determine 'how' these test cases will be tested. Each test will describe the test inputs and expected outcomes. A script may be used by several different test cases in order to fulfil the tests. Similarly, several different scripts may be required to fulfil a single test case. The purpose of breaking down scripts into reusable subtests is to increase maintainability and decrease effort in reworking scripts to keep them in line with any system changes.

Test execution

The tests are grouped together into a schedule and then assigned to individual tester to be executed as a work package.

A test can be automated or run manually.

Having built the test schedule, the next step is to execute it. This may involve running the software in the designated test environment, physically creating or identifying the prerequisite test data, completing the inputs, observing the behaviour of the system and capturing the outputs.

Tests should be executed according to the day's schedule, defects from expected behaviour recorded and the defects logged. Testing will continue until the exit criteria defined in the test plan are met or until major defects occur that require the suspension of testing.

Test recording

Test recording links the actual outcome of each individual test script back to the original requirement. All incidents and potential defects will be logged, assessed for priority and severity and assigned to an owner for investigation and resolution. When the defects have been resolved the test must be repeated. It is important to schedule sufficient time for development to support the test team in this activity.

The scope of retesting and the regression testing of any 'fixes' will be determined by the root cause of the original defect, its assigned priority and severity, and an assessment of its impact on other parts of the system.

During this phase the test logs will be completed and kept for auditing purposes. This will enable test progress to be monitored and provide a traceability log at the end of the project.

Test checking

The concluding activity is to ensure that the entry and exit criteria have been met for each phase of testing. We need to ask ourselves the question 'can we move to the next phase of testing?' – 'Have we completed our testing at this phase?' If the answer to either of these questions is 'no' then we must consider producing further tests to satisfy the exit criteria.

A test summary report should be produced at the end of each phase of testing. Release notes must be produced when the software is handed over from the development team to test and from test to implementation.

MANAGEMENT OF TESTING

Good test management is not just about defining the approach and the process; it is also about monitoring and controlling the execution of those processes. When software passes from one stage of development to another, test managers should ensure that quality gates are in place to provide assurance that the testing in the previous stage has been carried out and that the entry criteria for the next stage have been met. The quality gates can take the form of a check-list or a formal meeting. The quality gates, and the criteria that have to be met, should be defined within your test strategy.

The test readiness review

The test readiness review is a quality gate that requires a formal sign-off before each testing phase can begin. The review is usually in the form of a check list and is designed to provide assurance to the management that all the necessary preparation has been completed and that the entry criteria, as defined in the test plan, have been satisfied.

The test completion review

The test completion review is a quality gate that allows a formal sign-off of a test stage prior to the software being released. The review is usually in the form of a check list and is designed to provide assurance to the management that all the necessary testing has been completed and that all test deliverables, including reports and metrics, have been delivered.

The test continuation review

The test continuation review is an optional management process that takes place between the high- and low-priority test activities in the test plan. The purpose of the review is to assess the quality of the software based on the initial testing of high priority defect fixes and changes. It acts as a Go/No-Go decision point before entering into full regression testing. If the quality of the software is found to be poor during early phases of a test cycle the test manager may wish to cancel the remainder of the test cycle and reject the software delivery without completing the test cycle.

Change control

All test documentation, test assets and test environments should be subject to a change control process. Testers must be confident that they are using the correct versions of test scripts and test data. They must also be confident that the components deployed to the test environment are the correct ones for the application under test. For example, a new build of code may require a change to the database structure and it is essential in this case that the correct code and database are deployed into the test environment. In many cases testing is carried out on stand-alone PCs in test labs or offices and there is often little control exercised over the test environment. By employing a suitable change control process, backed up by an effective configuration management system, errors caused by unscheduled changes or incorrect deployments can be reduced. An effective change control process also provides an audit trail for change.

Document storage

All test documents should be subject to some form of document management. This is usually linked to the change control process described above. A good document management system provides a single storage location for all test documents which means everyone knows where to find them. Test scripts, plans, data, metrics, reports, release notes – all these documents have value and should be centrally stored. Document storage should also provide version control and an audit trail for changes.

Defect management

Defect management is the process of removing defects from a system. It begins with a defect being identified in a system. Defect is not always the most popular term. Many organisations use other words, such as 'issue' or 'problem', to avoid the implication that every anomaly found in a system is a defect. We'll use the word 'defect' here to cover all the anomalies found.

When defects are found it is not always clear whether they are caused by errors in the system, errors in test scripts or a misunderstanding of the expected functionality. This is not important at the beginning of the process. The first action is to record the defect and, in particular, the record must contain enough information for another tester, or a developer, to recreate the defect. The test record should also contain an indication of the severity of the defect. Note that a defect can be raised against anything.

- The application
- A test script
- The test environment
- Test data
- Test workstation

Defect management interfaces with the change control process. Therefore defects must be reviewed before any changes are made to the system to resolve the defect. All changes made must be recorded against the defect to ensure that a change history is preserved.

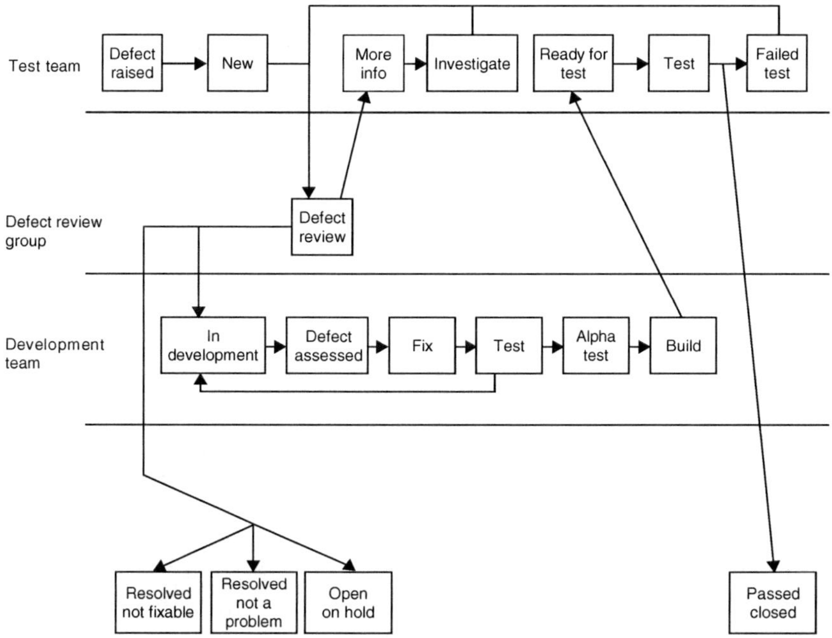

Figure 14.3 Defect tracking process

Source: T. Durham.

The defect resolution process is shown below.

Regular defect review meetings should be scheduled during test cycles. The defect review group will set the status of each defect and assign ownership. The members of the defect review group will be drawn from requirements, development, testing, delivery and QA. An example of the workflow for defect management is shown in the Figure 14.3.

RISK

In anything other than a very simple system you just can't test everything. There isn't enough time or enough money. So what do you leave out and how do you know what to test? Given that testers will not have all the time they need they will need to make the best use of the time available by identifying the parts of the system that, should they fail, represent the biggest risk to the business. This provides the test manager with the information he needs to make the most effective use of the time and resources available. The test manager can consider different types of testing, different techniques and different depth of coverage. The testing can be prioritised – the areas of highest risk are given a higher priority in the test plan and are executed first. Finally, the risk analysis helps the testing to be more objective by impartially describing the risk of delivering a system if testing is reduced or not done. When testing time runs out the sponsors need to decide if they can live with the risks and the test manager needs to be able to provide them with the necessary information.

In order to ascertain the most appropriate approach to testing, a process for managing risk must be followed. There are three stages to the risk analysis process:

- Risk identification;
- Risk rating;
- Action.

The risks to be identified relate to the business requirements as defined in the test specification. It is the success or failure of the application to deliver a business benefit that is assessed rather than the risk of a test failing. In a well-ordered test plan the individual tests will be linked to specific requirements and they will inherit the requirement's risk rating.

A review of the risks and the associated test priorities will take place prior to each release of code into testing. The priority of each test may change for each release as, for example, areas of functionality become more stable.

Risk identification

The way in which risks specific to testing can be identified will depend upon the type of project, the organisation and the culture. Some that should be considered are

- Statistical – Analysing metrics from similar projects, reviewing the existing project risks and issues log and identifying those that specifically relate to, or will have impact, on testing.
- Heuristic – Using the experience of the business sponsors, developers, business analysts, project managers and testers in a workshop environment facilitated by the test manager.
- Technical analysis – working with the developers and business analysts to identify probable points of failure.

All identified risks will be recorded in a risk log. This can either be one overall log for all of the projects or one specifically for testing that will provide regular feeds into the log maintained by the project manager.

Types of risk

There are various types of risk. The following (Table 14.1), though not an exhaustive list, should be considered when identifying and analysing risks:

Table 14.1 Types of risk

Technical	**Complex** – is there a module or function that has caused the development team or design teams a problem?
	New – are there any new bespoke elements to the application?
	Change – is there an element of the software that has been subject to numerous change requests in the release?
	Installation – is it possible to test the installation?
Political	**Precise** – is there a service level agreement or specific customer entry criteria that must be met in order to go live?
	Core – Is there a core business function or process that is used daily or is imperative that the business must have? company For example, there would be little purpose in a motor insurance not being able to produce a motor insurance quote. This could be determined by establishing the number of transactions being completed.
	Third party – Has any of the software been purchased from a third party? Is there any exit criteria that must be tested to ensure that the product is acceptable? Does this testing have to be completed by a certain date?
	Standards – Are there any project standards that must be achieved, for example ISO15022?
Economic	**Market** – Does the software release need to be completed by a certain date in order to maintain or enhance the company's market position?
	Advertisement – Has the company advertised features of the software release?
	Market – Is there a feature in the software that is crucial to the company's market success?
	Penalties – Are there any monetary implications for the delivery of the software or the quality of the software?

Continued

Table 14.1 Continued

Security	**Standards** – are there any industry standards that must be achieved, for example Data Protection Act?
	Penetration – is the software a target for potential hackers?
Safety	**Standards** – are there any industry standards for safety that must be achieved?
	Life – could the product endanger human life?
Management	**Resource** – Are there any resource limitations for the test team in terms of number or specific skill sets?
	Budget – Is the budget set, and is it possible to complete the testing within the budget? Has any contingency been allowed that could include overtime?
	Decisions – If there is a late delivery of code what is the approach that will be taken? (A reduction in the test coverage, additional resource, overtime etc.)

Source: T. Durham.

Risk rating

Once risks have been identified the risk rating values (the severity of the risk should it occur) should be assessed based on the likelihood of the risk occurring and the impact on the business if the risk did occur (see Table 14.2). Other factors may be included when calculating the risk rating including, for example, the time and effort required to resolve defects and the impact on contractual obligations.

Tolerance levels for high and medium risk are decided first. Then the impact of failure on the business is assessed and ranked from 1 to 4:

Table 14.2 Risk rating

	Impact
1	**Low** – limited number of users affected and/or no financial impact
2	**Medium** – manageable, a known number of users affected but impact can be controlled and workarounds put in place, and/or limited financial impact
3	**High** – significant number of users affected, and/or financial implications
4	**Business-critical** – all users affected, major financial implications

Continued

Table 14.2 Continued

Next the likelihood of failure is assessed and ranked from 1 to 3.	
	Likelihood
1	**Low** – for example a packaged solution and/or minimal dependencies and/or known technology.
2	**Medium** – for example a customised solution, and/or some dependencies (e.g. interfaces, external systems, etc.), and/or technology used elsewhere.
3	**High** – for example a customised solution, and/or key dependencies and/or unknown technology.

Source: T. Durham.

These two numbers are then multiplied to create a risk factor. The risk factor is compared with the tolerance levels and then the results can be given a high, medium or low risk. The standard approach to risk analysis is shown in Figure 14.4:

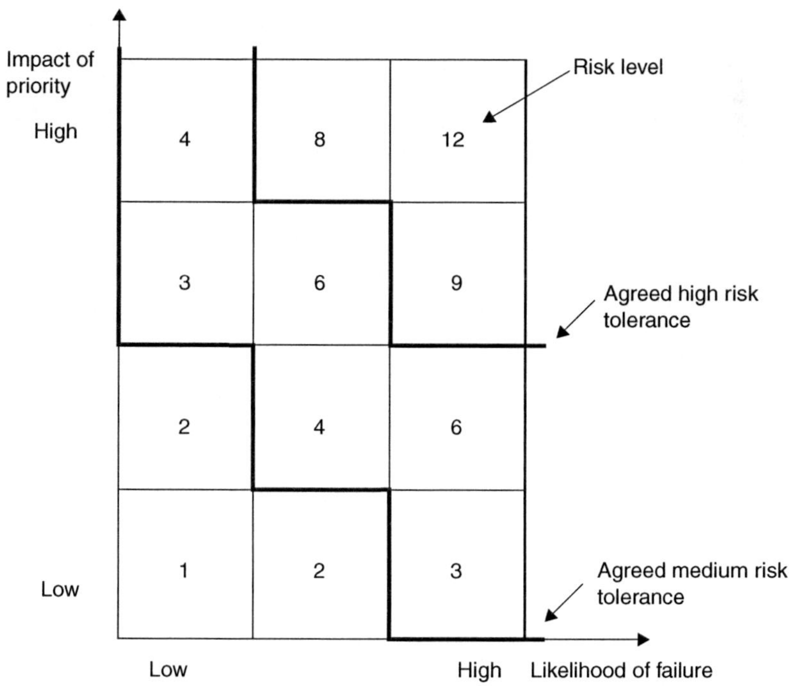

Figure 14.4 Risk evaluation

Source: T. Durham.

Risk actions

The output of the risk analysis provides a priority for the tests to be run in each cycle of testing. Running the high priority tests first allows testing to find the most significant defects as early as possible within the test cycle.

The test priority is considered to be

- High (must be tested)
- Medium (should be tested)
- Low (could be tested at a later date)

High priority tests will always be run first.

If time is limited and it is unlikely that all tests can be completed the prioritisation of requirements and their associated tests ensures that the most important tests are completed.

Weaknesses

There are a number of weaknesses when undertaking risk-based testing that must be taken into account when considering it as a viable technique:

- The analysis is a lot of work;
- The analysis may not uncover all the risks;
- The analysis may deliver an incorrect rating;
- All identified risks appear equally ranked and consequently have the same priority. The test manager should consider a weighting technique, where particular items or features in scope are allocated a weighting factor depending upon their importance (the higher the value the more important).

Despite the potential weaknesses the risk-based approach is an excellent technique on which to build a test plan, and it allows testing to be more effective and to comply with the fail-fast principle.

It must be remembered that there are different objectives for different phases of testing; for example the goals of integration testing are very different from those of acceptance testing. In addition, objectives will vary over time; for example in highly competitive markets getting the product to market quickly will always be critical to success but as the market share becomes more established the quality of the product being delivered becomes more important. This means that the risks identified may change over time and must be reviewed at each stage of testing.

TEAM STRUCTURE

There are various different roles to be considered when creating or managing a test team. These roles can all be carried out by a single person or can be allocated to individuals within the team. An understanding of these roles helps managers to understand the test process and how it is delivered.

On small test projects the team may simply consist of two or three testers, one of whom takes responsibility for the team lead and test manager role. On complex projects the test team could be extensive and managed by a test project manager and several discreet test managers.

Tester

A tester is responsible for executing tests and recording the results in accordance with the test plan, specification and/or test schedule. They also ensure that the defects found are raised and documented in accordance with the agreed procedures. They may also assist in the development of test scripts and the production of progress reports as directed.

Testers report to a test team leader.

Test analyst

A test analyst will analyse business requirements and other project documentation with the aim of producing the necessary documentation to support the test execution activity. The may also discuss the application with developers and users to build a clearer understanding of the test needs. From this information the test analyst will create the test requirements and map them back to the business requirements. Once that is complete the analyst will identify the test cases for each requirement. A requirement may contain a single test case but is more likely to contain a large number. Once the test cases have been completed the analyst will create the test scripts required to exercise the test cases and specify the expected result for each step.

During testing the analyst may be required to provide assistance to the less experienced test team members. The test analyst reports to the test team leader.

Test engineer

The test engineer's role is confined to test automation. The test engineer is responsible for the creation and maintenance of automated tests. There is no differentiation within this role for functional or non-functional (e.g. performance) testing.

The test engineer reports to the test team leader.

Test team leader

The test team leader coordinates the work of several testers. The test team leader reports to the test manager.

Test manager

The test manager is responsible for delivering the testing or a subset of the testing required. There may be more than one test manager working on a project if it is of sufficient size. Test managers are responsible for delivering test plans and managing the process of test execution.

The test manager will report to a business manager or, in a more complex environment, to a test project manager.

Test project manager

A test project manager is a project manager responsible for the delivery of several streams of test activity. A test project manager may plan and coordinate the work of many test managers each of whom is responsible for different types of testing. On a large programme there may be test managers responsible for

- Functional testing
- Performance testing
- Fail-over and resilience testing
- Security testing
- Service readiness testing

The test project manager will have responsibility for budgeting and resourcing and will report to the programme manager.

Measurements and metrics

Metrics are quantified observations of the characteristics of a test process or the object under test. They are the 'barometer' that provides business managers with a clear indication of test progress and the quality of the application being tested.

Acquiring and using test metrics will allow for management by facts rather than by opinion and will reduce the potential impact of risks to the project.

The collection of metrics and their subsequent analysis can demonstrate success and provide pointers towards improvement. Metrics collection plays a significant role in cost containment as well as providing valuable statistics such as time-scales, budget and resources.

In order for metrics to be meaningful, it is first necessary to understand

- What metrics need to be collected
- How the metrics will be used
- Who will use the metrics?

The recording of metrics should be regarded as an investment in the quality of the test process. They need to be reliable and useful. Recording metrics is of little use if they are not reported, understood or used, or if they are inappropriate. Metrics can be misinterpreted and need to be used wisely over a quantifiable period of time and comparisons need to be regulated.

However, appropriate test metrics will support the monitoring and controlling of

- Test progress
- Test costs
- Thoroughness
- Software reliability
- Productivity
- Effectiveness
- Improvements

Benefits

The appropriate collection and use of metrics is expected to provide the following benefits:

- Provide confidence measures on progress, process effectiveness and delivery probability;
- Provide visibility of effectiveness and early warning of issues requiring management action;
- Allow prediction of potential problems through trend analysis;
- Allow objective measurement of effectiveness of management initiatives for process improvement;
- Allow for informed decision making in respect of initiation of mitigating actions and contingency plans;
- Reduce the potential impact of risks to project time-scales, costs and quality;
- Provide improved basis for future estimating and planning.

Example test metrics

When collating test metrics, it is important to bear in mind the principles of testing, as detailed earlier.

There are different objectives for different phases of testing. Objectives will vary over time; for example, in highly competitive markets getting the product to market quickly will always be critical to success but, as the market share becomes more established, the quality of the product being delivered becomes more important.

Testing, and thus the test metrics collected, should be directed towards the most appropriate objectives at any given time. Detailed below are some metrics that should be considered for implementation (Table 14.3).

Reporting

A standard method of reporting open and closed defects during any test stage provides an effective summary of the status of the application. The report should contain the following parameters:

- Number of defects opened since the last report
- Total number of open defects
- Total number of defects raised

Table 14.3 Test metrics

Metric	*Type of measurement*	*Measurement frequency*
No. of tests planned	Testing thoroughness	Per project
No. of tests executed	Testing thoroughness	Per project
No. of tests passed	Testing thoroughness	Per project
No. of tests failed	Testing thoroughness	Per project
No. of unplanned tests executed	Testing thoroughness	Per project
No. of defects identified by test stage	Testing effectiveness	Per project
No. of defects by classification level	Testing effectiveness	Per project
No. of defects fixed in unit and integration	Testing effectiveness	Per project
Defect detection percentage[1]	Testing effectiveness	Per project
Defect fix percentage[2]	Testing effectiveness	Per project
No. of iterations of the test plan and test summary report	Testing effectiveness	Per project
No. of testing activities completed to the effort estimated	Testing effectiveness	Quarterly
No. of system testing projects completed to the time estimated	Testing effectiveness	Quarterly
The outputs have been developed to the agreed standards	Quality assurance	Per project
All deliverables have been reviewed as indicated and signed off by the appropriate bodies	Quality assurance	Per project

Continued

Table 14.3 Continued

Metric	*Type of measurement*	*Measurement frequency*
All deviations from the test plan have been recorded in the test summary report	Quality assurance	Per project
All test defects have been recorded	Quality assurance	Per project
All defects have been managed to an agreeable conclusion	Quality assurance	Per project
Quality review points have been defined and carried out at the frequency indicated	Quality assurance	Per project

[1] DDP = No of defects identified in unit and integration/No of defects identified during system/acceptance testing.

[2] DFP = No of defects fixed before release/all defects found (Where 'all defects found' is defects found in unit and integration and fixed + defects found in unit and integration and not fixed + defects found during system/acceptance testing.

Source: T. Durham.

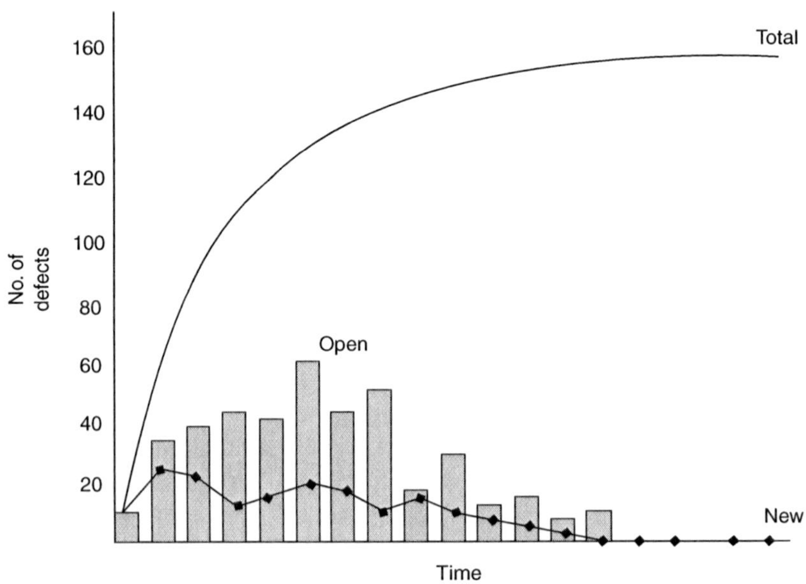

Figure 14.5 Defect tracking

Source: T. Durham.

When charted against time this produces the following (Figure 14.5).

The standard result for a new AUT is an initial steep rise in defects as testing begins. As the application becomes more stable the total number of defects levels off.

Testing is an industry in its own right and the complexity levels can only be indicated in this chapter as a guideline to financial services practitioners.

CHAPTER 15

Benchmarking Value

We've spoken a few times about the need to benchmark value in technology management. This is an entirely different concept from benchmarking the nuts and bolts of a deployment such as a software application. The latter can be done to a large extent numerically – does the application do what its supposed to do, if not to what extent does it not fit the requirement? What are its metrics in terms of response speed? and so on. All these can be identified and measured. I have to say, however, that even in this area, practice is polarised. One European bank has a 6-month test cycle for new software which costs €150,000 each time an application enters the pipeline. New vendors must submit to this test routine even before their software is delivered into a user acceptance testing (UAT) phase. Any change made or fault identified is logged and any fixes that are required must be built into a new version and resubmitted into the 6-month test cycle. This gives you a very clear picture of the level of conservatism in financial services. Another company I came across, a software vendor, had no quality control at all for the first ten years of its existence. Bugs found by clients were reported, fixed by the programmer that wrote the original product, tested by the same programmer, documented by the same programmer and released to the client by the same programmer. As a result, because different clients found different bugs, essentially this company was writing code 'on the fly' and maintaining over twenty different variations of the same product since the programmer couldn't fix the problem in someone else's code. So, my comments regarding quality control of deployments themselves must not be taken to imply that there is nothing to be said about this subject.

From a technology acquirer's perspective it is essential to have a deep grasp of the degree to which any solution, bought, built or outsourced fits the need and how any element that is not directly within your control, is managed. Chapter 14 provided more insight into this area.

In this chapter we will be focusing on the benchmarking of technology management, not the benchmarking of the technology itself.

There are four phases to benchmarking the performance of management:

1. Planning
2. Budget control
3. Delivery
4. Ongoing maintenance

Now, part of the problem is that a benchmark, as opposed to a target, makes a presumption about the efficiency of a process in relative terms, usually relative to market practice. So, without knowing the particular kind of technology deployment – communications level, systems level or application level, let alone the expected size of the deployment which could range from a simple application to the implementation of a global communications network – it is going to be impossible to give absolutes.

We should consider this a bit like the relationship between budgeting and planning. If I set a budget ‘x’ within my overall plan of action and I ultimately come in under budget by 50%; in most businesses, looking just at the expenditure, this would be looked upon as a good thing. We would need of course to check to make sure that the budget underspend did not materially impact any of the other variables, particularly quality of product. But this highlights the point I am trying to make from a management perspective. An underspend will have created a completely new task caused by some fear of failure and that task will take time and energy. So, from a management perspective the underspend is a bad thing. It highlights one of three possible management failures:

1. the planning wasn’t good enough;
2. the budgeting wasn’t good enough or
3. both weren’t good enough.

In a good project underspends are just as bad as overspends. I look on this scenario from the perspective that if my staff managed to calculate the budget that inefficiently in all likelihood the actual deployment was flawed as well – in ways that I can’t yet know.

The big issue is: How good are the planning and budgeting skills?

While I’ve used these in the same sentence, and the benchmarking model below uses budgeting as its template, planning skills are (i) a separate and just as important issue as budgeting and (ii) the IC model below applies in all its principles, to planning skills as well as budgeting skills. The measurement parameters will be slightly different. In any benchmarking exercise of this nature we seek to give managers an iterative process. How close the management come to the benchmark and in what manner are key areas of interest.

Typically we would want to employ managers that are already excellent practitioners of both. The reality is that these are fluid issues. So, I will take them from the perspective of a clean start. Readers may assume for their own financial firms a start point somewhere along the line.

Wherever the managers start, its to be expected that expenditure on planning, budgeting and training will deliver results that improve performance which asymptotically approaches some given benchmark. If the performance of a manager at the start is low, that is, budget planning versus reality has large differences, then more money will need to be spent on oversight activities. What is important here is that if you don't let the manager learn and get better at his craft in your environment (loyalty means reduced staff turnover) you won't reap the rewards. However, it is clearly unacceptable to have these people making critical mistakes. So senior managers need to understand how to juggle these issues successfully.

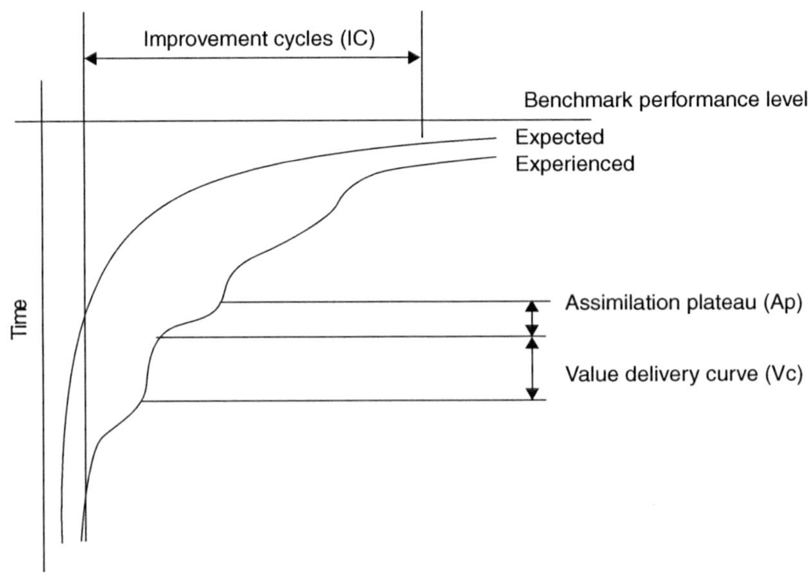

Figure 15.1 Benchmarking management performance

Source: Author.

Figure 15.1 above shows how this works. Let us presume that we take one performance measure – budgeting skills. The manager will have a set of skills in this area from historical projects which can be tested and analysed. For this purpose however we will assume no previous knowledge. The benchmark may be, often is, that the manager should be able to budget to within a 95% confidence interval. This means two things. First that the manager must be able to budget a project and have the actual measured spend be within 95% plus or minus an acceptable margin of error. Second, the manager should be able to reproduce this performance with consistency again in the 95% confidence interval.

This methodology acceptably deals with the most common mistakes of middle and junior managers, that of 'contingency building'. The feeling is that all projects must come in under budget and that overspends are bad. This is simply not reasonable in financial technology deployments. The issue is actually how consistently can a manager calculate the various variables and create a budget that is a reasonably accurate estimate. This, when successfully delivered, builds trust between senior and middle/junior managers. This has far-reaching consequences. Those project managers that can sow reliability in budgeting will naturally be given the more sensitive and critical projects. They are also more likely to be given the larger-cost projects where a percentage point overrun could mean millions of dollars.

Training is of course the key, as with so many things.

Figure 15.1 shows two lines. The first represents what would be expected in a perfect world. The second represents the real-world situation. Each improvement is associated with a plateau. The plateaux represent a consolidation period where skills learnt in the previous cycle are embedded in the manager and training takes place to address those areas that need improvement. Figure 15.2 shows how the plateaux can be deconstructed into a simple cycle.

For technology management projects, financial firms need to view the delivery of value holistically. This first element is looking at how well the firm performs over time. One of the interesting things about this type and level of benchmarking methodology is that it is very rare for the top levels of management to be subject to it. This is a C-level issue and the benchmark system if implemented correctly starts with C-level staff being assessed as to their ability to improve the cycle. Effectively this means that in a more efficient organisation, the number of plateaux in Figure 15.1 and the distance between them are minimised by effective training and analysis. The net result is the business becomes much more effective than its competitors at delivering value to the business when measured as a function of efficient planning. I say this because at middle and junior management levels, this type of benchmarking is more common. These levels expect to be measured and expect to go through a 'professional development' cycle. C-level staff

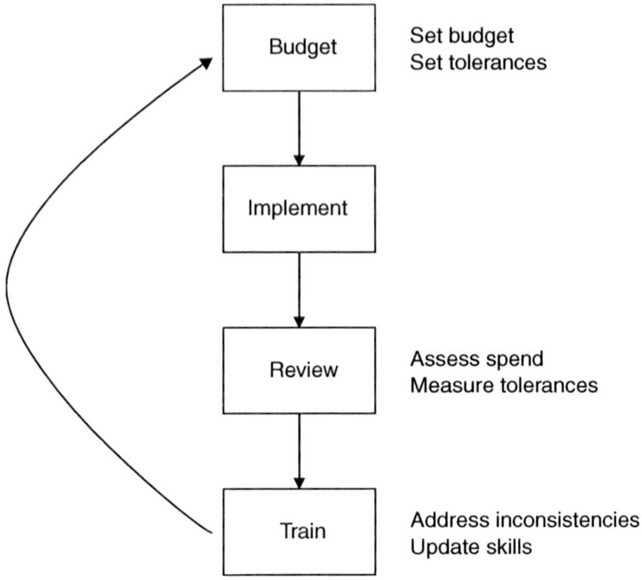

Figure 15.2 Benchmarking and improvement cycles

Source: Author.

often avoid this and, as a result, all the work done down below can be lost or at least damaged in its effectiveness.

The above gives rise to a series of numeric benchmarks.

$$\text{IC}\left(\text{the Improvement Cycle}\right) = \sum_{l}^{n} \text{Ap} + \text{Vc},$$

where Ap is a measure of the assimilation plateau, Vc is the value delivery curve and n represents the number of such cycles lying between the start of the assessment period and the achievement of the 95% confidence benchmark.

There are different features of this model. First, it gives numeric analytical ability to a management function. Second, it allows for a number of sub-levels of possibility for senior managers.

Here are some examples:

1. The larger the number of Ap events, the smaller the time horizon of the individual technology manager. In other words, their attention span is short and they need multiple small events to achieve a higher level of skill. This may be a retention issue.

2. If the first derivative of the Ap or Vc curve is taken, that is if we measure the rate of change of curvature in the graph, this represents the rate at which training is effectively being absorbed and translated into value.

3. IC itself is an effective measure of performance improvement indicating how quickly a 95% confidence can be assigned to a project manager's budgeting or planning skills.

We must remind ourselves here that we are, at this point, only discussing value delivery in terms of the firm's use of its resources to deliver technology projects. We have yet to come onto the actual measurement of the value of such projects to the business activities of the firm in terms of what the deployment actually does. The key measurables in the above model are of course (i) how much do you predict this will cost and (ii) how much did it actually cost. The effectiveness of this tool is directly proportional to the granularity with which it is deployed. If you just apply the test at the top-spend level, you may achieve the 95% confidence in your project management, you just won't know why or how. If you take the model down to lower levels of granularity and then reaggregate them into the top figures, you will have both a better understanding of why your projects are getting better budgeting and a better use from your professional development expenditure.

When it comes to planning, the same rules apply, the measurables are different. Many firms use project management software to improve project delivery and certainly most of these have some budgeting and time measurement elements to them. Few, if any however, provide any intuitive improvement tools. In other words, the project manager can input project elements and move them around within certain constraints; usually certain project elements cannot start until a certain stage has been reached in others. This hides an important flaw in delivering value from planning. The constraint management gives the impression that the end result plan is actually the most effective use of time and materials to achieve the objective. Actually this is very far from the truth. The reality is that there is no information whatsoever in these tools to prove that any given plan is the best. They merely prove that all the constraints have been met. In other words its 'a' plan, not the best plan. In my time at university studying materials technology I came across this principle many times when researching the packing of atoms in a molecular structure. If you're given a bucket of sand and you pour in into a measuring jug, it may appear to show a certain volume. But we all know that if we shake the jug around, the volume will appear to decrease as the sand granules find, through gravity, a more effective way to pack themselves together. So if the plan is to put sand efficiently into a measuring jug, we know that 'pour it in' is 'a' plan, but its not the best plan.

The best plan would be 'pour it in then shake it'. Following the analogy from a technology management perspective of course the question then becomes how long must I shake the jug before I get no further improvement in packing.

So, please don't assume that because you have project planning applications, you don't need to pay attention to planning as a possible improvement area. Let me use another slightly more direct analogy to highlight the issue that project planning applications hide.

Say you have ten programmers, twenty-five people in the UAT team, three business analysts and a documentation and specification person (aka administrator). Typically, you would take a business specification and begin the planning process to assess scale and scope, then flow into the deployment processes themselves. Whatever process you've used, it falls over the same unwarranted assumption – that your staff are all equally capable and properly trained to do their jobs within the project. As I hope I've shown earlier in this chapter, the fact that any given project manager, when budgeting, is unlikely to be close to the 95% limit, all your staff will also be at different levels of knowledge, ability, experience, enthusiasm, skill and political sensitivity. With the exception of the last in this list, every project manager and C-level executive I have ever met, falls into the trap of assuming a consistent and usually high level of all of these factors. When you think about it, this is clearly an untenable position. So, at the more granular level, you have a plan to create and it needs three programmers. Two have been with the firm for three years and are highly skilled. One has been with you six months and while he/she has good skills, he/she isn't familiar with your systems yet. From a planning perspective, how would you deploy the team to achieve its objective? If you put the experienced people on the job and give the new guy a simpler job, you run the risk of disillusioning him or her which will ultimately mean a shorter employment, greater spend in HR to find someone new and train them up. This may seem like a very narrow case, but it is important t understand the principle. All you have to do is look at the variables within your resource base in any project to understand that if you assume a constant high level of each, you, as a planner, are not going to be delivering value.

SUMMARY OF BENCHMARKS NOTED ELSEWHERE

I have summarised the benchmark formulae provided elsewhere in this book so that an 'at a glance' table can be reviewed for use in practical situations.

Ergonomic Fit (Ef) (see Chapter 8) – This measures the degree to which the different variables in the deployment have been factored in. Since there is a degree of judgement involved here, the measure uses the results of sub-group pre- and post-deployment analyses to provide an indication of both absolute fit and relative fit, that is, in the latter case, the degree to which the spend on ergonomics has delivered value.

$$\text{Ef} = \sum_{1}^{n}(p-q)$$

where p is a result score generated from a questionnaire given to a focus group post-deployment, q is the result score generated from a questionnaire to the same focus group pre-deployment and n is the number of groups (i.e. if age and gender only are grouped then $n = 2$)

Integration Coefficient (see Chapter 8)

$$Ic = \int_{1}^{n} f(x)$$

where f(x) is the function that describes for each group involved in the project the historic and future trend of resource availability.

So, now we have looked at benchmarking value from the budgeting and planning phase. However, most C-level executives will want to focus on the value that the technology deployment has had in the business. Again, where management focuses on one element, there are actually more than one. Of course, any competent business level specification should include some very direct identification of the expected output from a financial technology development. The more obvious high level questions are

1. At the top line
   a. Is it faster? Does it let me do things more quickly and therefore improve my ability to compete?
   b. Is it cheaper? Does it let me do things for a lower per event cost enabling me to be more competitive?
2. At the cost line
   a. Does it make me compliant? Does it reduce liability and/or risk by controlling processes more efficiently?
   b. Does it mitigate risk? Does it reduce the opportunity for error giving me a way to reduce costs
   c. Does it reduce the number of people needed to perform tasks?

3. At the bottom line

   a. Does it combine top line and cost line benefits to create bottom line benefit?

I chose the title for this chapter very carefully. It is about delivering value. But that can be interpreted in more than one way. From a technology management perspective, delivery means 'it is there', 'it exists', 'you asked for it and now we've delivered it'. The delivery, in other words, is the act of putting the deployment in the hands of its commissioners. For the commissioning team of course that's just likely to be the start of delivery not the end. The development team have already moved on in their own minds to issues such as maintenance and updates and upgrades while the users are figuring out how to use the deployment. So we have three constituencies – commissioners, users and developers. Each has a direct or indirect interest in delivering value, but each has a different perspective on what that means.

Developers, and by this term I mean anyone who isn't a user and who isn't one of the commissioning business team, are generally short-term thinkers. This would include the project management, program developers, trainers, psychologists, consultants and so on. While I believe my statement above to be true, that for the developers the act of taking a deployment live equals delivery, this is a view that needs to be tempered by the risk that's associated with that short-termist approach. Its failure lies in the fact that it dissociates the development team from any of the occurrences post-launch. From their point of view in other words, they developed and deployed what was asked for. The implied comment being 'so if the users screw it up, its their fault either for not using the system correctly or the commissioner's fault for not specifying correctly'. A common enough dissociative ploy. Of course a user's view is even more short-termist. As far as a technology deployment in financial services is concerned, more so than in almost any other industry, if the users can't see obvious and clear changes to their working day from any new system, their approach to it is likely to be somewhat jaundiced. At C-level, the commissioning level, there is a degree of medium-term thinking and a recognition that some elements of value delivery may be both longer term and not necessarily delivered all in one go. Additionally there may be an understanding that the degree of value that can be extracted from a technology deployment may also be affected by other things in the business and indeed the market.

Figure 15.3 shows the way in which the different constituencies perceive the delivery of value. The concept being described here is a 'time horizon'. This is the longest time period over which any constituency member thinks and plans. It is important because any deployment which mismatches value

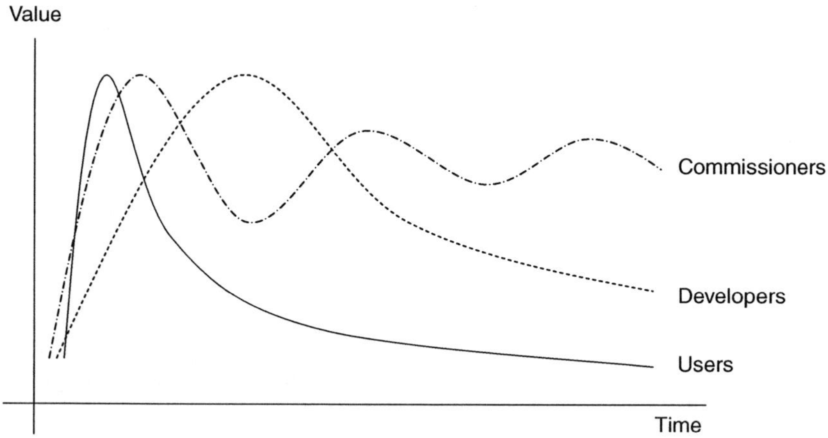

Figure 15.3 Value delivery perception by consitituency
Source: Author.

delivery to the time horizon of the constituencies is almost doomed to failure before it starts.

Typical users have short time horizons. This may be a daily target, a monthly target or more typically a three-month review. Certainly the longest time horizon for many will be one year, which represents their time horizon to the next performance (and pay) review. So all their attitudes and general thought processes in and surrounding their work are codified by this time horizon. So, as shown in the graph in Figure 15.3, once a deployment is launched, users will very quickly and naturally test out those parts of the deployment that affect them the most and come to a conclusion as to whether their lives will be easier as a result. Their enthusiasm rapidly decreases with time as the benefits of the deployment are quickly assimilated into their day-to-day activities.

In a similar vein, developers have a longer time horizon, often starting at six months and sometimes going out as far as two or three years depending on the size of the team, whether they're working in the retail or wholesale sector and where the next project is coming from. They have a better grasp of the strategic benefits of technology not least because it is in their interests to do so. However, their vision of value is sometimes clouded by the fact that their work often continues beyond the first deployment phase into maintenance and support issues. With several projects in different stages contemporaneously in most financial firms, this causes a lattice effect which can make it difficult for developers to see the truly big picture.

The commissioners on this graph have the most complex pattern of all. If they are effective at their level, they will have a time horizon stretching out starting at a year and often going as far as ten to fifteen years. No-one is saying that they know the future that far ahead. At fifteen years out, the value delivery is cumulative on too many factors in between including the market changes that will have occurred. But in technology one thing is very very clear. Convergence is occurring in all areas of financial services. This is occurring at the market level where the large players are rapidly taking over the smaller; and at the technological level where deployments must use disruptive technologies more and more to survive. One of the key facets of disruptive technologies is that they are often visible as either an agglomerated platform ('this application is operating system independent') or as agglomerated hardware ('this technology works on TV, internet and mobile telephony'). I've drawn the commissioner curve deliberately with multiple peaks, to make two points. First, any given deployment is likely to deliver value in a non-continuous way. Second, most commissioning bodies either don't perceive the multiple value delivery or don't take account of it in their assessments.

So, after we have established how to assess value delivery inside the deployment and we have established some of the complicating factors surrounding post-deployment assessment of value, we are left with the question 'what is value?'. Well, I think we've established that value means different things to different people within an organisation. The only view left not discussed is the view from the organisation's perspective. In that regard, the shareholders represent that view since they 'are' the organisation. Undoubtedly, not many practitioners include share value (and by inference market value) into their calculations, but ultimately this is the only market by which the company is measured in the market. All other activities connect together to create that value – its people, its products and ... its technology.

I can cite the reverse of this scenario using an example of some relevance. I consulted for a major financial institution recently to help their management understand and implement technology systems to deal with the Sarbanes–Oxley Act. While they weren't a US firm they had figured out (unlike most) that the fact their shares were listed on the NYSE and that their global operations fell under the remit of the US act. During the project we discussed what constituted a 'reportable event', that is an event which, if not reported, had the potential to lead to a misstatement of the financial health of the organisation to the market. The Act requires 'timely reporting' and 'appropriate response'; so while a minor error could be reported up the normal chain of command and meet the terms of the act; a serious issue would require a direct communication with a C-level executive, usually CEO and/or CFO missing out the intervening command chain. The Act also requires assessment by auditors of the strength of controls in the organisation to identify, prevent or cure any given issue. In this case, the firm had appointed someone with only six months experience in the business, to be responsible for stock control in the vault – in which were £3 billion in bearer bonds. During the consult, this person admitted to having ‘lost’ the bonds for three days. They were showing on the stock record as being in the vault, but they weren’t there. The person had not informed anyone else, but searched the communication chain in a low-level way to try to find them again. This was successful. The point, unfortunately, was that (i) the stock control was clearly not good enough – no value delivery there; (ii) the person concerned, given the size of the issue, should have reported directly to the CEO within ten minutes and (iii) without a grounding in both regulatory issues, systems and management, this issue would have been swept under the carpet.

The point of this anecdote is that because this organisation had no concept of value delivery nor of its measurement, they placed their firm in a position where the share value would have been affected. Barings, Northern Rock and Societe Generale all stand as testament to what can happen when you think you have good technology in place, but don’t continually question its value. If you do question its value, because you understand the multiple peaks in Figure 15.3, you stand a better chance of surviving in a complex financial world.

PART IV

Regulation and Compliance

CHAPTER 16

The Role of Regulation and Global Regulatory Impact

There are a plethora of regulations that affect the use of technology in financial services: in the front office, on the buy-sell side of the business, the Markets in Financial Instruments Directive (MiFiD) ads well as SEPA, the Single European Payments Area; in the back office, not with the force of regulation, but of best practice, the Giovannini group works to create a level playing field on the securities side of financial services.

In my book *The New Global Regulatory Landscape* published by Palgrave, I outlined the nature, scale and scope of over twenty regulatory structures that can affect financial services and inter alia the management of technology. They are:

1. The UK Combined Code

2. Higgs

3. Turnbull

4. Money Laundering Regulations (MLR)

5. Freedom of Information

6. ISO17799

7. Companies Act

8. Operating and Financial Review (OFR)

9. Financial Services and Markets Act 2000 (FISMA)
10. Sarbanes–Oxley
11. US-NRA Regulation, s.1441
12. The Patriot Act
13. Gramm–Leach–Bliley
14. Safe Harbor Act
15. Securities and Exchange Commission Act 1934
16. Basel II and III
17. UCITS
18. EU Data Protection Directives
19. E-Commerce Directive 2000/37/EC
20. EU Framework Directive for Electronic Signatures 1999
21. Financial Transactions Reports Act (Australia)
22. International Financial Reporting Standards (IFRS)
23. IASC and IASB Frameworks

Because technology is so ubiquitous in financial services, most of these regulations, which only form a part of the total universe, have an impact on or are impacted by technology deployments. These interactions can become so complex that, for the management process it can look more like the technology is being deployed solely for the regulations rather than for support of a business need that has regulatory constraints around it. In certain cases of course there is a much closer relationship; for example, Sarbanes–Oxley's requirements for timely reporting of events, anywhere in the business, that could affect the firm's eventual financial statements (and/or share price).

It is essential to any technology management process to evaluate the applicable regulatory structures and the degree to which their constraints or freedoms affect the way in which a technology deployment is planned, specified, delivered or managed. See Chapter 17 on IT governance.

The requirement, right at the beginning of the management process must be an analysis of the business need in the context of applicable regulation. This is termed a Global Regulatory Impact Assessment (GRIA). This is a process that must have at least two iterations. The first iteration of the analysis is designed to create a matrix or table that identifies the basic functions or impacts of a proposed technology deployment. Again, I've used the proposition of an application here, but the concept applies equally to communications and systems layers.

An example of this first stage might look like this (Table 16.1).

This stage effectively identifies the actors in the organisation that will need to be involved if any deployment is to be effective and not put the firm at risk.

Table 16.1 GRIA Stage 1

Objective	*Impact*	*Affected*	*Regulation*
1. To improve corporate actions efficiency	1. Income processing 2. Relationship management 3. Account opening 4. Tax	1. Corporate actions 2. Sales 3. Compliance 4. Legal	1. US- NRA, s.1441 2. Double Tax Agreements 3. Sarbanes–Oxley 4. Data Protection Directives 5. AML

Source: Author.

Table 16.2 GRIA Stage 2

Objective	*Impact*	*Affected*	*Regulation*
1. To improve corporate actions efficiency	1. Income processing	Data feeds need to be STP Market reference data needs to generate golden record	AML
	2. Relationship management	Client communications need to be reviewed	Sarbanes–Oxley AML

Continued

Table 16.2 Continued

Objective	*Impact*	*Affected*	*Regulation*
	3. Account opening	Client documentation needs to be reviewed and made electronic	Electronic Signatures Act
	4. Tax	Tax processing must be STP	Double Tax Treaties US-NRA, s.1441 Data Protection Directives

Source: Author.

The *affected* group has the task to drill down to the next layer of the analysis taking each impact area and identifying those parts of the each regulation that are pertinent to the proposed deployment. Of course the good thing about such groups is that because they are, by definition, cross-functional, it is likely, even probable, that even at this stage there may be regulations that no-one had considered applicable or groups that could be affected that have not been identified straight away. So this first stage needs to be iterated until there are no further additions. The group can then move on to the second stage where actual requirements become clearer. Even at this second stage, additions can be made to the group as further granularity often brings to light unforeseen impacts. So a second stage analysis might look like this (Table 16.2).

As these increasingly granular levels are reached, the impact on what any given deployment can do, will do or is allowed to do will materialise.

CHAPTER 17

IT Governance in Financial Services

WHAT IS IT GOVERNANCE?

The contemporary business environment is totally reliant on its IT systems. Technological developments have not only made many forms of business activity more effective and efficient, they have created new forms of business. This applies to rational as well as 'new' markets. The birth and growth of the information economy has radically changed the way we run our lives. No sector has benefited from technology as much as the financial sector. Financial services are now inconceivable without the pervasive support of IT and communications. Local and global activities in near real-time, essential for oiling the wheels of all business activity, rely completely on the success of IT systems. It is no surprise, then, to find that the link between business interest and IT development is strong. This link is key to shaping the vital interface between business aspiration and IT reality, it defines the scope and central place of the concept of IT governance.

Historically there has been a gap, or time lag between the breathless opportunities pushed by rapid technological development and the slower, earthbound needs of business in general. This has led to a difference in culture, where IT systems have been grudgingly admitted as being necessary, but seen as a cost to the business, a cost which is detrimental and which should be reduced. Meanwhile the IT culture, carried by the wave of falling procurement costs, more realisable solutions and a growing complexity in business life and supply chains has pushed hard for budget. The lack of synergy between the IT and business functions has led to 'siloed' solutions, closed areas of discussion and inefficiencies in the way systems have been deployed. IT governance is, in part, a response to this cultural divide. It recognises the central importance of IT and insists that it is driven by business and for business interests. It places responsibility for the critical infrastructure of an organisation where it belongs – at board level.

Governance bodies talk of IT as 'essential to manage transactions, information and knowledge necessary to initiate and sustain economic and social activities. … IT is fundamental to support, sustain and grow the business.' No-one would argue with this now. What were once competitive benefits have translated into essential requirements for survival. As a consequence, the most successful organisations are those that have moved on to consolidating these benefits and preserving them while minimising any disadvantages. This is also part of the IT governance remit. Understanding and dealing with the risks stemming from implementing new technologies is a strong indicator of organisational maturity. IT governance widens this to include other challenges.

- It recognises the convergence of IT and business management.
- It points up ways of aligning IT strategies with business strategies.
- It indicates levels of responsibility throughout the organisation.
- It responds to the complexity of organisations by insisting on a systematic approach and looks to framework solutions rather than piecemeal fixes.
- Because business is accountable and success is represented in figures and other measurable parameters, it recommends that IT performance is also subject to measurement.

Ultimately, this bringing together of operational and technical interests for the good of the business is the responsibility of those who hold the future of the organisation in their hands.

BOARD RESPONSIBILITIES

At the apex of the organisation is the board of directors. Once, governance issues were low on the agenda and the responsibilities for it delegated to lower levels. As the focus for non-compliance shifted from persuasion to punishment, especially of those at the top of an organisation, the significance of good governance has increased. Measures aimed at addressing these top management concerns are now actively promoted by the governance layer of an enterprise. Boards and executive management now need to extend an awareness of governance, already exercised over the enterprise, to IT by way of an effective IT governance framework. This is the way to addresses strategic alignment, performance measurement, risk management, value delivery and resource management.

In the United Kingdom, the Turnbull Report was issued as a guide for company directors on how they should comply with the UK Combined Code. These guides covered internal controls and addressed the areas of operational, risk and compliance management. The report recognised the central role of IT and the dependency on information systems. Practical implementation of effective systems of control is seen as the way to ensure real governance. Through these, transparency and risk management are made real. For example, the application of standards, notably ISO standards, is an option. Implementing large frameworks can prove to be expensive. Every firm must judge for itself how far such frameworks are applicable, especially for smaller firms. However, as management models, standards and the frameworks they imply represent a form of benchmark.

One standard, ISO 17799, has been widely adopted for implementing an Information Security Management System (ISMS). The secure accessibility of information based on thorough risk analysis is a critical priority for any organisation in the information economy. This applies particularly to financial organisations. The information economy relies on a model of ecommerce where data is secure, accessible and reliable across multiple systems. Internet access and the ongoing struggle with fraud insists on this. In a sector where trust and confidence are paramount, any deviation from a high standard in these areas is too high a risk to tolerate; the integrity of an organisation's information is central to its future prospects. Consumer confidence in the security and accuracy of investments, savings and personal information is directly related to how the protection of that data is perceived. Failures in one sector can have adverse affects on others, as was the case with Enron – a failure in the energy sector has affected all others, especially finance.

RISK AND SECURITY

'*Every* deployment of information technology brings with it immediate risks to the organisation' (Calder and Watkins, 2004, p. 2).

At one time it seemed that the opportunities made possible by IT were so beneficial, it was only necessary to purchase a solution and implement it for the business to grow and expand into new markets. But, as with all business activity, the risks soon became apparent. In the age of mainframes, IT control was paramount, but it was a slow, limited development as access to business information was limited by dumb workstations and centralised processing. As local area networks, and wide area networks, introduced more and more power to the desktop control devolved to the user, information sources proliferated. By the advent of the Internet the interface to business life had morphed beyond recognition: personal computers, laptops,

PDAs and even mobile phones. The challenge for IT departments still charged with accountability for the storage and access to information is daunting. E-mail alone is a massive load on storage; business data accumulates at astonishing speed; for reasons of compliance and business need, all this information has to be retrievable, almost instantaneously. Running through all this is the balancing factor of risk. For every benefit there is a risk and the size of the risk matches the potential of the benefit. It is no surprise then that much of IT governance is concerned with identifying, prioritising and mitigating risk.

Effective IT governance has two fundamental components:

- First, the way IT is strategically deployed in an organisation, as a significant investment, managed and accounted for;
- Second, the way the associated risks of that deployment are defined and managed.

However, as we empower consumers by pushing more and more financial decision making on to them, providing more and more information to help form opinions, perception and reality overlap. The risk burden is also spread – the financial decisions made by individuals are the results of balancing qualified risks, which are, however, often poorly understood. For financial institutions their responsibility is to be more efficient, more accurate and more informative on financial matters. User access is widened, through Internet access and home ownership of personal computing. With this power comes risk as the weak links in networks and personal administration of systems is exploited. Security has been the Cinderella of the IT world. The emphasis has been on growth and access rather than discretion and control. Competitive business instinctively distrusts barriers and restrictions. Regulation, forced on corporates and the public is resented. The result is a compromise, which sometimes fails.

INFORMATION SECURITY

Traditionally, security has focused on inventories of hardware assets, but in the information age, assets are abstract. The real risks are not the office on fire, but the failing network or corrupted database. Information security is complex – it deals with confidentiality, integrity and the availability of data. IT governance is even more complex, placing these concerns in a larger context of business needs, partners, suppliers and the chain of activity that make a business function. Standards, such as ISO/IEC 17799: 2005, encourage a systematic approach, the only real approach to these issues.

Information security is a key component of IT governance. As IT becomes more strategic and information evolves into the real capital of business, so the management of information and similar assets becomes of greater concern to company boards.

ACCOUNTABILITY AND RESPONSIBILITY

Accountability is central to IT governance. The decision making process defines who makes decisions, who is accountable for processes, who changes them; all within the context of change management.

The initial decision makers in software development or procurement processes must be accountable for performance since they have established the criteria on which performance assessment is made. This is especially so since regulation, notably in the financial sector, is focused on accountability and the way this responsibility is acknowledged and acted upon within the organisation. Accountability permeates the entire organisation. No level is untouched. IT governance recognises this when it inherits the larger view of enterprise and corporate governance. These latter realms address confidence and transparency within and without the organisation, establishing credibility and trust in the market. IT governance does much the same but largely within the organisation.

However, when IT concerns link to the supply chain we see the extension of the enterprise; critical processes branch out into wider markets and chains of accountability. Governance at this point widens the scope of interest.

As we've seen, the financial sector spends huge sums on IT solutions. More than anything this investment reflects its dependency on technology to support its central role in the information economy. Firms now offer a large number of products and these are increasingly electronic in nature. Many companies encourage users to buy products and open acocunts on the Internet, using financial incentives and ease of access as market drivers. To not have this kind of solution is to seriously undermine a competitive position.

A report from Financial Insights suggests that capital market firms alone were projected to spend $95.5 billion on technology in 2007. IT infrastructures are recognised as being core to the delivery of services, and central for home banking, ATMs and trading systems. Regulation has responded to this by developing legislation that assumes firms have certain IT capabilities.

For many companies as the vertical sectors reshape in the face of changing market conditions, they merge and acquire each other. IT resources are combined and integrated to realise efficiencies of scale, pooling skills and consolidating platforms. These factors raise a number of specific sector issues.

- With the increase in IT-based products there is more to track and monitor.
- The size of IT spending requires high-level decisions and budgeting.
- IT infrastructures are used to link and integrate business activities such as home banking, ATMs, trading systems, call-centres and so on.
- The frequency and scale of mergers and acquisitions complicate IT integration and add extra levels of complexity to business.

Underpinning the succes of the sector in the context of these issues is the need to perform against targets. IT governance has a mission to shape the relationship between IT and business ambition. Closely linked is the requirement to ensure that business information is sound; the quality of business intelligenece (BI) cannot be understated as a fundamental issue. It is worth touching on all these issues to see how they interact as part for the IT governance picture.

TRACKING AND MONITORING

Within the business there are varying responses to these drivers. Tracking business activity is fundamental, as is monitoring processes for compliance and quality, through internal controls. The retail side often has an emphasis on tracking and monitoring. Marketing has to develop and roll out programmes into a volatile market under scrutiny with performance measured by results. Sales manage leads within a sales cycle, and project teams work towards greater market share. Tracked activities are primary inputs to BI and help decide on how best to deploy IT. All this has to be reviewed within an overall, consistent governance framework.

For regulators the need to track what is happening in their area of interest is reliant on deploying IT. The UK Financial Services Authority (FSA) collects information about product volumes, such as mortgage, insurance and investment products. This data helps a regulator to be efficient in the way it targets its own resources, identifying potential issues that may require action such as increased supervision of a sector or product type or production of consumer information. Collecting data on mortgages, life policies, general insurance, collective investment schemes and SCARPS (structured capital-at-risk products, such as precipice bonds) might be carried out on a quarterly basis. Crucially, the data is collected elctronically and covers direct sales and those made through an intermediary. Classification includes

- the type of product sold;
- whether the sale was advised or non-advised;
- property and loan value, buyers' status and repayment method.

Intermediaries and all retail firms, such as independent financial advisers and mortgage and insurance brokers, have to supply information about their financial resources, complaints received, training and competence and other matters. Pricipally this enables a regulator to focus resources on those areas that pose the greatest risk to effective regulation. To do this, it will need the big picture mapped out: a view of who sells what to whom; and the ability to spot potential problems in advance. The message form the FSA was that 'accurate, timely information will make the FSA a smarter regulator'.

While much emphasis is now placed on consumers to manage their own financial affairs, firms and financial sector organisations are now required to be seen to treat their customers fairly. Although different, the three main sectors of financial services – banking, capital markets and insurance – face many similar challenges in this area:

- they have to meet the demands of an increasingly informed and technology literate customers where satisfaction and service levels will determine customer loyalty;
- at the same time, they compete in a consolidating market where global institutions and niche businesses differentiate themselves through customer satisfaction.

Customer relationship management (CRM) systems are fundamental to the way financial service operations track and monitor their customers, big or small, retail or institutional investor. Many firms that have adapted contact management systems can no longer support the demands of the business or are outpaced by the rest of the company's IT infrastructure. This is often as a result of a number of factors:

- a shift in emphasis from products to clients,
- increased competition,

- the demands of regulation,
- the need to offer a broader range of products and
- an increasingly diverse and demanding client portfolio.

These lead to the use of technology as a tool to more effectively and proactively manage customer relationships.

Within the business there are varying responses to these drivers. The retail side often has an emphasis on tracking and monitoring. Marketing has to develop and roll out programmes into a volatile market under scrutiny with performance measured by results. Sales manage leads within a sales cycle, and project teams work towards greater market share. All this has to be reviewed within an overall, consistent governance framework.

Regulation is not only specifically financial, that is, driven by the FSA in the United Kingdom or the SEC in the United States. Other regional and national regulation requires the capability to track and monitor activities. For example, in the United Kingdom, since 2005 The Freedom of Information Act 2000 (FOI), the Freedom of Information Act (Scotland) and the Environmental Information Regulations 2004, introduced new laws that gave anyone the right to request information from any public authority including central government, local authorities, NHS services, schools and colleges, courts and police. Data privacy is enshrined in many regulations, generally through data protection legislation. Again, in the United Kingdom, the Freedom of Information legislation extends the right of access to personal data under the Data Protection Act 1998, to include and allow access to all types of information held, whether personal or non-personal. This means the capability to make such information available and its use tracked, is fundamental to everyday business activity.

IT SPENDING

Traditionally IT has been seen as a cost centre. Over time, as the significance of technology has been reassessed, it has become accepted as an investment. Whenever the business attempts to modernise, explore new markets, meet regulation, become more efficient, it seems that this investment must be renewed. A number of companies have managed to recoup their investment by using their infrastructure as a business service for others, or extend their bespoke software to generate revenue. But this is often a distraction from core business. The end result is that as IT along with technology evolves rapidly, systems need to be replaced or upgraded. It is no wonder that IT budgets, while under scrutiny, are growing. The very size of such budgets requires high-level decision making, and so IT spending has high visibility at board level. An aspect of IT governance is its focus on business needs and IT serving those needs through balanced budgeting. In Spring 2007, the research organisation Datamonitor noted that IT budgets have increased by an average of 11% in the trading, brokerage, fund management, investments and securities, and hedge fund sectors during 2007. The prediction is for a big spending year in 2008 for financial service organisations looking to boost their IT infrastructures.

LINKING AND INTEGRATING BUSINESS ACTIVITIES

The advances in IT in general and infrastructures in particluar have transformed the way financial services do business, such as home banking, ATMs, trading systems, call-centres and so on. For many customers IT-based solutions are a given – they expect near instant access to their money and investments and immediately available facilities for transfering funds and trading. Customer satisfaction is the dominant theme.

The integrated nature of the financial sector market is such that products are often hydrids of components from different sources. When cross-selling financial products a company might be promoting a package that has input from many underwritten sources. A call-centre employee might be selling a product supplied by another company on behalf of a third company; the product itself might consist of components from multiple sources.

Increased competition has led to seemingly contradictiory trends such as consolidation. This is also cited as a key factor to the focus on customer relationships. An important additional trend is impending regulatory changes to the sector. For example, the Markets in Financial Instruments Directive (MiFID) in Europe requires financial institutions to review their IT infrastructures. MiFID is a driver for close scrutiny of what is achievable with existing infrastrcutures; IT is being assumed as the means of delivering a more open, transparent trading system. The future for trading in the sector for everyone involved is electronic.

Integration, within a firm, between firms, across markets and globally, relies overwhelmingly on the successful implementaiton of IT solutions. All the challenges of budgeting, effective choice and measured assessment of potential come together in a comlex arena. Integrating IT solutions is a major cost and resource activity. Getting it right is difficult; making sure it works well for the business is even harder. Without a framework that monitors and measures this effectiveness it is likely to fail.

IT GOVERNANCE AND PERFORMANCE MANAGEMENT

Performance is a key indicator, a guide to how well things are going for all aspects of business. The difficulty in managing performance is measuring it. How do we define good and bad performance and in what terms? A process may be performing well against its stated aim – to manage and deliver so many transactions per hour – but its usefulness to the business is inappropriate. In other words, when it was created, the measures were not related to business needs, merely to a quantitative view of its activity. Assessing the links of IT activities to business needs is what IT governance is about, and linking an IT process or activity to business is the critical ingredient often missing from performance management.

Poor performance can be considered in a number of ways: the way the program is coded may be inefficient and perhaps ineffective, the system design may contain unanticipated bottlenecks. When initially introduced the product may well have been suitable for the task at hand but incapable of scaling when the business expanded or it is too inflexible, unable to adjust to a change in business direction. A common issue is the inability to integrate well – an aspect of the insularity of developing applications separately from real business environments, solutions that 'fix' a problem but do not fulfil a role in a bigger solution.

How are these issues identified at an early stage of the software development or procurement cycles? Functional testing has a place in ensuring a working product, but matching products to the realities of turbulent business life is not easy. Once resolved, how do we ensure that the IT processes that underpin business success remain effective? The path towards this ideal is defined by concepts such as more frequent testing to the point of continuous monitoring.

Especially in financial services, the expectation of users is such that very high levels of performance are assumed. When introduced, IT solutions are expected to cope with loading and often untested use. They are assumed to cope with this all with integrity and reliability. Contemporary firms deal with very large volumes of data cumulated from internal sources and the markets in which they operate. They work through this data instantaneously and are expected to deliver accurate information for critical decision making. Shortfalls in performance are immediately noticeable. The drive towards being ever more competitive requires these solutions to be flexible and capable of adapting to the constant switching of market of direction. Responsiveness is now an important aspect of performance. Trading environments are particularly demanding. They need speed, lots of bandwidth, heavy loads of data all delivered reliably and processed accurately.

In a world in which performance is now taken for granted, bundling traditional performance measuring activities as a strategy for delivering effective systems is no longer enough. To bridge the gap between IT activity and business focus we need a more encompassing approach. This is all the more pressing when we factor the need to manage the escalating risks of working in heavily regulated markets.

IT governance establishes itself as a means of determining value from IT systems. At board level it provides assurance about execution. Many vendors have introduced 'dashboard' tools to help executives maintain a high-level but quantitative view of business performance. That is, these tools provide quantitative data to allow executives build a picture of the key performance indicators of their business – critical Business Intelligence (BI) elements presented as a 'snapshot' of how they are doing. They are not a substitute for full analyses, but a representation of the main trends. Dashboards, such as these, have had variable acceptance among customers. They have the virtue of often being graphical in the way they represent complex data. But in their very simplification of the data that had led IT departments to be wary of them they do not provide a full picture. They are often 'fixed' and not easily changed to reflect the real interests of the business. They might even reinforce the disconnect between IT activity and business needs. The need to integrate complex information into levels of representation appropriate to levels with the business has been a function of BI.

BUSINESS INTELLIGENCE AND IT GOVERNANCE

Often analytical applications focus on specific business issues and information and also tend to focus on a department or function such as finance and accounting.

Strategies will vary – some organisations will build in-house solutions, bespoke, or use consultants to develop integrated solutions, others will use point solutions. What these BI applications do have in common is that they straddle the IT–business divide. In this way they sit well with the concerns and value of IT governance.

The Butler Group have produced a number of reports on this area; in one (Managing Costs in IT), they discuss the separation of IT management and the management of intelligence. Essentially the activities of managing data, its creation of storage, retrieval, transfer and destruction is different from the management of information, the transformation of data for decision making with context and meaning.

The way these activities are handled involves crossing the IT–business divide, using IT, the engineering side to support business, the information use side. IT governance attempts to ensure this management of information in both spheres is a quality process. Inevitably the culture of organisation comes into play. If the hierarchy of information transfer recognises the roles of all those involved, and their accountability and the need to understand processes, then it might be claimed to be transparent. This confers governance on the IT realm. The structures for decision making may vary. A contemporary financial services organisation may devolve decision making down to the call-centre, the trading desk or the branch operator. Wherever it stops it should be an informed process, information must be accessible and accurate. All the features of secure systems must be active. In fast moving markets, flexibility trades with control. IT governance makes this happen in a way that is in line with the risk profile of the organisation and accountable to it.

Formal IT governance, defined and established through refernce models, is an effective way of finding solutions to the business issues that face financial services (discussed earlier).

In the United States, The Sarbanes–Oxley Act of 2002 (SOX), which can also apply to companies outside the United States, has mandated a high standard for corporate governance and accountability in IT. In the United Kingdom, The Turnbull Report and other guides, such as the Combined Code, have, like SOX, emphasised frequent auditing, and the monitoring of systems of controls over business processes. IT directors are now answerable to boards of directors that are directly accountable to regualtory bodies that threaten heavier penalties. They are responsible for the security, accuracy and reliability of the systems that manage and report their companies' financial data.

A significant aspect of this regulation is that it assumes IT capabilities that can deliver information in near real-time, that is, almost instaneously. We have seen that MiFID assumes a lot from the technological base. All trends point to an intensification of the IT effort to meet modern business needs. Firms need to report on compliance with complete confidence in the accuracy of the data they provide. That demands up-to-the-minute accuracy and availability. The current level of competitiveness with the financial sector is such that IT solutions that deal with these issues can make or break a business. Above all, it is the company with a coordinated approach to IT management and governance that will survive and grow.

So, as well as integrating IT and business interests and supporting effetcive business decision making within the known risk profile of the firm, IT governance adds value by being a natural response to

- the increased demands of corporate governance,
- the automation and increased frequency of auditing,

- the exposure of the security of a firm's intellectual capital and data,
- the higher profile lines of accountability and
- the need for real-time information in a dynamic business environment.

IMPLEMENTING SOLUTIONS

The implementation of a solution follows a familiar path for IT procurement.

1. Draw up in-depth business requirements;
2. Get sign-off, budget and commitment at the highest level;
3. Search for a suitable solution;
4. Narrow down to a short list of vendors or integrators depending on whether the answer is an integrated solution with best-of-breed (BOB) point solutions, frameworks or single solutions such as common-off-the-shelf software (COTS) and
5. Selection of solution, including on-site product demonstrations, submission of tender documents, detailed project timelines, budgets, and further risk analysis.

Factors driving selection might include:

- the flexibility of the system to meet the company's current and future business needs,
- an ability to be implemented in a phased way,
- the level of customisation possible,
- the ease of integration with existing solutions and
- end-user ease-of-use and acceptance.

Driven by the strategy this may be a short-term or long-term solution. The natural project for IT governance is a large-scale, complex implementation. It seems that the larger the solution the greater the need for governance. But in reality, even smaller-scale endeavours need the rigour of an IT governance discipline. So the larger framework is applicable to almost any scenario.

One view of IT Governance, which takes an optimistic slant on the overhead it represents, is that it has, at heart, the intention of maximising the value of IT to the organisation. By monitoring and managing against a risk regime, and ensuring that budgets are built around real business interests, IT is evidently beneficial. The Butler Group, in a report on IT governance, concludes that

- IT plays a significant role in creating value for an organisation.
- Without this governance, the contribution to business of IT is greatly reduced.
- Effective IT Governance defines a clear framework for all IT-related decisions.

This last point is particularly important. The need for reference frameworks is largely a function of the complexity and scale of the way IT now underpins the financial sector.

FRAMEWORKS FOR IT GOVERNANCE

When evolving an approach to integrating business and IT interests it makes sense to examine best practice. An IT governance framework, such as Control Objectives for Information and related Technology (COBIT) is a well-known example of such a framework. COBIT is, by intention, a comprehensive solution. It seeks to provide a set of guidelines on how best to achieve the synthesis of business and IT interests. It is systematic in approach and thinks through the scope of processes and activities that need to be addressed to achieve a working solution. It implicitly recognises a number of the issues discussed earlier; it ensures that responsibilities are recognised and allocated and accountability is built into a reporting process. Its main focus is on information systems, processes and systems of control that ensure these processes and systems are effective. It doesn't dictate how they are to be made effective, but it does indicate how this might be achieved.

The final step is for the firm, or business to think through its own well-known processes and apply the framework, thoroughly. Such application can lead to a very comprehensive portrayal of how the business operates and how IT makes that possible.

How this is applied will depend on the strategy the organisation chooses to achieve its business objectives. There are three categories of strategy.

- Operational excellence – This strategy has an emphasis on cost reduction using highly efficient business processes throughout the organisation and into the supply chain. IT is seen as the tool for realising process management and automation.

- Customer relations – Focusing on the benefits of good customer relationships through excellence in customer service IT maximises the benefits of customisation. It extends customer reach and generates business intelligence for developing further products.

- Product leadership – This sees IT as the prime instrument for product and service innovation around a strong brand image. IT delivers knowledge management and supports collaboration on product design and marketing.

Whatever strategy is chosen, a framework like COBIT is essential. The way decisions are taken will depend on the strategic approach and the risk analysis, or resulting risk profile, for the firm. The IT Governance Institute sees this balancing of interests as the business of IT governance, ensuring proper control and governance over information and the systems that create, store, manipulate and retrieve it.

LATEST TRENDS IN IT GOVERNANCE AND BEST PRACTICE

SOA

Service Oriented Architecture (SOA) is a new definition of what we might expect from a practical framework for managing IT and bridging the gap with business functions. Essentially an SOA places the business drivers at the heart of IT architectures and systems. It sees the internal divisions and disciplines of IT as linked through service arrangements which are measurable and accountable. This overall service architecture provides a visible entity onto which business demands, as processes, can be mapped. As a layered architecture it marries well with BI, which seeks to concentrate business information in the right places within an organisation. Each discrete service area, by being seen as separable and therefore manageable, can be subject to appropriate performance measures. Linking complex IT systems in a web of defined relationships broadens accountability and management capability so that the architecture can reflect and adapt to changing business needs. But at heart it must maintain transparency, ensure compliance and not be tempted into a siloed approach to maintaining IT standards.

The breakdown of systems into manageable parts allows problems to be identified at an early stage and resolved locally. For issues that affect several functions an overall managed architecture means these can been seen in their wider context.

Certainly SOA has its appeal for the financial sector. As an IT framework with services at its core, where services have standardised IT functions within a business so as to be used elsewhere, it has its attractions. Recent reports noted that just under 10% of surveyed IT initiators in financial services had deployed SOA with almost double that trialling solutions that might be described as SOA. The figures start to become impressive since nealry double that again, near 40% were evaluating such frameworks.

Vendor approaches

In 2006, Microsoft announced an SOA architecture for developers and integrators in financial services. The Microsoft Insurance Value Chain Architecture Framework (IVCAF) contained tools, libraries and workflows for building and integrating applications and services using Windows and '.NET'. Focused on workflow, specifically in the insurance sector, IVCAF is a major platform serving as a blue print for how developers and integration staff can build software and services for applications and back-office activities. Microsoft yoked MS Office software to SAP's enterprise resource planning (ERP) software. Recognising the central role of workflow in financial services, this SOA strategy features Visio process models and web services messaging recommendations, platform-specific implementation guidance and integrations.

A number of software vendors have moved to be part of this framework. For example, suppliers of policy administration systems have evolved their insurance workflow products to deliver straight-through processing across multiple insurance applications. Collaboration between specialist vendors within an SOA context enable insurers to rate, issue and service commercial policies. SAP, in particular, talked of enterprise service-oriented architecture and an application 'landscape', with a design driven by business needs and service types in an overall architectural plan.

- SAP's approach to enterprise service-oriented architecture (enterprise SOA): Software layers, service design, process platform, component clusters, process platform

- Standards-based business applications: Semantic, technical and portability standards

- Transition to enterprise SOA: Critical success factors

- Enterprise SOA checklist: Steps to successful deployment

One of the most valuable aspects of SOA is its encouragement of reuse, the holy grail of best practice, as a basic principle in the development of services. It can radically reduce the time-to-market for a new service and cuts the costs of strip down and recreate practices, also dealing with that great escalator of costs – project overrun. Inevitably, new initiatives require new software; and this software has to work with existing solutions. The result is the complexity and challenge of integration. SOA is a natural platform for building integration.

Generally business is reactive, howevermuch it aspires to being proactive. Markets mutate and organisations respond. The key is in the way they respond and how fast. Flexibility, to mergers, acquisitions, new regulation and competitive moves, is essential. Matching the relative inflexibility of elderly, but still essential, mainframes with agile desktops sets a process of extreme junctions. Wrapped around this is the need for governance. The SOA approach has governance as a central tenet – matching business and IT needs, shifting the focus from technology to business process. Centralised IT management, which is aware of existing infrastructures modified by standard frameworks for governance, can absorb new elements more easily. Responding to business needs, such as making it easier to acquire accounts across various business platforms, is made easier.

Perspective is also significant. The IT manager who has the task of integrating new software and managing IT governance will have a different perspective to that of a board member who sees only a cost factor in the delivery of a new service. The business manager who has to ensure that staff build effective client relationships through reliable, integrated solutions is a further factor. Satisfying all perspectives is a real challenge. Providing a clear return on investment (ROI) is a natural contribution from an SOA. Having the patience to wait for it is another thing. Patience is a virtue often lacking in business. But if we consider that many IT infrastructures and carefully integrated environments have been constructed to meet IT rather than business priorities, the transformation to the SOA approach might be more complex than originally imagined.

Combining the skills and disciplines associated with business process management (BPM) with those of SOA under the umbrella of IT governance is a way forward, as BPM adds a degree of flexibility to service change and an awareness of how automated systems can be modified. Getting to grips with the effort involves working with software tools. They have to be managed through governance channels – change management, upgrade paths, security wraps and so on. Like a number of vendors, SAP has introduced its industry value network (IVN), focused on banks and their processes. It assumes there are common processes that can be leveraged in a SOA context. Defining service types and metrics to make their performance measurable is an important step. Then refining these types by the their degree of reuse for further services helps prioritise efforts. This is especially important for an environment where change is constant. Maintaining a discipline of governance throughout this activity is critical for ongoing success. The need to maintain levels of service, enforce new behaviours and policies, even oversee culture shifts is a governance issue.

Security and SOA

Security increasingly dominates our reaction to financial services – security as an investor, as a borrower, as an online, interactive user of accounts, or as an organisation managing the vulnerabilities of systems to internal and external attack. The increase in access, its variety and method, has led to an unparallelled increase in the number of vulnerabilities and the potential for them to be translated into threats. Measuring this in the context of risk management means thorough assessment within a recognised, practical framework. Security policies have to be enforced consistently; their timing can be critical – often at run-time. Compliance to regulation is particularly sensitive to these issues. To be successful, the large financial organisation has to work within suitable, scaled responses. SOA adds to an understanding of how this can be achieved allied to good IT governance.

Managed services

From the IT perspective, managed services means a number of things; this is because it has so many manifestations. Generally this is a selective process, where specific functions of IT are identified as being amenable to cost reduction by having another, normally eternal, organisation to look after it. This does not mean that responsibility for the whole IT activity is passed over. It tends to be specific aspects. For example, web sites are passed to providers who may host and develop the sites; the skills within the organisation may be lacking or the cost of doing this in-house is too great. The key IT functions of managing desktops, servers and networking may still be managed internally. Managed services are used to reduce costs, avoiding recruiting additional skills, improving availability, improved performance, greater resilience and often security. The selection of a service or sub-function will depend on the required benefit, which is not always that of reduced cost.

Such service provision is well suited to any size of business, not just the large firms. It is a useful way of responding to the pressure of maintaining

24 × 7 services in a supply chain or where IT skills are thinly spread. Often it is part of plan to release IT resources from the mundane to strategic activities. Managed services are also seen as a response to a particular issue or opportunity and not necessarily a permanent transfer.

Outsourcing

Outsourcing normally has a much bigger scope. It is used to describe the strategic decision to pass over the entire IT function to a third party to maintain and manage. It often means IT staff are also transferred and become members of the third-party team, and so includes HR and other sectors. This is a major step, difficult to rescind and very strategic in outlook, generally taken for the impact the outsourcing has on the profitability of the business through operational cost savings.

Best practice

The IT Governance Institute (ITGI) issues a number of yearly reports which gives an insight into the way companies operate. This is true of firms and the financial sector. The IT Governance Global Status Report – 2006, noted a number of developments that may influence our view of the direction IT governance is taking. Some of the findings reinforce the trends noted.

The significance of IT was such that it was a frequent item on the board's agenda. Given that all IT initiatives translate into budget requests this is not surprising. However, at a senior- and middle-management level, IT is seen to be critical and an assumed component of operational success. As intellectual capital and the information economy is closer to the interests of the financial sector, firms are seen as being more committed to IT governance than other sectors such as manufacturing and retail. A significant trend is that around outsourcing; in essence, the problems that drive outsourcing are not necessarily seen as being addressed by outsourcing. Recognising that problems exist and attempting to deal with them in-house, often through a more disciplined approach, such as one based on effective IT governance, is the way forward.

IT governance helps establish transparency as part of its portfolio. It is a way of demonstrating the value of IT to the business and the board. While firms are now more aware of the frameworks that have flourished in the wake of more punitive regulation, the implementation of these frameworks to realise governance does not seem to have become any easier. This is partly a result of the increase in the complexity of fully implementing governance. Deriving good practices takes time, effort and skills and the need to think-through the implications of frameworks such as COBIT before selecting appropriate models to match the firms' needs. To cover the many areas that IT addresses, its wealth of technological developments and increasing areas of practice, without a reference framework such as that introduced by IT governance means the institution will be hard pressed to make sense of business direction and meet its regulatory requirements. Bringing business and IT together for the benefit of the business and the customer is more than ever the most pressing priority.

CHAPTER 18

Conclusion

This book has been fairly wide ranging in its scope, which fairly mirrors the state of the industry and its management today.

Decisions about what technology to deploy, how to deploy it, when to deploy it, what regulatory constraints, risks and liabilities may be consequent and finally how to make sure that the firm derives some value from it – all are neither easy nor stand-alone decisions.

I have tried within the constraints of reasonable time and space to give an overview of some of these issues and some flavour of the issues that are likely to be coming over the horizon.

The conflict, will always be between the speed with which technology can be invented and deployed and the conservatism of the financial services sector which prefers tried and tested solution with a high degree of safety and resilience.

From a security viewpoint, an issue of ever greater importance we must remember is that what science can invent science can circumvent and therefore security within technology management is perforce always going to be lagging behind those entrepreneurial souls who seem to derive some value from undermining technology.

That said, I hope that in this work I have provided some ideas and some insights that might help technologists plan better for the future. I can't hope to have covered everything in the field, but I do hope to have generated some value through discussion of the most important issues of the day.

APPENDIX 1

Template Request for Proposal

The template below is reproduced with permission from TConsult Ltd. Content includes sample text where possible and guidelines for content where sample text would limit the usefulness of the template. TConsult Ltd makes no representations or warranties with regard to the legal acceptability of this template which is provided for reference only.

OVERVIEW

An overview of the issuing company's status, market position and need.

Proposal scope

A more specific definition of the project. What is and what is not covered within the terms of the request.

Proposal guidelines

In order for Issuer to evaluate each service provider proposal in a similar fashion, respondents to this RFP should adhere to the guidelines and deliverables as stated within this document. Failure to comply with these guidelines may be grounds for disqualification.

Activities and key dates

Key activities and target completion dates for the Request for Proposal and service provider selection process are set forth below.

Activity	Date
Distribution of the request for proposal (RFP)	
Question and answer session to clarify scope (if required)	
Written proposals submitted by service providers	
Selection of preferred service provider	
Contract negotiation/signing	
UAT testing commences	
Testing completed	
Production initiated	

Proposals must be submitted by < date >.
Issuer reserves the right to change these dates at its sole discretion and convenience.

Contacts and filing requirements

Issuer has designated a single point of contact, i.e., a prime contact, for all service provider inquiries during the proposal development and assessment process. Issuer's prime contact is:

< < Issuer's contact information > >

Service providers should submit two (2) hard copies and (1) one soft copy of its proposal inclusive of its pricing. Providers should also provide the name, title, address, and phone number of the individual with the authority to negotiate and contractually bind the vendor, and who should be contacted during the proposal evaluation period. An authorised officer of the service provider must sign the service provider's proposal.
The service provider's proposal and pricing responses must be received on or before < < date > >. Issuer will not accept delivery of a proposal by facsimile. Issuer may reject proposals not received at the above address, in the number of copies specified, in the format specified, and by the time and date specified. If a service provider chooses not to respond to this RFP, X requests written confirmation of that fact on or before < < date > >.

Proposal format

All proposals must be organised to follow the format of this RFP (i.e., when framing responses, all service providers must use the same section/subsection

designations). The service providers must respond to all stated requirements posed by Issuer and indicate whether the service provider intends to comply or not comply with the stated requirements. It will be assumed that a specific requirement will not be satisfied by the service provider's solution if this specification is not addressed within a service provider's RFP response. Service providers should not defer responses to requirements/questions until a later date (e.g., during contract negotiation). The service providers should identify any material assumptions made in preparing its proposal.
Please note that in responding to this RFP, when the word 'must' is used within a question, it is mandatory that the service providers meet the standard or requirement described. Where information requested in this RFP uses the words 'should' or 'may' within a question, it is optional, but advantageous, that the service providers meet the standard or requirement described.

Proposal preparation costs

The service providers will assume all costs associated in responding to this RFP and providing any associated analysis required by including, but not limited to, additional information required and site visits. The service provider selected will also assume all costs it incurs during the process of contract negotiation.

Best offer

Service providers are advised that they should submit the most favorable pricing, terms, and conditions they are prepared to offer in response to this RFP. The selected service provider's proposal (including pricing) remain valid for < number > > months from the RFP response due date, and all or any portion of this RFP and the service provider's proposal may be incorporated into the final contract.

Service provider evaluation criteria

Proposals will be evaluated on the basis of how they advance X's objectives and on the following criteria, which include (in no particular order):

- **Effectiveness**. The effectiveness of the solution in meeting or exceeding stated objectives;
- **Creativity**. The service provider's ability to advance proposals which knowledgeably, creatively, articulately, completely, and specifically address objectives and concerns;

- **Knowledge**. The service provider's demonstrated understanding of the business and technical requirements put forth in this document, and
- **Responsiveness**. The service provider's ability and commitment to complete negotiations on a timely basis in accordance with the schedule and to establish and maintain a flexible relationship.

Service provider details

(a) Please provide the following general information about your firm.

Company name

Address of your Local Office

State of incorporation

International offices

Authorised signatory

Marketing representative

Number of years in business

Total number of employees

(b) Describe, if any, the extent to which your company has formed alliances or relationships with other organisations that impact the services to be delivered.

(c) Provide a minimum of six (6) references with at least three (3) in the financial services industry.

Company name

Division

Contact name/title

Address

Telephone number

Email

(d) Describe any litigation involving your company which may be pending.

(e) How long has your organisation offered the services which are the subject of this RFP?

(f) How many clients do you have? Please distinguish between clients for other services or products you offer and those which have purchased essentially those that are the subject of this RFP.

(g) Please detail the size and geographical breakdown of your clients?

(h) What is your market share by country?

(i) Name some large clients, if any, who use your services. What are the major issues you've encountered in implementing your services with these clients? How have you dealt with these issues?

(j) Are all your services handled internally by your company? If not, please explain where subsidiaries or outside service providers are used and provide an example of the process.

(k) Please provide an organisational chart showing the structure of the organisation identifying responsibilities and reporting lines.

(l) Please provide a full list of countries in which you offer services.

(m) Under what circumstances would you consider offering services in a new market?

(n) Do you actively benchmark your performance against that of your competitors? Do you share the results with your customers and offer plans for improvement in deficit areas?

(o) How does your firm handle the initial account set-up and maintenance function (e.g. – manual, automatic, etc.)? To what extent would a client be able to control this function?

(p) Please provide a case study that highlights your most technologically advanced products and services in use today. Please include details on the size of the client and volume of business handled.

PROJECT OVERVIEW AND REQUIREMENTS

Project overview

A more detailed description of the project than that given in section 1 with attention given to details of the project that have particular importance or are business level constraints. This section should also contain any general constraints on the project caused by limiting factors in the issuer's business.

Project requirements

The following section provides specific product or service requirements.

Distribution rights

If information forms part of an RFP, a section detailing the rights of the issuer to distribute the information internally or re-distribute the information, perhaps to other customers, should be added here.

Help desk

If support is required for an application details of the requirements should be included here with particular reference to time zones and response speeds.

PRICING

General

If the issuer wishes to apply any constraints or limitations on pricing or offer guidance as to what may be acceptable or viewed favourably, it should be placed here.

PERFORMANCE STANDARDS

Service level commitments

Vendor should describe their approach to service level management including:

- proposed service levels;
- measurements;
- methods for documenting service levels;
- measuring customer satisfaction;
- performance against such service levels; format and frequency of reporting;
- monetary penalties for failure to meet the service levels.

Service level measures should include:

- Timeliness
- Accuracy
- System availability

Business continuity procedures

Vendor must explain its business continuity plan (BCP) and the measures in place to address situations where the vendor is not in the position to support the contracted business practices. The response should include but not be limited to the following:

1. Detailed BCP
2. Client notification procedures in the event of the vendor not being able to meet service levels
3. Back up procedures employed to mitigate the possibilities of the above conditions existing, and
4. Problem resolution procedures, including classifications of problems, response levels, and times for resolutions of problems.

OTHER TERMS AND CONDITIONS

No representations or warranties

Each service provider must perform its own evaluation of all information and data provided in this RFP. Issuer makes no representation or warranty regarding any information or data provided. Issuer makes no commitments, implied or otherwise, that this RFP process will result in a business transaction with one or more service provider(s).

Confidentiality

This RFP is confidential and the property of Issuer. Issuer will, in turn, respect the confidentiality of proposals submitted by the service providers.

News releases

The service providers will not make any news releases pertaining to this RFP, or the project, without prior written approval from Issuer. No results of the RFP process are to be released without Issuer's prior written consent, and then only to designated individuals.

Use of third parties

Issuer anticipates that the selected service provider will perform all the services described in this RFP. The service provider will not delegate or subcontract any of its responsibilities without the prior written approval of Issuer. Any subcontractor will be required to adhere to the standards, policies, and procedures in effect at the time, whether these are Issuer's or the selected service provider's or both. Confirm if the service provider plans to use subcontractors, and if you do, that the service provider shall remain responsible for all obligations performed by subcontractors to the same extent as if such obligations were performed by the service provider.

Termination of the RFP process

Issuer reserves the right to discontinue the RFP process at any time, and makes no commitments, implied or otherwise. Issuer's engagement of the selected service provider is subject to mutual agreement on a definitive contract.

Due diligence

This RFP is intended to provide service providers with enough information to prepare their proposals. It is the service providers responsibility to obtain any additional information deemed necessary by it.

APPENDIX 2

Typical Business Continuity Policy Statement

The following represents a typical example of a business continuity plan.

RESILIENCE

1. Backups are validated nightly immediately after backup completion to ensure the accuracy of the backup.

2. Random files are restored and compared at least weekly to further verify backup integrity.

3. Cluster servers are brought down at least once per month in order to ensure that the switch over is performing properly.

4. The end-of-month backups are 'restored' to off-site servers monthly. Functionality of those servers is then verified.

5. Internal database logs are kept with test results and exception handling.

6. E-Mail dial-up switchover is the last choice safety option.

7. Border Gateway Protocol (BGP) Lines, One local area network and one T1 have been implemented to protect internet connectivity; Switchover

is tested on the first Saturday of each month. Under normal operation, switchover is invisible and switch back occurs upon restoration of the local area network. Internet Switchover to alternate sites requires 24 hours.

8. In-house phone lines are services by dual-redundant T1s and backup standard telephone lines. All phone service can be diverted to an alternate site within 24 hours.

9. Uninterruptible power supplies are tested every Friday through built-in battery tests; marginal batteries are hot swapped within 72 hours.

10. External connection to the Internet is protected through dual-redundant hardware firewalls with anti-virus scanners. Network Active Translation (NAT) has been implemented on all machines not needing Internet visibility.

11. A Scout server monitors and tracks all Internet traffic, blocks malicious web sites, along with providing Intrusion Detection System (IDS) capabilities. A Scout SPAM Virus Server scans all incoming mail blocking all spam and most viruses. A server centralised, anti-virus has been implemented on all machines (updates are automatic and performed nightly).

12. All machines are locked down and controlled from centralised Win-2000/2003 servers implementing Active Directory. An external mail server, independent of the primary mail server, further protects against malicious mail and hacking prior to delivery. All servers are maintained in dual locked, independently air-conditioned, anti-static, server rooms. Access to the server rooms is restricted to authorised personnel.

SYSTEMS SUPPORT TEAM AND THEIR FUNCTIONS

The company maintains in-house technical support team of technical experts. Specific areas of expertise include network installation and maintenance, system design and integration, software development in numerous languages and systems, Microsoft products, Unix based internet servers, etc.

BACKUP SYSTEM LOCATION/LENGTH OF RECOVERY IN THE EVENT OF A SYSTEM FAILURE

The disaster recovery plan encompasses the following components:

1. Hardware failure

a. Communication
   i. Telephone lines can be forwarded to an alternate site within hours.

   ii. E-mail can be switched to an alternate dial-in SMTP provider, maintained under current contract, within 24 hours at any alternate location.

   iii. FTP and HTTP servers can be switched to an alternate site within 24 hours.

b. Servers
   i. Critical data servers are set up in redundant configurations in either a fall-over or cluster arrangement. All servers are standard off-the-shelf PCs containing standard, off-the-shelf, components. In the event of a critical server failure, a secondary server would take over processing within 45 seconds. Additionally, in house PCs can be substituted for a failed server. Finally, virtually any part can be obtained in short order from retailers located nearby.

c. Disk drive failure
   i. In addition to the redundant configuration of critical servers, primary file servers are equipped with level 5 raid arrays. Error correction allows the servers to continue to function with a single drive failure. The failed drive may be hot swapped with a replacement drive.

d. Ethernet switch/router failure
   i. Multiple switches are in use, all critical users can be moved to an unaffected switch. The failed hub can be replaced in short order. Spare switches are maintained on-site as emergency backup.

e. Power outage
   i. All servers are connected to one of multiple APC un-interruptible power supplies (UPS). The primary servers communicate to their

UPS through a serial connection and vendor supplied software. In the event of an extended power loss, the file server will be notified. The server will then execute an elegant shut down, thereby preventing data loss or corruption.

f. Logical disk corruption
   i. Nightly backups are made of ALL servers in a grandfathered tape rotation scheme. Lost or corrupted files may be restored from the tape backups.

2. Site disaster

a. General system backups:

   i. Daily, weekly and monthly backup tapes are rotated off site to allow for a full system restoration, either on site or off site, in the event of disaster.

   ii. Three alternate off-site locations containing needed power, internet and telecommunication facilities have been identified.

   iii. All necessary computers, high volume printers, network equipment, and other peripherals are either available off site or can be obtained within one business day thereby allowing for the rapid resumption of operations from an alternate site. Site functionality restoration benchmark is within 1–3 days and full operation within one week (Critical functionality required to meet immediate deadlines will be restored within 24 hours.

3. Documentation

a. Critical operational documents are scanned into an electronic documentation system. The files are maintained on a standard, off-the-shelf, server in standard Tiff format. Backups of this server are rotated off site daily, weekly and monthly.

4. Critical software

a. Copies of all critical software, whether developed in house or purchased, are maintained at off-site locations.

5. Validation of the disaster recovery plan

a. File comparisons are done regularly between the backup tapes and the system files. Files are regularly restored from the backup system, as tested and as needed.

Further Reading

BOOKS

Calder, Alan and Steve Watkins (2004) *IT Governance: A Manager's Guide to Data Security & BS 7799/ISO 17799*, 2nd edn, p. 2. London: Kogan Page.

Christensen, Clayton (1997) The Innovator's Dilemma: When New Technologics Cause Great Firms to Fail, Harvard, Business School Press.

McGill, Ross (2003) *International Withholding Tax – A Practical Guide to Best Practice and Benchmarking*, Euromoney.

WEB SOURCES

Actuate Survey

The Actuate 2007 Open Source Software Survey, conducted on behalf of Actuate by Survey.com. Available from www.actuate.com

www.cert.org

The CERT Coordination Center (CERT/CC) is the most widely known group within the CERT Program, and addresses risks at the software and system level. CERT supports software developers and systems engineers so they can make security a top priority. CERT's Secure Coding initiative helps software developers eliminate vulnerabilities that stem from coding errors, identify common programming errors that produce vulnerabilities, establish standards for secure coding and educate other software developers.

Datamonitor Report, published Monday 02 April 2007.
IT Governance Global Status Report – 2006'. IT Governance Institute. Available at http://www.itgi.org/

OpenForum Europe

A not-for-profit, independent organisation launched in March 2002 to accelerate, broaden and strengthen the use of Open Source Software (OSS) in business and government. OFE pursues the vision of an open, competitive European IT market by 2010 in line with the European Commission i2010 Strategy with the mission of facilitating open competitive choice for IT users.

The GNU Project was launched in 1984 to develop a complete Unix-like operating system which is free software: the GNU system. Variants of the GNU operating system, which use the kernel called Linux, are now widely used; though these systems are often referred to as 'Linux', they are more accurately called GNU/Linux systems. Some GNU/Linux distributions are dedicated to freedom and do not distribute or promote non-free software.

http://www.opensource.org/

The Open Source Initiative (OSI) is a non-profit corporation formed to educate about and advocate for the benefits of open source and to build bridges among different groups in the open-source community. One of our most important activities is as a standards body, maintaining the Open Source Definition for the good of the community, creating a focus for cooperation for developers, users, corporations and governments.

SourceForge.net

SourceForge.net is an open source software development web site. SourceForge.net provides free hosting to open source software development projects with a centralised resource for managing projects, issues, communications and code.
Available at **http://www.sourceforge.net**

Index

1441 NRA, US, 198–9

ACH, *see* Automated Clearing Houses
ADBIC
  additonal destination BIC, *see* Bank Identifier Codes
adopter stance, 21
  and maturity, 22
AIX, 71
alternative investment industry, 40
Apache (web server), 59
Application Service Provider, 37
applications, *see* technology, layers of
ASP, *see* Application Service Provider
asset servicers, 37
  and custodians, 35
Association of Global Custodians, 39
ATM, 6, 25, 122, 205–6, 209
Automated Clearing Houses, 125

back office, 11, 12, 25, 33, 35, 41, 48, 73, 81, 96, 101, 104, 120, 138, 197
  and client documentation, 41
  functions outsourced, 36
  open source upgrades, 70
  operational efficiencies, 39
  and settlement, 33
  tasks, 34
Bank Identifier Codes, 50
Bank of America, 113
Bank of New York, 7
Bank of New York Mellon, 7
banking
  wholesale, 24
Banking Act of 1933, *see* Glass-Steagall Act
banks, 6, 21, 24–5, 29, 34–8, 40, 43, 73, 79, 86, 105, 113, 123, 134, 218
  activities, 7
  custodian, 48
  and ISO15022, 43
  and liquidity, 127
Barings, 193
Basel II, 198
benchmarking, 26, 29–30, 182–4, 186
beneficial owners, 36, 49–51
Berkley Software Distribution, 66
best of breed, 32, 38, 96
  bureau, 96
best practice
  and benchmarking, 31
  defined, 26
Betfair
  gambling platform, 123–4
BI, *see* business intelligence
BICs, *see* Bank Identifier Codes
big bang, 105–6
Bilateral Key Exchange, 46
BKE, *see* Bilateral Key Exchange
board responsibilities
  and IT governance, 202
BPM, *see* business process management
BSD, *see* Berkley Software Distribution
BSP, *see* business services provider
  and innovation, 38
BT Radianz
  and messaging connectivity, 44
budget control
  and software projects, 82
bureau, 50, 96, 97
business intelligence, 57, 206, 211, 215
  and SOA, 215
business language, 27
  models, utility style, 111
business process management, 217
business services provider (BSP), 38

C level
  understanding of technology, 27
Capital One
  and de-coupled credit, 125
Central Securities Depositories, 141
Christensen, Clayton, 112
  and disruptive innovation, 110
Citigroup, 34
Closed User Groups, 44
COA, *see* constraints on action
COBIT, *see* Control Objectives for Information and related Technology
code
  reviewing, 158
Combined Code, 197, 203, 212
common off the shelf software, 213
communications
  standards and messaging, 43
Compaq, 115
concierge services, 41
confidence, 30
  benchmark, 186
  limit and business specifications, 30
conglomerate
  as a business model, 127
consolidation
  and convergence, 24
  cycle, and market pressure, 24
constraints on action, 142
constructive overlaps, 27
consultants
  as interpreters of jargon, 27
contingency planning, 68
Control Objectives for Information and related Technology, 214
convergence, 192
  and fragmentation, 25
  defined, 24
  mobile telephony, 43
copyright
  and open source, 69
corporate governance, 100, 104
cost and benefit, 26
  real cost over time, 37
Cost of Full Time Employees, 102
COTS, *see* common off the shelf software
CRM, *see* customer relationship management
CSD, *see* Central Securities Depositories
CUGs, *see* Closed User Groups
custodian
  bank, 101; and software integration, 81
  definition debated, 35
customer relationship management, 207

Data Protection Act 1998, 208
defect management, 168
defect review group, 169
Defence in Depth, 142
Dell, 115
Depository Trust and Clearing Corporation, 141
destructive overlap
  in regulation, 27
DiD, *see* defence in depth
disaster recovery, 24, 159
  and convergence, 25
  and resilience, 142
disintermediators
  Betfair, Zecco and Zopa, as, 124
disruption
  features of, in financial services, 111
  low-end, 115
  market disruption, 113
  and resources, processes and values, 114
  taking advantage of, 33, 109–13, 117–18, 121, 123, 125, 127
disruptive
  innovation: defined, 110; issues, 112; as a threat and opportunity, 109
  technologies, 14, 73, 107, 192
document
  business specification, 131
  compliance specification, 135
  contract, 137
  functional specification, 132
  management, 24; and fiduciary responsibility, 42; the importance of, 42
  pre-business case analysis, 129
  project control, 134
  review, 157
  risk profile, 136
  storage, 168
  strategic business case, 131
  technical specification, 134
documentation, 20, 41–2, 67–8, 85, 107, 128–32, 137, 151, 157–8, 160, 188, 200
  categories of, 128
  change control, 137, 167
  and contracts, 149
  in the planning process, 128
  project, 175
  and software code, 68
  and testing, 155
Dollar Financial, 113
Double Tax Treaties, 49, 200
DTCC, *see* Depository Trust and Clearing Corporation

EasyJet, 112
Ebay, 125
  reputation management system, 125
E-Commerce Directive 2000/37/EC, 198
Egg, 123

enterprise resource planning, 216
Environmental Information Regulations 2004, 208
Ergonomic Fit, 80, 189
E-Trade, 123
EU Data Protection, 136
EU Data Protection Directives, 27, 198
Euroclear, 141
extraterritorial jurisdiction, 103

FaceBook, 6, 23
fail-Fast, 160
fast moving consumer goods market, 5
Federal Financial Institutions Examination Council, 67
Federal Reserve System, 67
FFIEC, *see* Federal Financial Institutions Examination Council
FI, *see* financial intermediaries
finance industry
  and automated trading exchanges, 113
  vulnerabilily to disuptive innovation, 110
financial intermediaries, 18, 49
financial services, 13
  and convergence, 192
  conservatism of, 221
  and distributed risk, 123
  firms, 5–11, 19, 22, 29–31, 35, 48, 80, 86–7, 91–2, 102, 110, 122, 136, 181, 216, 218; access to liquidity, 118; electronic messaging, 47; outsourcing and competition, 75; resilience to change, 122; SOA deployment, 216
  and the front office, 18, 33
  and innovation, 14, 109
  and IT governance, 201
  Markets Act 2000, 198
  and open source, 56
  and outsourcing drivers, 100
  processing needs, 77
  projects, 17
  and quality control, 153
  regional culture, 13
  and regulation, 17, 197
  retail, 5, 22, 30; regulation, 6
  small exchanges, 127
  structures, 7
  technology: adopters, 21; deployment, 190; myths, 15
  three basic divisions, 32
  vendors, 98
  wholesale, 5, 6, 22, 24; and risk mitigation, 7
Financial Services Authority, 89, 206
financial stability
  and software vendors, 92
financial supermarkets, 35
FMCG, *see* fast moving consumer goods market
force majeure, 148
forking, 65
  code variations, 66
FOSS, 56
Free Software
  defined, 57
The Freedom of Information Act 2000, 208
front, middle and back office
  client facing, 32
  defined, 32
  front office, 18, 33, 36, 104, 197
  and Linux, 70
  as profit centres, 32
  spend on IT, 36
FSA, *see* Financial Services Authority
FTE, *see* Cost of Full Time Employees
fund manager, 41
funds
  US, organised as partnerships, 41

General Public License, 66
geopolitics, 21, 23, 24
Germany, 57
Glass-Steagall Act, 34
Global Crossing, 7
global hedge funds, 40
Global Regulatory Impact Assessment (GRIA), 199
Global Security Services, 35
GlobeTax, 48–54, 117
GNU, 57
Google, 6
governance
  and financial services, 104 *see also* IT governance
GPL, *see* General Public License
Grameen Bank, 113
Gramm-Leach Bliley Act, 34, 198
GRIA, *see* Global Regulatory Impact Assessment

Hewlett Packard, 127
Higgs, 197
HP, 71, 115
HP-UX, 71

IBM, 114, 115
ICSD, *see* International Central Securities Depositories
independent financial advisers, 207
India, 6, 136
information
  communication options, 45
  security and IT governance, 205
Information Security Management System, 203

innovation
  disruptive, 109
integration coefficient, 189
  and software integration, 81
Intel
  and innovation, 110
  Gordon Moore (co-founder), 119
intellectual property rights, 74
International Central Securities Depositories, 141
International Financial Reporting Standards, 198
internet, 5, 14, 24, 45, 82, 120
  banking, 6, 25
  and deployment confidence, 30
  service providers (ISPs), 141
  TV, 192
Investment Act of 1940, 34
investment chain
  players in, 18
iPod, 119
IPR, *see* intellectual property rights
ISMS, *see* Information Security Management System
ISO
  15022, 43, 44, 45, 49, 50, 171
  20022, 44, 45, 55
  7775, 43
  IEC 17799:2005, 197, 203–4
  messages and standards, 41
ISPs, *see under* internet
IT
  as a cost centre, 208
  governance, 199, 201, 202, 205, 211; and business transparency, 219; deriving value from, 211; frameworks, 214; fundamental components, 204; linking IT to business, 210; and performance management, 210; and quality processes, 212; sector issues, 205
  trends, 215
  spending, 36, 206, 208, 209
IT Governance Institute, 215, 219
ITGI, *see* IT governance institute
iTunes, 119
IVCAF, 216

JP Morgan Chase, 35

Keynes, John Maynard, 109
key analysis points (KAP), 130

legacy systems, 86
liability
  remedies and limitations, 145
License Review Process, 66
licensing
  and maintenance of acquired software, 92
  and open source, 65
Linux, 58, 59, 64, 69–71, 133
  Red Hat, 69, 71
  SUSE, 69
localisation, 78
  and design differences, 79
low-end disruption, 115
  and market disruption, 113

maintenance control document, 129
  issues within a contract, 151
management, *see* technology
managers
  and technology layers, 23
manipulating code, 61
Markets in Financial Instruments Directive, 197, 209
MCD, *see* maintenance control document
message
  sample message, 47
  types, 37, 51
Message User Groups, 44
methodology
  testing, 185
metrics, 177, 180
  benefits of, 178
  collecting, 177
  test, 178
Microsoft Insurance Value Chain Architecture Framework, 216
middle office
  and pre-settlement, 33
MiFID, 118, 133, 135, 212
  see also Markets in Financial Instruments Directive, 209
MLR, *see* Money laundering regulations
Money Laundering Regulations, 197
morphology, 3, 5, 8
  defined, 7
MUGs, *see* Message User Groups
Muhammed Yunus, 113
MySQL, 58, 59

Napster, 126
New York, 7, 24, 39
Northern Rock, 110, 193
  high risk model, as a, 110
NPW (Not Proceeded With), 88
NRA tax regulations, 51

OAT, *see* operational acceptance testing
OFR, *see* Operating and Financial Review

open source, 3, 56–8, 66
and financial services, 57
and OSI, 57
platform architectures, 62
product maturity, 63
and risk management, 58
Open Source Initiative, 66
OpenForum Europe, 57
Operating and Financial Review, 197
operational acceptance testing, 159
OSI
and open source, 57
outsourcing, 28, 100–2, 104, 106, 219
main categories of, 100

The Patriot Act, 198
Paypal, 123
PC, 19, 70
desktop, 119
IBM, 114, 115
PDA (Personal Digital Assistant), 119
peer to peer (software), 126
pre-settlement activity, 33
product maturity, 63

QA, *see* quality assurance
quality assurance, 30, 153, 182

Radio-frequency ID, 118, 119
rates of taxation, 36
Rational Rose, 83
RCA, 119, 121
real-time pricing, 35
Red Hat
Linux version, 69, 71
Rediffusion, 119
redundancy
resilience protection, 29
technology defined, 29
regulation
data protection, 6
and document management, 24
and technological developments, 198
relief at source, 49, 101, 132
regulatory compliance with, 103
reputation and creditworthiness, 125
Requests For Proposals
types of, 93
return on capital employed (ROCE), 98
reversion, 94
and model changes, 95
RFID, *see* radio-frequency ID
RFPs, *see* Requests For Proposals
risk
analysis, 59, 71, 90, 161, 170, 173–4, 203, 213, 215
and buying software, 91
and early adoption, 21
identification, 170
rating, 172
security, 203
types, 171
ROCE, *see* return on capital employed
roll-out, 84–5
and delivery, 85
integration with existing systems, 86
and software production, 84
Royal Bank of Scotland, 126

Safe Harbor Act, 198
Salomon Smith Barney, 34
SAP, 216, 218
Sarbanes-Oxley, 9, 27, 135–6, 192, 198–200
SCARPS, *see* structured capital-at-risk products
Section 1441, *see* NRA tax regulations
securities processing, 44
security
and the information life cycle, 33
protection and websites, 30
SEI, 96
semantic web, 14
SEPA, 135, 197
September 11 2001, 24
servers, 16, 23–4, *see* also technology, layers of
service level reporting, 143
service oriented architecture
IT governance, 215
and Microsoft, 216
services
mortgages and pensions, 6
short-termism, and firms today, 26
SIBOS, 35
SIV, *see* Special Investment Vehicles
Skype, 118, 126
SOA, *see* service oriented architecture
Societe Generale, 6, 193
Society for Worldwide Interbank Financial Telecommunications, 11
alliance gateway, 140
copyright in business process, 45
and ISO, 43
and message routing, 43
software
business requirements, 61
categories of, 59
leasing, 37
spread, 91
warranties and indemnities, 67
Solaris, 71
Sony, 119, 120, 121
Special Investment Vehicles (SIVs), 40
SSADM, 83

standards
  the need for, 37
  software compatibility, 62
State Street, 35
static testing, 156
Statutes of Limitations, 105
STP, *see* straight through processing
straight through processing, 7, 48
structured capital-at-risk products, 206
structures
  granules, 11
  layers, 9
  siloes, 10
  tiers, 9
Sun Systems, 71
SUSE, 69
SWIFT, *see* Society for Worldwide Interbank Financial Telecommunications
System Analysts, 165
systems,16, 23, 24, *see also* technology, layers of
  mirroring, 24

tax, 106
  and IPR, 150
  withholding, 117, 129, 143
technology
  acquisition, 73
  approaches to acquiring, 73
  best practice, 26
  client-facing, 35
  as a combined discipline, 30
  developments, 31
  disruptive, 6, 23
  environment, 13
  'event' driven, 24
  and financial services, 7
  flexibility in, 6
  and the front office, 32
  inward-looking solutions, 20
  jargon, 27
  layers of, 16
  management, 7; benchmarking, 29; and context, 17; fundamental questions, 14; issues, 13, 21; principles of, 16
  model, overlay, 20
  modelling content flow, 19
  strategist, role of in, 22, 26
  as a tool, 16
  type, silo, 20
Tesco
  as a financial intermediary, 126
testing, 30
  appropriate, 28, 29, 84, 155, 162, 171, 172, 179–81
  the business case, 164
  business critical systems, 28
  collaborative, 163
  cost-effective, 160
  cycle, 174; cycle resilience, 26, 28
  defined, 153
  and design, 87
  for fitness, 84
  functional, 156
  integration testing, 157
  load and performance, 158
  management, 21, 163, 176
  methodologies, 107
  metrics, 178
  non-functional, 157
  open source, 59
  principles, 159
  and quality control, 153
  recording, 166
  resilience and fail-over, 158
  risk based, 161
  roll-back, 31
  scheduling, 166
  scripts, 162, 165, 167, 168, 175
  standard techniques for, 161
  system evaluation, 153
  team, 176
  and timing, 154
  types and methods, 156
  user acceptance, 62
trading
  cross border and convergence, 24
  cycles, 24
  rooms:and Linux, 70
training
  assumptions for deployement of software, 87
  and software development, 87
  and software implementation, 84
transaction types, 40
trust gained through test, 98
TTT, *see* trust gained through test
Turnbull, 197, 203, 212
Turquoise, 7, 118

UAT, *see under* user
Unix, 59, 69
  brands, 71
unserved market, defined, 115
upgrades, 93, 151
US S 1441 NRA, 198–9
user
  acceptance testing (UAT), 78
  interface design considerations, 77

value
  benchmarked, 107
  in business, 114
Value Added Resellers, 67
value chain, evolution of, 114
value node, GlobeTax processing
    solution, 52
VARs, *see* Value Added Resellers
version control, 84
V-STP, *see* straight through processing

Wal-Mart, 112
waterfall model, 154
wholesale services, 6
withholding tax, 48, 50, 101–6

Y2K, 73

Zecco.com
  online financial portal, 123
Zopa, 124